The
COASTAL KAYAKER'S
Manual

Help Us Keep This Guide Up to Date

Every effort has been made by the author and editors to make this guide as accurate and useful as possible. However, many changes can occur after a guide is published—establishments close, phone numbers change, hiking trails are rerouted, facilities come under new management, etc.

We would love to hear from you concerning your experiences with this guide and how you feel it could be made better and be kept up to date. While we may not be able to respond to all comments and suggestions, we'll take them to heart and we'll also make certain to share them with the author. Please send your comments and suggestions to the following address:

The Globe Pequot Press
Reader Response/Editorial Department
P.O. Box 833
Old Saybrook, CT 06475

Or you may e-mail us at: editorial@globe–pequot.com

Thanks for your input, and happy travels!

The COASTAL KAYAKER'S *Manual*

Third Edition

A Complete Guide to Skills, Gear, and Sea Sense

by
Randel Washburne

The Globe Pequot Press

OLD SAYBROOK, CONNECTICUT

Library of Congress Cataloging-in-Publication Data

Washburne, Randel.
    The coastal kayaker's manual: a complete guide to skills, gear, and sea sense / by Randel Washburne. —3rd ed.
    p. cm.
    Includes bibliographical references and index.
    ISBN 0–7627–0168–4
    1. Sea kayaking. I. Title.
    GV788.5.W37 1998
    797.1'224—dc21   98-13603
                                                          CIP

Illustrations 18.2, 18.5, 20.1, and 20.4 courtesy of the Canadian Hydrographic Service; not to be used for navigation. Remaining illustrations by Randel Washburne. Photographs by Randel Washburne except when credited otherwise.

Manufactured in the United States of America
Third Edition/Second Printing

Contents

Acknowledgments

This book had its origins with Tim Davis at Pacific Water Sports of Seattle, Washington, who pestered me over a number of years to write a manual oriented to North American entry-level and intermediate hardshell kayak paddlers. Having tried that, Tim's inspection of my manuscript brought it much closer to the mark. I could not have muddled through writing about kayak performance and design without the help of Lynn Senour, Lee Moyer, and Matt Broze. Individuals who helped with other particular aspects were: John Meyer and Dan Lewis on bracing and surfing skills, Lee Moyer on wave paddling, Chris Mork on accessories, Leo Shaw and David Arcese on marine mammals, and Dixon Stroup on the behavior of ocean swells. Ted Steudel suggested valuable additions for the new editions. I thank Wayne Marsula for introducing me to the use of a double bent-shaft canoe paddle and his unique way to stow it as a spare.

Linda Daniel's influence goes far beyond her help with writing over the years. Many is the road I would not have taken without her encouragement and support. Her cooking has enriched our paddling adventures, and her humor has enriched my life.

And I owe special thanks to my friend Audrey Sutherland, who I came to know after being taken to task for my wholesale dismissal in *The Coastal Kayaker* of inflatables as serious sea craft. My kindred spirit for solo adventuring and actualizing dreams, Audrey has shown me that there are many ways to explore the coastal wilderness.

About the Author

Since 1973, Randel Washburne has kayaked much of the coast between southeast Alaska and Puget Sound, usually solo. His earlier books were *The Coastal Kayaker, Kayak Trips in Puget Sound and the San Juan Islands,* and the annual *Washburne's Tables,* which is used by Pacific Northwest mariners to predict tidal currents.

1

Introduction

Fig. 1–1. Eagle Cliffs in Washington State's San Juan Islands.

The skin-covered hunting craft of the far north are the ancestors of modern sea kayaks, but today's models assume shapes and uses that the Aleut and Eskimo creators never could have imagined. They would scarcely recognize some of the colorful vessels that we call kayaks, and they would be amazed at the numbers plying the North American coasts and waterways. The sea kayak's renaissance began in Britain and spread to Australia and New Zealand. But the greatest numbers of paddlers and manufacturers of boats and gear are found in Canada and the United States.

Sea kayaking's popularity has brought specialization to fit all sorts of people and their boating preferences. A skillful paddler might choose a sea kayak as nimble, but tippy, as the original skin hunting boats. Others go for the big, stable sea kayaks that safely accommodate an entire family with children. Some kayaks are designed and used exclusively for competitive events in settings from city lakes to mid-Pacific channels to winter surf. A salmon fisherman can customize his boat with an electronic fish finder and a bait-preparation station.

Most people like the kayak simply as a nice way to be on the water, and they choose it over other boats because it brings them closer to the marine world. Compared to powerboaters or even sailers, the kayaker's experience is as different as hiking through a forest is from driving through it. Paradoxically, the main difference has a lot to do with the shoreline.

Kayaks are in their most charming element when skirting along shores. For most sea kayakers, paddling out into open water for the day is as interesting as hiking on a treadmill. (This popular misconception of sea kayaking as being *out to sea* is exemplified by the question of how one endures an all-day trip without a chance to relieve oneself.) Instead, kayakers delight in being literally within arm's distance of things near or below, perhaps reaching out to touch the worn planks of a beached hulk or down to stroke a starfish or feed a bit of leftover lunch to a tiny crab. Stops ashore are easy, and kayakers can see and explore coastline features that other boaters miss.

Perhaps I can best show what sea kayaking means to me through fond recollections.

Most February afternoons in Mexico's Sea of Cortez are breezy, but this afternoon's has not materialized yet. Paddling south along this rocky island, we have seen few inviting landing sites in the last hour's paddling, so lunch was impromptu in the cockpits. And now the noon heat and post-eating lethargy militate against our forward progress. No matter, we have no particular goal for camp tonight, and we will take whatever comes.

An hour and scant miles pass, and still no wind comes. It is time to energize ourselves. Now we appreciate our beamy folding kayaks, made more stable by a month's camping supplies and the eighty pounds of drinking water lying in bags along the keel. Sitting on the deck, I shed my cotton sun shirt, wriggle into fins, and pull on my mask and snorkel. Rolling over the side, I drop into a cool world where meters of travel assume the dimensions of miles. Tiny blue fish and big green ones, both iridescent in the sunlight, cruise the coral a dozen feet below. Above, my boat's hull looms as a dark reminder of my origin. I swim forward to grasp the bow toggle over

*my shoulder and, after a fashion, am traveling again. A glance aside
shows three other similarly propelled kayaks.*

*After a half hour of sightseeing, we resurface, steadying each
other's re-entries to the cockpit. The sun's heat is now welcome as I
stretch out on deck, legs straddling forward of the cockpit, head on
the life vest folded aft of it so that I can see ahead while lying flat
and peeking under the brim of my big straw hat. My paddling
cadence is far from efficient in this position, but who cares?*

If marine mammals were to initiate communication with
mankind, sea kayakers would be their likely choice. We already
know them better than most, sharing intimacies that teach us such
little things as the importance of eye contact with the harbor seal or
the sound of the humpback whale's intake breath as it readies to
dive deep. In certain Northwest waterways, where they congregate
to fish and palaver, the giant dolphins called orcas (misnamed
"whale" and maligned as a "killer") may tire of the kayakers that
flock to see them, but elsewhere entire orca family groups may go
out of their way to spend a moment with some awed kayakers, and
to this date, never with malice.

*For the paddler traversing Vancouver Island's west coast, the
Brooks Peninsula is the most formidable of several obstacles. Jutting
like a hitchhiker's thumb, it has a reputation for accelerated winds.
I start the twelve-mile open-water run for its cape early to beat the
inevitable afternoon winds, but nearing there at 1100 hours,
twenty-five knots are already blowing at my back. The seas and my
adrenaline build together. I will find protection ahead, but now I
am on an awakening ocean in a lonely and notorious end of the
earth. My attention is ahead. Otherwise, I might have noticed the
dozen orca overtaking me before they were all around me. Three
pull in close alongside, the nearest a bull longer than my boat and
with dorsal fin towering above and just beyond my high paddle
blade. There is a bullet hole through the fin. Shaken, I stroke along
with my escorts. Soon the bull rolls down and beneath my hull, and
for an instant his eye gazes up at me. Then they go about their
business, fins shearing around the rocks and kelp off the cape. The
seas flatten as I enter the kelp beds inside Solander Island, and I
raise my sail. Slithering and bumping over rafts of bull kelp, I relax
and reflect on my encounter. Though awed at the time, I am left
feeling reassured by their checking up on me during a rough and
lonely crossing. They held me in their power, but I was never*

threatened. That night I share a moonlit beach with two timber wolves, peeking from my tent at dark forms trotting their rounds through the sand, skipping nimbly over the piled logs, and sometimes pausing nearby to watch me silently. A howl echoes from down the beach. What a day!

Some kayakers, struck with a wanderlust for distant shores and the desire to use their own power to get there, have become distance paddlers. Kayaks have crossed the Atlantic on two occasions. Ed Gillet paddled the length of South America from the snow squalls of southern Chile to subtropical Ecuador. Another year he kayaked from California to Hawaii, also alone. In the Northwest, at least a few kayak parties (Gillet included) each year follow the summer-long, thousand-odd mile Inside Passage route between Washington and Alaska.

For those with the inclination and time for it, the sea kayak becomes *home* for weeks or even months. Packing everything essential (and even nice to have) beneath the decks, wherever we happen to be is where we live.

My tent flaps are tied back for a panorama of the squall's passage across the sound. New snow dusts the seaside peaks, a nearby island glows in sunset leaked through the clouds, and a half inch of hail lies fresh on my beach. This is waterfront living-room

Fig. 1–2. Traveling with comforts of my tent and little wood stove requires a larger volume kayak than my friend's in the foreground.

comfort—sipping tea just inside my tent while my little woodstove warms my back. Such early April evenings draw me back to off-season paddling on Vancouver Island's west and north coasts. I remember similar times camped under tarps less fondly—sought out by cold breezes bearing drizzle through the eddying smoke. As dark falls I will zip the door, light the lantern, and strip to a light shirt as the interior temperatures climb to the seventies and dinner simmers on the stovetop. Tomorrow I will be gone. My little stove on its short legs will leave no scars at this tent site. Scarcely a foot in any dimension, it slides into the kayak's cockpit ahead of my feet. My three lengths of pipe wedge into my rear hatch; my light, floorless wall tent fits through my seven-inch forward hatch, poles and all. There's even room for a few Presto logs to augment the wet winter driftwood.

Besides being a vehicle to transport me to distant and remote places, my kayak can give me the thrills to last a lifetime. It is particularly at home in the Pacific Northwest's legendary tide races. Washington's Deception Pass is a place of powerful moving water that sometimes resembles a large, deep white-water river, except that this is moving salt water. With it close enough to my home in Seattle for a day trip, we often spend hours playing in its eddies, swirls, jet currents, boils, and whirlpools. With a wet or dry suit for cold water protection and sometimes an outboard inflatable for backup, it is a fine place to extend our boat-handling skills and experience the power of the sea.

Far to the north, we occasionally visit Nakwakto Rapids. Deception Pass generates currents up to eight knots; Nakwakto's are at least twice as fast, and this awesome place is not for play. Instead, we haul out during the brief intervals between flows on Tremble Island, a tiny rock pinnacle in midstream providing a ringside seat to watch what may be the fastest-moving salt water in the world.

City-bound, I find other delights from my sea kayak, like my regular up-close inspections of the busy harbor waterfront. Or my own kind of escape on a hot August Sunday afternoon.

Working around the house has bogged down to a stalemate of lethargy. I have just enough energy left to load up the kayak and head for a city lake. Thinking of a swim, I bring along my mask.

The park is as crowded as I expected. Ski boats swarm; becalmed sailboats swelter. I choose a languid route along the tree-

shaded shore where mallards paddle and mumble quietly. A capsize is a cooling solution to the day's heat. On goes the mask. Placing the paddle alongside the hull, over I go.

I hang inverted in the cockpit and gaze through my mask at fish wandering through the weeds below. I extend my arms, paddle in one hand. Relaxed and seemingly weightless, I expend no energy and am amazed how long I can hang there, chuckling silently about the nearby sunbathers wondering if I am dead. Eventually I will Eskimo roll up to rejoin their world. But for now, this timeless one is mine.

This book is designed to help you make kayaks your own special link to the sea. My frame of reference is the North American paddling environment and boats and equipment commonly available in Canada and the United States. My perspective is that sound equipment that you know how to use is critical for safety, but security in sea kayaking depends on skills and knowledge. Learning these occupies most of the space in this book.

Suggested Reading

Sea Kayaker magazine. Six times a year. 7001 Seaview Ave. N.W., Seattle, WA 98117; (206) 789–9536. Articles on technique, equipment, designs, destinations, environment, and safety. Does a strong trade in back issues. Periodic subject indexes.

Canoe & Kayak magazine. Six times a year. 10526 N.E. 68th Street, Suite 3, Kirkland, WA 98033; (425) 827–6363. A general paddling magazine with frequent articles on kayak touring.

2

Skills for Safety

To protect themselves from sea hazards, kayakers need knowledge and skills to help in threatening conditions and acute boat-handling crises. All of the skills are important, though learning them may be bewildering at times for the new paddler. The following will help the kayaker make sense of these skills and assist in organizing an approach to learning them.

Think of the skills as four concentric rings of defense, starting with the first or outer ring and moving inward: *(1) avoid trouble* by anticipating tidal current or weather conditions bringing rough seas; *(2) survive rough seas* by keeping upright and continuing on course to safety; *(3) recover from a capsize* by either an Eskimo roll or re-entry following a bailout; and, when all else fails, *(4) signal for help.* Beginning with the first outer ring of defense, the failure of any one of these brings into play the skills associated with the next inner ring, and weakness in any one skill burdens the rest.

The outer defense rings are the most effective, and the fewer rings you can prevent from being breached, the better your chances of survival. For example, assuming proficient skills, *preventing* a capsize in rough seas will always be easier than *recovering* from one in the same conditions. Ironically, postcapsize rescue techniques are easier to learn in short class or clinic swimming pool sessions than capsize-prevention and wave-handling skills, and many new kayakers focus their skill-building on this third defensive ring at the expense of skills in the first and second rings.

Instead, learn skills in every ring while developing as a sea kayaker, but give priority to the outer ones. Most of the skills important to each ring are included in this book. My explanations will help you get started; gaining proficiency will be up to you.

Below is an introduction to the kinds of factors and skills associated with each ring of defense.

Defensive Sea Kayaking

Avoiding Trouble

Unlike the river kayaker, who can scout and reliably predict the challenges he will encounter along a route, the sea kayaker faces routes that are changeable, and to some extent, unpredictable. This is due largely to the fickleness of weather. Unless you opt to stay on shore most of the time and to paddle very selectively, you must accept some uncertainty about what will happen on the water. Knowledge of the weather and the water can reduce this uncertainty to a calculated risk for each outing, making it possible for you to reject odds not to your liking.

Rough water is the prime concern, and wind is the common cause of rough water (hence, wind is the focus of marine weather forecasts). Though impending weather developments can be gleaned from visual cues like clouds, it may be most helpful to learn the local patterns for your waters, particularly the wind directions associated with bad weather or strong fair-weather winds (which may be an entirely different direction). (See "Trip Planning and Travel Safety" for sources of local weather forecast information and common weather patterns.)

Some coastal waters have significant tidal currents, which can produce rough water on their own. These special hazards and their causes (included in "Tides, Currents, and Weather") are worth careful study if you paddle in such areas. The hazards from tidal currents depend on their direction and speed, which are roughly synchronized with the vertical movement of the tide. "Tides, Currents, and Weather" also shows how to predict flows at a given time and how to assess the potential for hazard associated with it.

On the coast exposed to the ocean, rough water can come from *ocean swells*. These large waves may be coming from thousands of miles away, and their size may have nothing to do with the local winds and the waves that local winds cause (called *seas*). Since ocean swells are such a powerful and potentially dangerous factor in the outer coast areas, paddling such coasts (and getting through shore surf) deserves a separate chapter of its own (see "Paddling the Outer Coast").

Finally, a knowledge of skills using nautical charts, a compass, and a trained eye give you a critical edge over trouble. These skills will help you keep track of where you are, your destination, how long it will take to get there, and what hazards lie along the way. Because you may be paddling in waters also traveled by big ships that cannot easily see kayaks and cannot turn or stop in short distances, yielding the right of way is your responsibility. (See "Nautical Charts and Navigation" and "Trip Planning and Travel Safety.")

Surviving Rough Water

When a new kayaker first begins to capsize, he instinctively puts out a hand, which does no good at all. But the same reflex using the paddle can stop any capsize. These *brace strokes* are simply variations on either forward or reverse paddling, swept across it for support. Used in combination with paddling, braces provide an extraordinary degree of stability when you need it. *To be effective, bracing must be practiced enough to become an automatic reaction whenever you sense a loss of stability.* The chapter on bracing includes some suggestions for teaching yourself to brace effectively and also some exercises to build into your paddling routine to help braces become a well-established reflex.

Though basic braces are best learned and practiced under controlled conditions such as in a swimming pool, paddling and bracing technique in waves is harder to program, and you will have to take the lessons when and where nature offers them. The chapter on paddling in waves will give you some ideas to build on when you encounter the real thing. But to become proficient in this ring of defense, you will need to seek or invent more opportunities for practice than the challenges that normal outings provide.

Recovering from a Capsize

Once flipped, you can either roll back up (with the assistance of a nearby paddler's boat or via your Eskimo roll) or bail out and then re-enter.

Though the Eskimo roll is by far the more effective recovery, it is not a reliable line of defense for every paddler. One survey shows that most sea kayakers end up bailing out after a capsize. Some individuals simply cannot get the hang of the roll; others learn it but do not practice it enough to make it "bomb-proof" in real conditions. Rolling double kayaks is particularly difficult as both paddlers must coordinate underwater. Learn to roll if you can, and practice diligently. If not, compensate by being more proficient in other lines of defense.

The "how-tos" of Eskimo rolling in this book are limited; it is difficult to learn without hands-on assistance, and few readers of average ability can be expected to learn it solely from a book. Hence, I suggest that you take a class or prevail on the expertise of a friend willing to get in the water with you as you learn.

If you must bail out (called a *wet exit*), there are well-developed procedures for re-entering your righted kayak, either with the assistance of another paddler or alone. These are detailed in the "Wet-Exit Capsize Recoveries" chapter. Assuming that your boat has the essential flotation at *both* ends, it may be partially emptied of water before you re-enter or pumped out after you are back in the cockpit. The assisted-recovery methods require a companion who pulls alongside to steady your boat while you re-enter. The solo paddler can steady his own craft by fitting a special float to the paddle, which in turn attaches to the deck as an outrigger (see "Additional Accessories").

These procedures need a lot of practice, as they require prompt but careful and purposeful movement. Rough water and a cold, tired paddler make them even more challenging. Practice with likely paddling companions, and be sure that you each take both victim and rescuer roles. The person in the water should play dumb, as if he is hypothermic or inexperienced, in order to give the rescuer experience in directing a muddled victim. For partners of unequal size, a special sling technique helps to stabilize the boats so that a 100-pound woman can easily assist the re-entry of her 200-pound male friend.

Proficiency with the paddle-float outrigger system is a must for the solo paddler. There is no lonelier, more desperate maneuver when you are far from shore and help. Whatever can go wrong will do so, made worse by cold, fumbling hands. Yet the paddle-float recovery has worked for many paddlers in nasty conditions.

Signaling for Help

The situation is dire by the time you reach the last ring of defense, so preparation is all the more important. Before setting out be sure that you have signaling devices accessible on your boat or on your person (usually in a life vest pocket). The options for attracting help are many; some are quite expensive, and their reliability and effectiveness depend greatly on their shelf life, how well they are maintained, and sea conditions. This subject is important and complex enough to merit a chapter of its own (see "Emergency Signaling").

The other important part of this last ring of defense is surviving until help arrives. Most likely, you will be swimming with your capsized boat, so hypothermia from cold water is a threat. Hypothermia has been the primary cause of fatalities among sea kayakers. There are ways to forestall hypothermia (through nutrition and clothing), techniques to slow its progress while you are in the water, and critical procedures for treating a hypothermic paddler. If you paddle in cold water, the chapter on hypothermia should be priority reading.

Developing your rings of defense can be done with the aid of manuals such as this one and through basic sea kayaking classes offered through many retail stores, outdoor education centers, or kayak tour operators. A white-water kayaking class is excellent for developing your capsize-prevention skills.

The best school is the real one. There is no substitute for paddling experience. Actively working to extend your skills adds a rewarding dimension to each outing and pushes your development even when the sea does not. You may be lucky and paddle for years without once having your skills challenged. Unfortunately, this lack of challenge builds false confidence based on "experience." The sea, however, eventually sets that record straight. Its lessons are sometimes harsh, and regardless of your paddling experience, it will occasionally remind you that you have received no diploma.

Good judgment is the hardest thing to learn. Even with full knowledge of your environment and your skill level, ambiguous situations will arise when the risks ahead are unclear, and the temptations to go ahead are strong. Your own personality will influence your decisions, which may be different from someone else's under the same circumstance. If you are leading a group, your burden is to assess whether conditions could overwhelm the least capable members, who may lack the knowledge to judge that for themselves. (See "Trip Planning and Travel Safety" for some thoughts on group travel.) If you paddle solo, you must decide how much risk you are willing to accept. Are you willing to test your limits?

Such judgment cannot be reduced to rules that apply to every situation. It depends on your understanding of your skills and limits—giving the appropriate weight to whatever factors enter the sometimes murky equations of sea kayaking decisions—and intuition. Over the years you likely will make regrettable decisions, and these will become your best teachers.

Sea kayaking is predominantly a quiet, contemplative activity. Times of challenge are rare. But preparing for the worst adds an exciting dimension to paddling and an exhilarating sense of accomplishment for passing the sea's occasional quizzes.

3

Sea Kayaks: Types and Features

Considering the diverse ways in which kayaks are used, the variation in the craft called "sea kayak" is no surprise. In fact there are disagreements about what is or is not a sea kayak. Exact boundaries are not important, but in general, a sea kayak is a boat in which you sit with your buttocks only slightly higher than your feet and that you propel with a double-bladed paddle. Some decked canoes (the British call all sea kayaks "canoes") are used in sea paddling; they have a slightly higher seat and a single-bladed paddle.

Fig. 3–1. These wave skis at a Honolulu shop include an inflatable one *(second from left)*. *(Audrey Sutherland)*

Special kayaks have been developed for particular parts of the ocean world, especially for the surf zone and warm seas. One type, called a *wave ski* (see fig. 3–1), looks like a surfboard and is 6 to 10 feet long. The paddler sits on it. His feet hook under straps and he often wears a seat belt across his lap. The boat is used like a surfboard, though control is extended by both paddle and weight shifting. The *surf ski* (see fig. 3–2) is quite a different craft. It also has an open top, but it is narrow and up to 20 feet long. Though originally designed in Australia for surf rescues, surf skis are made to catch rides on open-ocean swells, and they can reach amazing long-distance speeds on the annual Moloka'i Channel race in Hawaii. Offshoots include recreational "sit-on" kayaks of intermediate length and width that are very popular for warm-water paddling and play in moderate surf. You will often see white-water kayaks playing in the same surf.

Another sea kayak is the so-called folding one. These have a framework with a tough fabric skin stretched over it, making a very seaworthy craft that quickly disassembles into compact and easily stowed bags. They are great for people who travel to distant paddling places by air or live in apartments that lack the space to stow a rigid kayak. Other globe-trotters like inflatable kayaks, which have thousands of miles of sea travel to their credit.

Hardshell Kayaks

Composed of either fiberglass, plastic, or plywood, hardshell kayaks are the most common sea kayaks. Hardshell kayaks are available in models for one paddler (called a K-1 or single) or for two (known as a K-2, double, or tandem kayak). Typical hardshell K-1s are 16 to 18 feet long and 20 to 25 inches wide. K-2s can range from the same length up to more than 20 feet long and to over 30 inches wide. A few have an additional center hole for kids, dogs, or cargo.

The tough skin of a hardshell kayak allows it to take abuse from scrapes, blows, and gouges. Construction techniques, particularly fiberglass, allow almost any design feature. Although a few hardshell sea kayaks are built from plywood or wood strips glued and covered with epoxy, most are fiberglass or plastic.

The hardshell K-1 is the primary focus of this book. If you are new to sea kayaking, a tour of the parts of a typical hardshell single may be helpful (see fig. 3–3).

At the bow, or front, is a rope or webbing loop (perhaps with a

Fig. 3–2. Surf ski. *(Photo courtesy of Valhalla Products)*

handle toggle) called a *grab loop.* There is an identical one at the other end, or stern, and these are used to carry the kayak and to secure it to the top of a vehicle for transporting. Toward the rear from the bow, many kayaks have a bow *hatch*—a tightly sealing door that gives access to a separate compartment, which is partitioned off from the cockpit area by a wall called a *bulkhead.* Most kayaks have hatches and bulkheads at the rear or at both ends, which provide flotation and dry storage for camping gear in case the cockpit area becomes swamped following a capsize. Boats without bulkhead systems rely on air bags for flotation.

Roughly in the middle of the boat is the *cockpit,* which is surrounded by a *coaming,* or lip. When seated in the cockpit, a kayaker wears a *sprayskirt,* which is pulled over the torso and then fitted onto the coaming to make the boat and the paddler a watertight unit. There is no danger of being trapped in the cockpit should you capsize; the spray skirt pops off the coaming easily.

The feel and fit of the seat in the kayak is vital, as one spends a great deal of time there. An adjustable seat back helps with comfort, and it can be removed or folded forward for access to the area behind it. Forward of the seat are *footbraces*—adjustable pedals to rest your feet on. The position of the footbraces is important, as your feet transmit paddling force and also help keep you firmly secured in the cockpit.

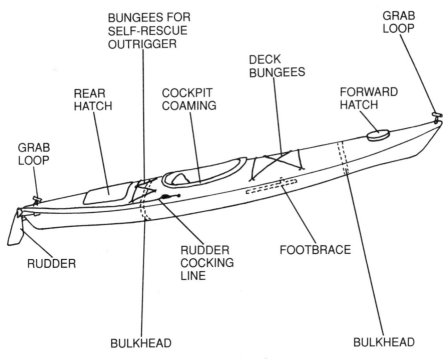

BUNGEES FOR
SELF-RESCUE
OUTRIGGER

GRAB
LOOP

DECK
BUNGEES

REAR
HATCH

COCKPIT
COAMING

FORWARD
HATCH

GRAB
LOOP

RUDDER

RUDDER
COCKING
LINE

FOOTBRACE

BULKHEAD

BULKHEAD

Fig. 3–3. Components of a sea kayak.

Many sea kayaks have a *rudder* on the stern. The rudder, which is connected via cables to the footbraces, is used to steer the boat. You manipulate the rudder with your feet by sliding the footbraces forward or backward. A kayak should steer perfectly well without a rudder, and it is often paddled with the rudder out of the water. (A *cocking line* allows you to lift it in and out of the water.) The rudder is most useful in wind and difficult seas, when carrying a heavy load of gear, or when you are tired and want to put all of your paddling energy into moving ahead, letting the rudder keep you on course.

Also on the deck may be a network of *bungees,* or elastic shock cord. These are used to hold all sorts of things on the deck, such as your nautical chart, a bilge pump, or a spare paddle. Just aft of (behind) the cockpit may be a specialized arrangement of bungies used for the *self-rescue outrigger,* a system using your paddle and a float that allows you to re-enter your boat should you be capsized while traveling alone.

Fiberglass Kayaks

The typical fiberglass sea kayak is made from a mold, a concave form in two halves—one for the deck and one for the hull. After coating the mold with a releasing agent, a gelcoat color coating is sprayed into the mold. This coating produces the smooth outside surface and is also an important barrier that protects the inner layers from the damaging effects of ultraviolet light. Next come sheets of glass fiber impregnated with resin. Most boats have one layer of *mat* (an unwoven sheet), then *roving* (a coarse woven fabric), and perhaps an inner layer of glass cloth. Either polyester or (somewhat more resilient but expensive) vinylester resin may be used, and either serves equally as well.

A good balance of resin to glass material with no air bubbles in the lamination is an essential part of the workmanship that goes into fiberglass boats. Too much resin adds excess weight and makes for brittleness; too little resin results in leaks and weakness. Builders are divided about whether a lay-up done by hand is better than one done by *vacuum-bagging*. In the latter, a plastic sheet is sealed over the mold while the vinylester resin is still liquid. The air is sucked out under it, and the resulting vacuum helps to get the excess resin out and pull the fiber layers together into a thin but strong lay-up. Consequently, vacuum-bagged hulls are a bit lighter (though a highly skilled hand lay-up specialist might do about as well). They also have a smoother inner surface, which makes cleaning the inside of your boat much easier (though it is harder to bond to for glassing in gear tie points). On the negative side, "bagged" lay-ups are a bit more flexible, because they are thinner (given the same material content) and may need reinforcement that offsets the weight savings. Stiffening may be needed on any flat surface in either lay-up type, particularly along the keels of flat bottoms or under decks near the cockpit.

Super-strong Kevlar cloth (developed for bulletproof vests) may be substituted for other glass fabrics in order to save weight, though at substantial additional cost. Lightness is possible because Kevlar is strong enough to take the place of much more standard fabric (and the resin needed to saturate it). But a thinner lamination flexes, and Kevlar hulls usually need more stiffening, though well-executed reinforcements with special sandwich materials can still allow a much lighter boat. Since gelcoat is heavy, many Kevlar hulls are covered with a thin but clear gelcoat layer that shows the gold color of the fabric while still protecting against ultraviolet light. Kevlar can be difficult to repair once damaged, and a lamination made with too little resin (easy to do with this material) may leak if the gelcoat is cracked.

After curing in the molds, the hull and deck parts are removed and then joined and seamed together. Some builders use a plastic extrusion on the outside of this joint, reinforced with fiberglass on the inside. Others prefer to use a fiberglass tape covered with gelcoat on the outside for additional strength. Whatever the method, this joint must be strong and leak free.

Next, the kayak is stood on end to receive an "end-pour" (resin mixed with chopped fibers or glass bubbles) in both bow and stern, which reinforces these critical areas and provides a solid base for installing grab loops and rudder fittings. (Check these carefully, as end-pours cracked from excessive heat buildup during curing are often the source of leaks.) A thicker resin putty is then used to install the cockpit coaming.

Plastic Kayaks

Plastic sea kayaks are cheaper to produce than fiberglass boats (and sell for about 25 to 40 percent less). Since they require a very large initial investment for the molding equipment, plastic boats tend to be aimed at the mainstream market and less toward specialized uses such as competition. The molding process has some limitations that require more rounded shapes than in some fiberglass kayaks. Developments in plastics and molding techniques promise to someday produce plastic kayaks with the same fine lines as fiberglass kayaks. Plastic boats are usually about 10 to 15 percent heavier than their fiberglass counterparts, but again, developments in plastics have begun to narrow the differences.

Plastic roto-molding construction involves placing plastic powder inside a two-piece aluminum mold, which is then sealed together and rotated at high temperature until the melted plastic coats the inside. After cooling, the mold is separated and the one-piece kayak is removed. Finishing involves installing a keel stiffener in some models (a plastic *pod* surrounding the cockpit does this job in one model) and the seat, hatches, or other fittings.

Either cross-linked or linear polyethylene plastic may be used in roto-molded sea kayaks. Cross-linked plastic has better impact resistance but is more flexible (and hence, needs more support). Linear polyethylene is stiffer and may resist abrasion better; it is also easier to recycle. Though either kind of plastic is very unlikely to be holed or broken, linear polyethylene is easiest to repair by plastic welding. Cross-linked polyethylene melts at a lower temperature than it bonds at, so welding is very difficult.

Blow-molding is another method of manufacturing plastic boats. During this process plastic pellets are fed into a screw-driven extruder that puts extreme pressure on the pellets, making the plastic semimolten. A tube of the plastic is then released from the extruder, and hydraulic rams clamp the two halves of a boat mold tightly over it.

When comparing the two methods, the most noticeable difference is that blow-molded hulls are heavier and thicker. They also are stiffer and do not require internal braces for support.

One of the drawbacks of all polyethylene kayaks is that they will not hold their shape under long-term stress, particularly in hot weather. Care must be taken in storage and transport; they should be well-supported and stored in areas where there is not a lot of heat buildup. Some deformations may be temporary (the shape can recover on its own); others may be permanent, requiring a heat gun for repair, or perhaps not repairable in some instances.

Fig. 3–4. When not in use, this rudder can be rotated onto the rear deck to protect it from damage.

Wooden Kayaks

If the idea of making your own boat sounds appealing, you can purchase do-it-yourself kits from a number of companies. Some kits use thin strips of wood in order to make boats aptly called "strippers," but most consist of marine-grade mahogany plywood covered with fiberglass cloth and epoxy. It will take some time to construct your boat, but the result is an exceptionally light boat that is much less expensive than a prefabricated model.

How much time does it take to build a kayak? It will depend on your woodworking skills and the model you have chosen. Keep in mind that 80 to 100 hours of work is common for a first-time builder. However, "stitch-and-glue" construction has improved wooden boat building by saving time and by yielding a superior boat. Boats made using this process are lighter, faster, and stronger, and applying this process takes far less skill, not requiring any forms or frames.

Hardshell Kayak Options

Bulkheads—internal walls that separate the cockpit area from each end—have become the predominant means of flotation in most sea kayak models. Some builders use fiberglass bulkheads bonded to the boat, but most now use thick ethafoam sheet sealed and secured with adhesive. Truly watertight hatches are the continuing bugaboo of the industry, particularly for large openings.

Rudders are now stock components on the vast majority of hardshell K-1s and K-2s and are an option offered for most others (though a few builders still oppose them along with bulkheads). Though all rudders must cock out of the water when not in use or when grounding (also essential for backing out of a kelp bed), a few designs pivot almost 270 degrees to lie on top of the rear deck (see fig. 3–4). These are preferred by paddlers who use rudders only occasionally, as they stow out of the way and are less susceptible to damage. On the other hand, they require more deck rigging for the cocking lines and take practice to manipulate.

Take-Apart and Folding Kayaks

Though folding kayaks allow worldwide air travel and compact storage, you will pay much more for this kind of boat and will incur extra maintenance not required of the standard hardshell.

One option is the take-apart or "sectional" hardshell kayak. A number of manufacturers have modified their more popular K-1s to take apart in two, three, or even four pieces: bow, stern, and a center that sometimes divides in two. Each section has its own bulkhead, which mates against that of the adjoining one and is secured by bolts. The result is a craft that is just as strong and performs equally to the one-piece model, though is marginally heavier.

Sectional hardshells have not developed a large market. They are significantly more expensive, and they do not store (or travel) nearly as compactly as folding boats. Their rigidity makes them more vulnerable to damage during transport (particularly at the sharp corners where the hull meets the bulkhead). But if performance and storage capacity are your main criteria for a transportable boat, you may prefer a sectional hardshell over a folding kayak.

Folding boats occupy a special niche among touring kayaks, dating to the beginning of the century when they were folded up for rail travel between lakes and rivers in Europe. Military applications for commando and clandestine operations furthered their development. Manufacturers now make them in Germany, Japan, France, the United States, and Canada. Most cost several times as much as hardshells.

Most folding boats are shorter and wider (and more stable) than the average hardshell. The cockpit is usually large and covered with a *spraydeck,* or in some cases, a spraydeck that is

Fig. 3–5. Some folding K-2s offer enough stability for launches such as this.

semipermanently attached to the boat with a smaller sprayskirt worn by the paddler. Many folding kayaks provide a coaming arrangement similar to hardshell boats. The extra stability and large cockpit make the folding boat ideal in tropical waters, as they are cooler and easier to dive in and out of. See figure 3–5.

Folding boats are most commonly of a plywood or aluminum structure covered with a fabric skin. Most have air bladders, or sponsons, along the sides for flotation; inflating them may also serve as the final tightening of the skin during assembly in some models. Several manufacturers have substituted maintenance-free plastic and epoxy-coated aluminum for the traditional wooden framework.

Assembly can be tedious, and a few models require some forcing of parts, especially in cold weather or when the boat has been disassembled for some time. With practice, most models can be assembled in approximately twenty to thirty minutes.

At this writing, folding boats do not include bulkheads and hatches. Gear must be loaded through the cockpit (though some include a way to open the deck for loading), and the internal frames make it difficult to push bagged equipment all the way into the ends. Though many folding boats include some integral flotation, additional buoyancy in the form of gear or flotation bags should be included as for hardshells without bulkheads.

Though a folding boat will allow you the freedom to roam the world, you will give up some hardshell features. Folding boats are perfectly seaworthy but cannot offer the efficiency and performance of the hardshell. They require more care along shore to protect the skin from cuts and abrasion (depending on care, it may eventually need to be replaced). Because the inner structural members take space and block access to the ends, folding boats have somewhat less gear capacity than hardshells. And if the structural members have wooden parts, you will have to varnish them periodically.

Inflatables

In my book *The Coastal Kayaker,* I dismissed inflatables, saying they were best suited for swimming pools. Hawaii resident Audrey Sutherland has forced me to eat my words. This veteran worldwide coastal cruiser has paddled over 4,000 miles in Alaska and British Columbia alone, always solo and always in an inflatable. Her ingenious gear system allows self-sufficient travel for weeks at a time, and she regularly manages 20-mile traveling days.

Sutherland prefers an inflatable for many reasons: it is light (twenty-one to thirty-five pounds for the models she likes), it is portable (she is usually able to check gear and boat on an airplane with no overage charges), it costs from one-tenth to half as much as a hardshell, and it is easy to assemble (five minutes of pumping). See figure 3–6.

Quality inflatables are difficult to puncture and unsinkable when intact. Since they take on less water inside, they are easier to recover from a capsize. Inflatables can be "bounce-landed" through surf and rocks in conditions that would surely damage any other craft.

The range of quality and designs for inflatables is vast. Some are so lacking in durability that pools are indeed their best habitat. Others use a supported material with a fabric layer between the airtight surfaces (usually polyester/PVC or Hypalon/nylon), which is tougher and can take more air pressure (and is less of a problem if the boat is left inflated in the sun). A few models are now specifically made for touring. Being flat bottomed, almost all inflatables are difficult to steer in the wind and require a rudder in usual sea conditions. Most lack decks, and Sutherland adds her own, secured with Velcro along the sides. By their nature, all inflatables are slightly more sluggish than a comparable hardshell boat, but the newer models are surprisingly more rigid than earlier craft. For portability, an inflatable cannot be beat.

The load capacity of an inflatable is definitely more limited than in hardshell or folding boats; gear must be pared to a minimum. Sutherland does that by taking items that will serve at least two functions.

Fig. 3–6. Audrey Sutherland fishes from her inflatable kayak during an Alaskan trip. *(Audrey Sutherland)*

4

Performance and Design

Everyone would like to own the best boat on the market, but no particular design model is universally recognized as being that paragon. Performance in a kayak is a mixture of abilities and characteristics. No one kayak design can give you the best of all of them (in spite of what literature may claim).

For instance, most paddlers would like a boat that is stable, fast, and stays on course, yet is quick to turn, can shed waves and spray to keep you dry, has tracking unaffected by wind, has a lot of room, and is light to carry. Unfortunately, many of these features work against each other. Very stable boats tend to be harder to propel, and good tracking usually works against turning agility. Hence, in choosing a kayak you must settle for a combination of performance features that best meets your needs and then find the boat that most closely matches it.

Picking a combination of performance features requires some boating experience to figure out what sea kayaking should be for you. How a boat will function is difficult to tell merely by looking at it; taking a boat out is always the best way to evaluate it. Of course, all this requires that you have mastery of some basic paddling skills. Start out in a variety of rented or borrowed boats, work on your skills, and evaluate your particular needs and interests in relation to the boat features that can best meet them.

Personal Considerations in Choosing a Boat

Your Shape and Size

A good fit in your boat is essential; it affects your control of it and your comfort in it. Its weight and size affect whether you can get it to and from the water. Matching boat size and shape to the paddler is a topic throughout this chapter.

Skills

Are you (or will you become) proficient at bracing and associated paddling skills? If you have doubts, then perhaps you should consider trading efficiency and agility for stability (and recognize that you will be more dependent on your first ring of defense—avoiding trouble).

Paddling Partner

Do you always travel with the same partner? If so, consider a double (K-2) kayak. There are significant advantages to a double over two singles. It will cost you about a third less than two K-1s of similar construction. You will be able to go farther and faster on the average in most K-2s. If your partner has strength or endurance unequal to yours, your two abilities are averaged by sharing a boat. The stronger paddler in a double kayak can often "carry" a spent companion, whereas the only recourse for two K-1 paddlers in the same condition is towing (not practical in all sea conditions and sometimes humiliating for the "towee"). In rough seas, you may find moral support and mutual confidence in handling a boat together.

But many K-2 paddlers tire of being Siamese twins and of not being able to take the boat out solo with ease. Doubles are also heavier to handle, and most have less storage capacity per person than singles. They require more skill to self-rescue and to Eskimo roll (since both paddlers must coordinate their actions underwater).

Activities with a Kayak

Fishing, photography, or sailing require a stable boat that takes care of you when the paddle is not at hand and when you are not attending to your balance. Though you may like other attributes of narrower and less stable boats, there may be occasions when you miss the security of a more forgiving hull.

If you are competitive or interested in adventure paddling (such as surfing or playing in tide races), you can opt for a boat that optimizes high-speed efficiency or has special design features such as good surfing characteristics.

Where Will You Paddle

Some individuals buy sea kayaks solely to exercise on

protected lake waters; their performance needs are quite different from those of people who usually paddle a rough and windy outer coast. Likewise, a boat used exclusively for day trips does not need the same volume as one that must accommodate gear for extended trips. And, if you are likely to travel to paddling destinations by air, consider a sectional hardshell, folding, or inflatable boat.

Having reviewed your particular boating needs, you must engage in the not-so-simple task of finding a design that best matches your ideal. Sea kayak design is an art rather than a science, and designers and sales people disagree about how boat shapes affect performance. Below are some relationships between design features and boat handling as I understand them and some suggestions for testing boats.

Stability

Though hull shape has some effect on stability, the beam (width) of the kayak and the height of the seat above the bottom are most responsible for it. Hence, only so much can be done to make a narrow boat as stable as a wider one. Single-seat kayaks range between about 20 and 26 inches in beam and doubles between 28 and 36; this seemingly minor range makes an enormous difference in the characteristics of each boat.

Seat height in relation to the water level affects how much the paddler's center of gravity shifts with a given degree of tipping. Seats in most sea kayaks are located very close to the boat's bottom to maximize stability. A higher seat may be desirable for other reasons, particularly comfort and better arm clearance for paddling in deep hulls (though a shallower cockpit would be a better choice if the latter is a problem). Canoes used for sea cruising have a characteristically higher seat, though the legs are extended forward as in kayak seating. These are usually wider to compensate in stability.

Though the overall width dictates stability limitations, hull shapes and length have some effects. Boats with *rocker* (a curved bottom profile from bow to stern when the boat is viewed from the side) are somewhat more stable than those with a straight keel profile, because the center section sits lower in the water and in turn lowers the seat height. For the same reason, a heavy person sitting in a shorter boat may find it more stable than a longer one of the same width (a lighter person might not feel as much difference). All kayaks become more stable when properly loaded with gear, because it lowers the overall center of gravity, and the laden boat and its paddler sit deeper. Regardless of loading, a longer boat is inherently more stable than a shorter one of the same width, as is one with fuller ends.

Some boats have *flare;* they are much wider at their beamiest point (usually several inches above the waterline) than at their waterline. The amount of flare affects stability at varying degrees of heel (tipping).

Flared hulls, which have a narrower waterline, typically have less resistance to minor amounts of heel. The degree of resistance to minor amounts of heel is called *initial stability.* Boats with low initial stability have a somewhat precarious or tippy feel, which a new kayaker might find disconcerting. But most of these boats increasingly resist tipping farther as the hull above the normal waterline enters the water. This resistance to increased amounts of heel is called *secondary stability.* Boats with little flare and a waterline nearly as wide as the overall beam (usually a quite flat bottom also) have high initial and secondary stability. Round-hulled boats fall somewhere in between, with moderate or low initial and secondary stability.

For casual paddling in smooth water, the widest, least-flared flat-bottomed boat would seem preferable. But there are other dimensions to sea kayaking. Many paddlers prefer a narrower, flared hull because it is easier to edge or lean for turning; it takes very little weight shift to bring the boat over on its side enough to help with sweeping turns (described in the paddling and maneuvering chapters). And, the strong secondary stability of a flared hull provides a "cushion" of resistance, making the boat stable against capsize in the leaned position.

A round hull allows for the same kind of turning maneuverability but has even less secondary stability, which makes it easier to lean radically. (The hull's volume is most important for leaning the boat far onto its side. When on its side, a big, wide hull raises the paddler's lower body above the water and makes the boat very unstable in that position.)

Avoiding excess stability is another reason some paddlers prefer a narrower, flared, or rounded hull. A small paddler may not have the weight to effectively lean a wider flat-bottomed boat, and he might not be able to control it without a rudder in all conditions.

Stability keeps a boat flat on the water surface. But what if the water is not level, as on the side of a wave? A stable boat can be aggravating when paddling parallel to waves (called *beam seas*). In these conditions an unflared, flat-bottomed boat is termed "lively," meaning it rolls abruptly and constantly as the waves pass under it (with tiring consequences for the trunk muscles). A flared hull with less initial stability is less torqued by such beam seas, and a round-hulled kayak hardly at all. This is one of the reasons that British sea kayakers have traditionally opted for rounder and narrower boats for their stormy waters.

At worst, too much stability can result in a capsize! If the wave is steep enough, a flat-bottomed boat can be thrown over on its side, particularly if the paddler is too light to counter with a lean and brace toward the wave or if the kayak is heavily laden.

Paddling an unflared, flat-bottomed boat with a heavy load of gear, I once encountered steep and breaking beam waves that required me to lean and brace as far as I could reach just to keep the boat flat! In my newer boat, which is slightly narrower and more flared, I find that even with heavier loads little lean is required in the same seas.

To test a boat's stability, you need either an effective brace or something to hold onto. You will feel the initial stability immediately, and you may need time to get comfortable with the wobbly feel of a boat with low initial stability. What happens with increased tipping is more interesting. Do you encounter strong resistance at a certain degree of heel, or does it continue to build more gradually and then diminish slowly as a capsize becomes imminent? If you are a small paddler, there is a simple way to test if the boat is too big for you to keep stable by leaning into steep waves: can you tip it over in flat water? If the result is no, or only with an effort, look for something smaller.

Efficiency and Speed

The relationships between "efficiency" (ease of paddling to maintain a pace) and "speed" (how fast you can go) are complex. It is important to understand that the ease with which a kayak can be propelled at normal cruising speed may have little relation to how fast it *could go* if paddled hard by a strong paddler. For instance, kayak model A may go slightly faster than model B at an average paddler's normal cruising pace, but B could be driven faster than A by the strong paddler in a race. Thus, a boat that is designed to go fastest with maximum energy output might actually be slower when paddled at most people's comfortable paddling rates. Adding the weight of camping gear may slow down one model more than another at normal cruising output. Reasons for these relationships have to do with the boat's resistance to moving through the water at different speeds.

Resistance is affected by different factors depending on speed. Kayak speeds have a somewhat hypothetical limitation called *hull speed*. Hull speed is partly a function of the boat's waterline length. Hence, longer boats have a theoretically higher maximum speed potential, assuming that the paddler has the strength to push the hull to that limit. As one approaches this hull speed, the kayak begins to plane (to lift out of the water by the force of sliding over it). Exceeding hull speed takes much more energy than a paddler can deliver, though kayaks may approach it when surfing down wave faces. Long surf skis attain their great speeds in ocean races by approaching their hull speeds periodically on ocean swells; their hulls are shaped for planing efficiency.

For normal cruising, the average paddler propels a sea kayak at speeds far below the hull speed, regardless of waterline length. In this speed range (three to four knots), efficiency is affected by friction against the wetted surface area and resistance through turbulence and wave creation. At cruising speeds, wave-creation resistance is about as significant as skin friction, but the former becomes many times more important when the speed increases another knot. Rounder hulls have the least wetted surface area. Fullness at the ends affects turbulence. A sharply tapered bow and stern below the waterline (called *fine entry* or *exit*) are considered best by some designers.

Comparing speeds of an average K-2 to a K-1 (20 and 17 feet long, respectively) provides an interesting example of energy output and speed in different hulls. Paddling each one solo, the longer K-2 would be much slower, because the paddler does not have the energy needed to drive it. But with two paddlers, the K-2 will go faster than the K-1, because the paddlers' combined energy is sufficient to push the hull at its best speed, and the wetted surface per unit of paddling energy is least. Hence, many paddlers choose a K-2 for covering long distances, and K-2s usually finish races in less time.

Primarily because of reduced wetted surface, a shorter K-1 might actually be faster than a longer one for a paddler who is not particularly strong or not willing to paddle hard, even though the longer one *could* go faster if pushed hard. But the longer one might be the better choice for carrying a heavy load of camping gear, since the shorter boat would sit so deeply when laden as to become inefficient. This and added stowage capacity are the primary reasons that longer boats are chosen for expeditions.

Where the volume is placed along the hull also affects efficiency, though these effects are difficult to pinpoint. Rockered hulls (deeper volume in the center, higher in the ends) tend to be a bit slower than boats with straighter keels. Most sea kayaks use a *Swede-form* hull, which is considered more efficient. The Swede-form hull has more volume aft of the midpoint (a few, called *fish-form,* have the reverse distribution and perform well enough). In smooth water, the shape *at and below the waterline* is what counts; whereas a view of the hull from above shows the shape at the widest point well above the waterline. This buoyancy above the waterline does become important in rough water. Suffice to say that all kayaks become harder to move as the water gets rougher.

Because the subtle differences in efficiency are difficult to detect, the best way to test a boat is by comparing it with another. With a companion, try out different kayak designs and switch off frequently, especially if sea conditions change.

Tracking and Turning

The better a boat tracks (stays on a straight-line course), the more difficult it is to steer to a new heading. Kayaks that turn very easily often wander slightly to one side with each paddle stroke, thus reducing efficiency. Of course, a rudder can overcome the steering problem in any design (though perhaps inefficiently), but each kayak should be examined for a balance between tracking and turning with the rudder (if there is one) cocked out of the water. Rudders do break, so be sure that you can handle the boat comfortably without it.

The amount of rocker in the keel affects the turning/tracking relationship. Boats with little rocker (a straight keel) turn slowly. A V-shaped bottom enhances tracking, especially if it is carried toward the ends, and can improve the tracking of boats with a fair amount of rocker. The deeper the V, the better the tracking and (as a side effect) the less the initial stability. A fish-form hull tends to track a bit better than a Swede-form hull.

Weight distribution of the paddler and gear affect the hull's end-to-end *trim,* and a poorly trimmed boat may be inefficient or difficult to steer. A few designs have cockpits located slightly too far forward with respect to the center of buoyancy, making the boats *yaw*—initiate unintended turns that are hard to correct. To check for this, paddle ahead at cruising speed and then rest, watching for turns in either direction (many boats will start gentle turns as they slow). Of course, using the rudder or fixing the trim by placing weight aft of you will correct such problems.

All boats are easier to turn with sweep strokes when they are edged or leaned to one side, because the underwater hull shape changes. Tipping drives the central part of the hull's side down into the water, creating a hull with more rocker and lifting the keel ends out of the water slightly. A few kayaks will initiate the turn on their own (without sweep strokes) when edged away from the desired direction of turn. This is called a *carved* turn, as opposed to the edged turn, which is initiated by the paddle stroke. To test this, paddle ahead to cruising speed, stop paddling, and observe whether the boat turns away from the direction you lean it. If it does, then lean the other way and see if it stops the turn. Only a few have this handy ability.

Carved turns are caused partly by a hand chine (a sharp corner just below the waterline) in the hull. A chine on a fairly wide stern is particularly important for carving; it acts like a curved keel that turns the boat when the hull is edged (though the angle of the stern itself can generate turning force when leaned by creating different resistances on each side). In rudderless kayaks, this turning ability can be used to counteract wind or wave forces pushing you to one side by leaning the hull toward them. It is handy for countering broaches (turning sideways to waves) in following seas by leaning into the wave.

One of the most pervasive problems in rudderless boats is the tendency to turn upwind or (less commonly) downwind. Such *weather-cocking* occurs because the center of the boat's mass in the water does not match its center of wind resistance. Many designers try to keep the ends of the boat low to reduce the windage and to concentrate the wind resistance at the center where it will have the least effect on steering. Boats with high ends have difficulty balancing wind and water forces because these change with both wind and boat speeds. A few designs try to adjust for this by using a sliding seat, which allows the paddler to balance the trim against the wind's effects.

Wave Handling

Kayak design can directly affect the way a boat handles waves. The object is to stay on course through waves and ride them efficiently, comfortably, and dryly. Head seas—paddling into wind and waves—are the most common wave conditions. They often get the paddler the wettest because of the spray blown back or the waves that run back along the deck in bigger seas.

Knifing and Lifting Bows

Designers have two approaches to head seas: the knifing bow and the lifting bow.

The *knifing bow* is made to slice cleanly through a wave without throwing spray. The deck is peaked to shed water immediately instead of carrying it back. Such bows are an advantage because they also can be low and thus reduce windage.

Other kayak designers prefer a *lifting bow,* which helps the kayak climb over waves rather than going through them. Such bows depend on *reserve buoyancy,* extra volume in the bow area above the waterline that provides lift as the bow begins to bury in a wave. Some kayaks use flared and peaked bows to achieve this reserve; others use an overhanging bow for the same effect.

Rocker in the hull is also important for lifting bows, as it concentrates buoyancy deeper in the water at the midpoint of the hull. With a rockered hull the stern can sink down when the bow tries to lift, allowing the hull to conform to the sea surface easily. A boat with little rocker is much more resistant to this fore-and-aft pitching. Make a comparison by raising and pushing down on the bows of two different boats with paddlers in the cockpit. The rockered boat's bow should be easier to move up and down. It will follow wave surfaces well if it has good reserve buoyancy in the bow.

It is difficult to determine which of the two bow designs is the more efficient. Any force that either displaces water (knifing) or changes the direction of the boat (lifting) is bound to detract from forward progress. Perhaps the worst is a compromise design that does neither well. To minimize the inertial effects of a lifting bow or the deep plunging of a knifing bow, concentrate your load toward the midpoint of your boat as much as possible.

On the Pacific Coast kelp strands are a potential problem for low bows. When the bow goes through a wave, even at normal cruising speeds, it might dive under several long fire-hose-size pieces of bull kelp that could end up across your lap before the boat can be stopped. In rough seas, the weight of the kelp can make you vulnerable to a capsize. Every kayak should be able to back up through kelp. This maneuver is not possible if the boat's rudder or skeg does not cock clear of the water or if the stern slopes forward.

Deck Shape

How wet the paddler gets when the bow encounters waves relates to how well the bow sheds water and to how it throws spray. A bow that goes through a wave may transmit water back to you along the deck. Solutions are a V-shaped (peaked) deck to shed the water or a bow that keeps water off the deck more readily (usually a flatter deck with higher edges at the forward part of the hull). If the waves get big enough, no bow will keep you dry. Features on the foredeck, including raised hatches, fittings, or items stowed on deck, can generate a great deal of spray by tossing even slight flows along the deck into the air to be caught by the wind.

Hull Shape

The detrimental effects of too much stability in beam seas have already been discussed. Given a good sense of balance and paddling skill, a narrower, deeper-set hull (with a rounded or V-shaped bottom) will have a smoother ride parallel to the waves. A deep-set hull is also less vulnerable to being blown downwind than a flat-bottomed hull, which can skim sideways more easily.

Running downwind in waves gives most sea kayaks the worst trouble, with the exception of those designed for surfing (the wave or surf ski). Plenty of rocker makes for best handling in this direction, as the bow is less likely to bury when the boat is poised on the front of a wave. Because the surface between the back of one wave and the front of another is curved, boats with little rocker cannot derive flotation in the center without digging one or both ends in deeply. Without this stability the boat is likely to *broach*, or turn parallel to the wave, in spite of efforts by the paddler to keep it straight (broaching is discussed in "Paddling in Wind and Waves"). Hence, boats with much more rocker, such as white-water kayaks, are preferred for surfing.

Personal Fit

Some kayak models are either too big or too small for your body. A forward area that is too cramped for your feet and favorite footgear will always give you problems. You may not like a cockpit size too short to lift your knees, because it makes entry and exit more difficult. If you are small, a boat with a wide and deep cockpit may require a long paddle to reach the water comfortably without hitting the sides (and this paddle length may be inefficient for you). And your elbows may rub the deck or coaming uncomfortably. Of course, a small person can pad the cockpit to fit, within limits. This might mean adding a foam cushion, which raises you enough to keep from hitting your elbows while you paddle but diminishes your stability. Instead, consider a smaller boat. (Some manufacturers can custom-build boats with a lower deck for smaller people.)

When you sit in a kayak, check for firm but comfortable contact at buttocks, lower back (seat back), hips (sides of the seat), knees and thighs (under the outside of the deck or special thigh braces), and balls of the feet (on the properly adjusted footbraces). Inability to make secure contact at any of these places will limit the boat's performance for you, though padding at sides and knees can make a proper fit. A long cockpit does not preclude good bracing with the knees; use the undersides of the deck just to the outside of the coaming. Some kayaks have specially molded decks in this area to improve secure knee bracing.

Discomfort, particularly from the seat, will probably not manifest itself until an hour or more into an outing, so give it time. Be alert for numbness in your legs (usually due to a seat front edge that is too low for even support of the upper thighs) or poor support for your lower back. Does the hull shape force you to twist your feet and knees outward in an uncomfortable position?

Double Kayak (K-2) Design Features

Almost all K-2s come equipped with a rudder, and many are difficult to keep on course without one, because paddlers must coordinate leans and sweeps for effective course control of a long and unwieldy hull (19 to 21 feet). Because the rudder is integral to most designs, many K-2s emphasize tracking ability with a largely unrockered hull.

Some K-2 cockpits are spaced just far enough apart for the aft paddler's legs; others in long K-2s are more distant. A widely spaced cockpit arrangement allows for independent paddle cadences without clashing. Most K-2 paddlers in boats with closer cockpits, however, have no problem with clashing, and they prefer being close enough to pass things back and forth between cockpits. Some designers claim that close cockpits have other advantages. For example, closer cockpits concentrate the load toward the midpoint and thus aid riding over head seas.

Widely spaced cockpits also allow the addition of a center hole that can be used for children, dogs, or bulky loads and increase storage capacity by concentrating it in the widest part of the hull. Some designs have bulkheads separating this area from both cockpits to provide a third area of flotation (the compartments at bow and stern provide minimal buoyancy by themselves in most K-2s).

Suggested Reading

Hutchinson, Derek. *Derek Hutchinson's Guide to Expedition Kayaking on Sea and Open Water.* Third Edition. Old Saybrook, CT: The Globe Pequot Press, 1995. The British perspective.

Stuhaug, Dennis. *Kayaking Made Easy.* Second Edition. Old Saybrook, CT: The Globe Pequot Press, 1998. The American perspective.

5

Basic Gear

Fig. 5–1. These are only a few of the accessories available for sea kayaking. *Top (left to right):* two sizes of dry storage bags, sprayskirt, life vest. *Center left:* sea sock, with bilge pump and VHF radio in waterproof bag on top. *Center right:* Chart case. *Lower (left to right):* paddle with leash, float for self-rescue, cart. *Bottom:* buoyancy bag (this one will not contain gear).

As you start out in sea kayaking you will quickly discover that purchasing a boat is only a fraction of your total outfitting cost. At this writing, the *basic* items essential to the operation of a kayak add about 20 percent to the cost of a new K-1 kayak. More sophisticated navigational and emergency signaling equipment can add much more. It may be better to economize on the cost of the kayak (buying a used one or cutting options) than to scrimp on the quality of essential gear.

The items described in this chapter are essential, regardless of where you go paddling. "Additional Accessories" presents optional equipment to consider, depending on what you intend to do with your kayak. Some of the items described in both chapters are shown in figure 5–1.

Paddles

Buying a good paddle may reward you in the long run. Sea touring paddles come in a wide range of styles, materials, and prices. The differences in paddles may appear subtle at first but will become more obvious throughout the countless thousands of strokes in your paddling career. Preferences for paddles are subtle and somewhat subjective, so rent a few models for at least part of a day's outing before making a purchase.

Feathered Blades

Feathered paddle blades are set at roughly right angles to each other. They are used by twisting the shaft with one hand to present each blade to the water while the opposite blade slices horizontally through the air. Feathered blades are also distinguished by which hand does the twisting: either right-hand or left-hand control. (They are not interchangeable because each blade has a front and a back face.) Some paddles also have slightly oval shafts in the grip area to help orient the blade position as you shift feathering positions.

Feathered blades reduce the wind resistance (particularly in head winds) of the horizontal blade that is in the air. There are also slight mechanical advantages of the feathered paddling motion. However, feathered paddles have a reputation for causing arm and wrist problems (popularly referred to as tendonitis) due to the feathering motion, and for a time many paddlers opted for unfeathered paddles. Paddling style can help eliminate much of that problem (see "Paddling"). A compromise blade feathering (such as forty-five degrees) can lessen the wrist movement and associated problems, except for the undesirable side effects of one blade diving in head winds while the other rises. Hence, most feathered paddles are now set to about eighty degrees for least wrist twist without side effects.

Unfeathered paddles have a few other advantages. They are easier to control in side winds, as the upper blade does not tend to lift the way horizontal feathered blades do. Going downwind, there may be a slight advantage from the unfeathered upper blade catching the wind (though minimal, since that blade is moving forward during the opposite one's paddling stroke).

All in all, feathered paddles have the edge in popularity. The best way to decide this issue for yourself is to try different paddles.

A good way to sidestep the feathered-unfeathered decision is by purchasing a two-piece *breakdown paddle*, which goes together at a center joint. A breakdown paddle can be set to unfeathered or feathered for either right-hand or left-hand control. They also are easier to store and can be stowed in the cockpit of most boats (an advantage for car-top transportation or when you dock somewhere and want to stow everything out of sight under a cockpit cover). The disadvantage is that the center joint is weaker and loosens in time, though it is probably repairable.

I once advocated switching, to suit conditions or mood, between feathered and unfeathered paddling with a breakdown paddle: feathered for upwind and unfeathered for across or downwind. I no longer feel it is a good idea, and now I always paddle feathered. Feathered paddling does not bother my arms, and I find little advantage to unfeathered for downwind paddling (though the side-wind blade lift can be a problem in strong gusts).

The reflex brace is a good reason to avoid switching between feathered and unfeathered paddling (see "Bracing"). For a reflex brace the relative position of your blades must be ingrained in your brain. You will not have time to check if your blades are parallel or perpendicular. It is best to decide on one way and stick with it.

Blade Shape

Some paddle blades are flat; others are curved or spooned. A hollow-shaped power face (the side pulled toward you through the water) grips the water better. Paddles with a ridge down the center reduce flutter or a tendency to slip to one side when the blade is slightly twisted. For fiberglass blades, spooning or ridges help to stiffen the blade and allow less material and weight. Spooned blades make bracing a bit trickier as blade angles must be more precise.

Many blades are asymmetrical in shape. Since blades are placed in the water diagonally and just deep enough to cover them, this asymmetrical outline puts the center of pressure along the centerline to eliminate twisting. The advantage is subtle, but quite striking when you switch from a paddle with asymmetrical blades to a paddle with symmetrical blades.

Paddles with smaller, narrower blades are modeled after traditional native designs; some are quite accurate re-creations, while others are more contemporary. Very long and slender blades are based on Eskimo and Aleut paddles, which were never feathered. Being slender, these blades are less susceptible to head winds. They also have a softer, quieter feeling in the water, and they produce a faster paddling cadence (an important topic discussed below under Paddle Length). Perhaps a bit easier on the arm muscles and joints, these may be the best choice for people prone to arm injuries from paddling.

The narrow-blade paddle has a faster cadence (compared to a wide-bladed paddle of the same length) because the blade slips through the water to some extent as power is applied to it. Acceleration is slower, but once you get going you go just as fast for the same energy output, though paddling faster. The Eskimo-style narrow-blade paddles, however, are produced in a longer length than most wide-blade paddles, and therefore do not produce a noticeably faster cadence.

Bracing and rolls are as feasible with narrow blades, though they take some getting used to. Braces may not be as powerful, and rolls require a quicker motion.

Paddle Length

Eight-foot and seven-and-a-half-foot (about 244 cm) paddles are equally popular, and together represent about 75 percent of those sold. Short paddles (7- or 7¼-foot [about 228 cm]) and long (8½- or 9-foot [about 258 cm]) make up the balance.

There is no universal rule for determining what length paddle you should buy according to your body dimensions. The paddle must be suited to your boat. Wide boats, particularly beamy doubles, require the longest paddles available to allow you to reach the water without hitting the shaft on the deck or requiring you to shift the paddle from side to side. The height of your torso in relation to the depth of the cockpit and deck shape also affect what you need; a short-waisted person in a deep boat requires a longer paddle.

Beyond that, length depends on preferences. Longer paddles help some people in bracing and rolling but hinder others. While paddling in steep seas, a longer paddle may minimize unnerving and potentially upsetting *air strokes*—missing the water with the blade. Though a longer paddle's feathered upper blade can be kept lower to minimize the wind catching it, the wind has less leverage when that happens with a shorter paddle.

The primary issue with paddle length is cadence. Longer paddles act like high gears and shorter ones like low gears. A paddle shorter than 7 feet will likely produce a cadence too fast for comfort at a four-knot cruising speed. Long paddles produce muscle strain, as with trying to ride a bicycle uphill in high gear. And just as bicyclists aim for "spinning" (keeping up a good cadence) to avoid knee damage, cruising kayakers should maintain their stroke speed to protect their arms, especially in upwind paddling when slower boat speed results in slower cadence. As a result, the trend has been toward shorter paddles or narrower blades.

Paddle Weight, Flexibility, and Feel

Though a few paddling experts prefer heavier paddles for their inertia, most agree that lighter is better. New (and some costlier) materials—plastic, fiberglass, graphite, carbon fiber, Kevlar—make for both lighter and stronger paddles than the traditional wooden ones.

Paddles can be made of fiberglass, carbon fiber, wood, or polypropylene, and each has its advantages. Fiberglass is flexible, durable, and is priced moderately. Fiberglass paddle blades glide well through the water since they are thin. Carbon fiber is lighter and a little more durable than fiberglass, but is not as flexible. Paddles made of wood are flexible and are the most pleasing to the eye. One benefit of wood paddles is that their shafts feel warmer in cold weather; however, they do require some maintenance. For an economy-priced paddle that is stiff, durable, and performs well, you might select fiberglass-reinforced polypropylene.

The less weight at the ends of the paddle, the better. Because paddles must move rapidly to bring one blade up and the other down between strokes, inertial resistance or *swing weight* affects the energy that is required to change from one side to the other. Hence, lighter blades are a big help (fiberglass are generally lightest and molded plastic heaviest). A shorter paddle has less swing weight than a heavier one that weighs the same overall. To compare swing weights, revolve paddles vertically to simulate the arc and cadence of changing from one side to the other.

Drip Rings

The rubber drip rings on the shaft of the paddle are fairly essential to sea kayaking. They prevent water from running down the shaft onto your hands, and they also make the water drip from the paddle far enough to the sides to miss you. Because white-water kayakers are almost always wet anyhow, they have little use for drip rings. But staying dry is definitely desirable for sea cruising.

Paddle Leash

Losing your paddle is something to avoid at all costs. Though you should train yourself to hang onto the paddle in any situation, whether you are still in your boat or capsized from it, you cannot always count on doing so. A paddle leash connects it to either your wrist or your boat. I prefer the latter. Make it from ³⁄₁₆- to ¼-inch line or elastic cord, or buy the commercial kind made of coiled cord.

For boat attachment, a paddle leash should be secured to the deck forward of the cockpit. Some paddlers prefer a long leash, most of which is coiled and secured under the deck lines for normal use, but long enough to allow attachment to the rear deck as a paddle-float outrigger (see "Capsize Recovery Skills"). I like it shorter, with a clip to my deck bungees just ahead of the cockpit. A leash that is long enough to just touch my nose while I am in a normal seating position is sufficient for normal paddling. By keeping the attachment loose enough to slide between my hands on the shaft, it adjusts enough in length to roll and brace. A quick-release buckle at the paddle end allows disconnection for setting up the paddle float or to escape entanglement.

Spare Paddle

Even with a paddle leash, some sort of spare is essential whenever you paddle out of urban waters alone, and every group should have at least one spare. Though paddle breakage is rare with today's strong synthetics, it does happen. Losing a paddle is more likely—whether from a big spring tide at your campsite or from a capsize. To be caught in your boat ten feet from your paddle with twenty knots of wind blowing is complete helplessness. I carry a light compromise spare on my boat. It is a short, single-blade, bent-shaft canoe paddle I can use to get to my dropped paddle or to the nearest shore. I often change off to this paddle in calm conditions, though my standard double-blade is more effective and secure when it gets windy or rough.

Double-blade spare paddles must be a breakdown model and usually are stowed on the rear deck for easy access from the cockpit. Many kayaks now have standard deck rigging for carrying spares. Consider a spare that complements your other paddle, either as a change of pace or for use in certain conditions: perhaps a narrow-blade and wide-blade paddle each the same length, a paddle of a different length, or even a short canoe paddle.

Canoe paddles are sized largely by shaft length: the handle should be at shoulder height with the blade just submerged (about 25 inches for me).

Sprayskirt

Your sprayskirt must fit both your torso and the cockpit coaming, and it must release easily from the latter in case of a capsize. Not all cockpits are the same size or shape, so be sure the sprayskirt is the right size for yours. Poor conformity to the coaming shape results in sag and water puddling on the skirt deck rather than running off. Some types of sprayskirts are adjustable to fit all body sizes, and most neoprene ones are sized for particular waist sizes (a few are adjustable to some extent).

Neoprene sprayskirts are the most expensive and are top-of-the-line. They seal better and leak less, fit more tightly on the deck, and are warmer. Nylon fabric sprayskirts are popular because they are economical, versatile, and cooler in warm weather. Some have a snug-fitting neoprene spraydeck and fabric tunnel. Most fabric sprayskirts have an adjustable tunnel top that can be drawn tightly around your body or left loose for ventilation (one size skirt fits most paddlers, though different coaming sizes are offered). Shoulder straps keep the tunnel high on your torso (without it being tight) to shed spray and keep deck water from running down into your lap. These also allow ventilation in warm weather. These sprayskirts, however, do not seal as tightly for rolling or bracing practice, and you may find the shoulder straps a hassle to deal with. Straps do not work with dry suits or dry tops that have a skirt designed to fit over the sprayskirt tunnel to reduce leaks.

Every sprayskirt should have a *grab loop,* a cord or strap at the front that is pulled to release the skirt from the coaming. Some designs have a grab loop sewn across the top near the front of the cockpit. This makes it easier to find and grab but harder to release, requiring a pull upward and to either side. All work fine with some practice.

Zippered sprayskirts are hard to find. They allow easy access below and safe ventilation without having to remove it from the coaming. The waterproof zippers add substantial cost to an already expensive neoprene sprayskirt, and they can end up leaking if not cared for properly. Without a zipper, ventilation and access still can be achieved by removing the front of the skirt while keeping the rear half in place; quickly rehook it onto the coaming when the need arises.

A small pocket on the front of the tunnel is convenient for carrying small items such as a hiker's compass or a folding knife. But keep in mind that it will be covered with your life jacket, so pockets on the latter are more usable.

Life Vest

Each person is required to carry an approved Personal Flotation Device (PFD) aboard his boat. Approval comes from the U.S. Coast Guard and the Canadian Department of Transport. Inflatable vests and divers' buoyancy compensators are not approved as PFDs for recreational boaters because they require maintenance to stay serviceable; some "hybrids" (part foam flotation and part inflatable) are approved (though they must be *worn*, not just carried).

The terms life jacket and PFD are often used interchangeably. Technically, the life jacket is a USCG Type I PFD, which will float an unconscious person faceup and will provide an adult with at least twenty-two pounds of buoyancy. The vast majority of PFDs sold for kayaking are Type III, which will not necessarily keep you face up and will provide at least fifteen and a half pounds of flotation for adults. The Type III is the most comfortable to wear. Avoid using any kind of PFD as a cushion to sit on, as it will gradually compress the foam and reduce the buoyancy; exposure to prolonged heat will have the same effect.

Many PFDs suitable for canoeing, rafting, or other boating do not fit kayakers because they are too long. Since the PFD is worn over the sprayskirt, it cannot extend down the body below the sprayskirt's tunnel. If it does, it either prevents you from putting the sprayskirt on the boat, or it rides up so that the jacket's shoulders are at your ears, and the sides are pushing into your armpits. PFDs suited to kayaks have flotation that is concentrated at the chest area or allow the lower row of foam ribs to be folded up out of the way of the skirt.

The PFD can also provide hypothermia protection in the water, and for this a snug fit also is important to minimize water circulation under the PFD. The sides of the torso under the arms are particularly vital, as this is an area of primary heat loss. Type I life jackets generally provide better hypothermia protection. (Also see flotation/exposure suits in "Clothing.")

Pay particular attention to underarm comfort. Constriction or excess bulk in this area will result in chafe. Some pullover PFDs concentrate the flotation in the chest area and have little or no flotation in the sides, which allows excellent arm freedom.

Some PFDs have pockets for carrying small items; adding your own pockets or making other modifications to your PFD will void its official approval. Adding a whistle on a short lanyard will not. Reflective tape sewn to the shoulders to increase your night visibility is not likely to get you a citation.

It makes sense to wear the PFD rather than carry it on deck. Do not count on being able to don it while in your cockpit when conditions get rough. Putting on a PFD in the water is a difficult task even in ideal conditions, and the fewer tasks you have to perform after a capsize the better.

Buoyancy Bags

Every kayak must have flotation at *both* ends, provided by bulkheaded compartments, buoyancy bags, or (safest) both, in case the hatches or bulkheads leak. For day trips in boats without bulkheads, simple inflatable air bags work fine. For longer trips, some flotation in the same space where gear is stored is required. Most paddlers choose to rely on their bulkheaded compartments to provide the flotation when the boat is laden with camping gear. In boats without bulkheads, gear can be enclosed in a number of dry storage bags (see "Additional Accessories"). Better still, use buoyancy bags that can be filled with gear and then inflated to fill the entire space. Essentially it is a bag within a bag; you fill it with equipment, seal the opening, position it in the boat, and then inflate the outer bag to fill the space and help hold it in place.

In boats without bulkheads, do not count on inflation to hold either air bags or gear bag in place. There have been a number of incidents in which buoyancy bags have popped out of the ends of swamped sea kayaks. Use a restrainer, such as a length of webbing clipped between tie points glassed inside the hull. (See "Cruising" for information on adding attachment points.)

There have been serious incidents in which kayaks have sunk (and in one case the kayaker died) because buoyancy bags were not inserted for a day trip during a multiday outing. In both cases, the kayaks had dry storage bags that had been left with the gear in camp. Carry some inflatable buoyancy bags if your standard flotation system works only with a large amount of gear.

6

Additional Accessories

Bilge Pump

A pump—electric, or either mounted or handheld and manually operated—is used primarily after a capsize, particularly by a solo paddler who has few other resources for getting the water out.

Compact, lightweight, battery-powered pumps developed for sea kayaks can bail out a boat rapidly and without the dexterity or energy of a paddler who is perhaps somewhat debilitated by hypothermia. They also free the paddler's hands to work on staying upright during bailing. The battery-powered pump is the most expensive alternative, and it requires that you keep the batteries charged (solar cells are available) and adds some fixed weight to the boat.

Deck-mounted pumps are popular on British-style kayaks, but few others. They allow you to pump with one hand and with the sprayskirt in place—handy for intermittent pumping. This would be especially valuable for keeping up with seepage from rough seas (when a few strokes may take care of it) or during extended rolling practice.

Lever-operating pumps, made for larger boats, can move water faster than handheld pumps, but most are quite heavy. The smaller pumps mounted on British-style kayaks will not move water as fast as handheld ones.

Handheld pumps are, by far, the most popular option, largely because they are inexpensive and do not add to the fixed weight of the kayak. Most sold to kayakers are less than 18 inches long, between 1¼ to 2 inches in diameter, and have plastic barrels. Metal pump shaft stiffeners are desirable to prevent breakage and, because most pumps are stored near compass mounts, are made of nonmagnetic aluminum.

Some hand pumps will sink if full from pumping. Add a flotation collar or, better yet, tether the pump to the boat so it cannot float away or down in front of your feet where the only way to retrieve it is by exiting the cockpit. The most popular stowage positions are between the seat and the side of the hull, or secured by bungees either on or just under the forward deck. I prefer a tether just long enough to reach from stowed position to pumping position so as to minimize entanglement problems.

A large sponge is nice for keeping up with sprayskirt leaks or the water that inevitably comes in with your wading footgear. Secure it under or next to the seat.

Sea Sock

The sea sock, a large bag that fits into the cockpit and is fitted over the cockpit coaming, limits the amount of water that can enter the boat outside of the sea sock. You sit in the sock and put your sprayskirt on the coaming over it.

Though sea socks should never replace other means of emergency flotation (buoyancy bags or bulkheads), they increase the boat's buoyancy and greatly reduce the water volume entering the boat in a capsize. For K-2 kayaks, which usually have a fairly low proportion of buoyancy to total volume and can take on an enormous amount of water when swamped, sea socks on *both* cockpits can make the difference for a successful recovery from a capsize. For heavily laden K-1s, a sea sock can make an important addition to what may be quite marginal flotation in the gear stowed in the ends of the boat. For an empty K-1 with average buoyancy in the ends, the use of a sea sock is less critical but will substantially reduce the volume of water taken on in a capsize.

Sea socks take getting used to. They are warm, and they are slippery at the contact points—seat, knees, and feet. You may wish to add some built-up knee bracing of glued-in foam inside the deck to improve security when the sea sock is used. Many people who wear rubber knee boots do not like the way they catch on sea socks, though I do not consider this dangerous from an entrapment standpoint. If you do not like the feel of the sock pressing around you when you get in the boat, pull the front of the sock off the coaming to allow air to escape, then move your legs apart and push out with your hands, thus "inflating" the sock in the cockpit area. Replace the sock on the coaming, and it will retain its inflated shape.

Paddle Float

The paddle float, a bag that fits on the solo kayaker's paddle, makes a stabilizing outrigger for aid in re-entering the boat after a capsize. Other items, such as water containers, can be used (if adapted in advance for this use), but this specialized float is very effective, easy to stow on deck, and relatively inexpensive. If you paddle alone, you should have some outrigger system and be proficient in using it (see "'Wet-Exit' Capsize Recoveries"). If you paddle in groups, then other assisted recoveries are usually more appropriate, and the float is less critical. The paddle float is a handy practical tool—for learning to brace or roll (best for nonsweeping rolls such as the high brace roll).

Compass

Every kayaker should carry a compass on anything beyond a "backyard" trip. Though I have used my compass only a handful of times in a dozen years of paddling, I would have had significant problems without it; I have cut short more than one trip because I left my compass at home. I now carry a compass whenever I paddle.

Fig. 6–1. This marine compass is dismountable and can also be used to take bearings by hand.

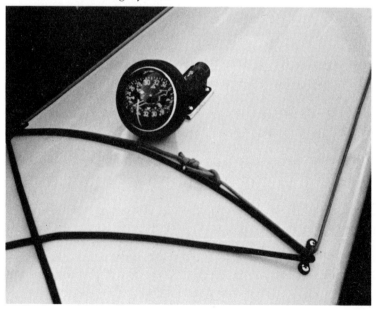

The choices are a small, inexpensive hiker's compass or the bulkier, costly marine compass (see fig. 6–1). The former serves fine, but a marine compass is convenient, easier to use, and generally more useful (see "Nautical Charts and Navigation" for using both types). If mounted permanently, however, the marine compass adds weight to the boat and is vulnerable to damage during boat handling. Some marine compasses can be dismounted from their installed base (or can be mounted on a removable compass mount available from kayak manufacturers or retailers).

As noted in the Nautical Charts and Navigation chapter, no correction for declination between true and magnetic north is needed if you are using marine charts for navigation, so neither type needs a declination offset device.

Since the marine compass usually is fixed to the boat and has a centrally rotating card printed with large numbers, steering a given course with it is easier than with a hiker's compass. The latter requires an extra step to adjust the compass to steer a particular course. With the marine compass always available for use, one can take bearings on a feature in clear visibility to aid navigation simply by pointing the boat at it. Doing the same with a hiker's compass requires that you cease paddling and adjust the compass.

A hiker's compass is nearly as accurate in calm waters for course steering, though in rough seas the boat's movement may cause the needle to hang up occasionally. (The marine compass is gimballed to accommodate boat movement.) The most useful hiker's compass has a clear plastic card with a straight edge used to align it with the boat's bow for course steering. The bezel on which the numbers are written should rotate to allow setting courses and taking bearings on land features.

Global Positioning System

The Global Positioning System (GPS) is an electronic device that can pinpoint your position anywhere on earth with amazing accuracy. It is small, battery-operated, and fits in the palm of your hand, and because of this many boaters find it useful when they tire of nautical charts and compass. A GPS is especially useful for jaunts along wilderness coastlines and during open crossings.

The GPS's receiver captures signals that are sent by satellites, digests this information, and gives you a reading of your current longitude and latitude on the LCD screen. There are different choices of GPS that vary in accuracy and cost, but a number of inexpensive, reliable models are now available. Keep in mind that a compass should always be carried as a backup—like all electronic devices, a GPS can fail.

Dry Storage Bags

As their name suggests, dry storage bags are used primarily to keep things dry; they provide flotation only if the volume inside weighs less than the same volume of water. They cannot be inflated to fill spaces. Nonetheless, putting as much gear as possible into dry bags (whether it needs wetting protection or not) will add to buoyancy if swamped. For instance, a set of pots and pans will provide excellent buoyancy if inside a dry bag, but none if they are loose and filled with water.

Bags constructed of thicker material last longer, as abrasion from sliding bags in and out of the boat will quickly wear through lighter ones. Most bags seal with a roll-down top and secure by bending the roll and clipping the ends together. They are quite waterproof *when* the top is rolled down at least four times and then bent away from the direction of rolling for clipping. Hence, do not put too much in a bag (filling it no more than two thirds) so there is room left for sealing.

If you are inclined to make your own dry bags, try heavy trash compactor bags. To seal, twist the bag shut, tie it off with a piece of line, double this twisted part over, and tie it off again with the same line. Put the compactor bag inside a cloth stuff sack for abrasive protection. Compactor bags last well, but periodically inspect them by putting the bag on over your head by a bright light to look for holes. Patch them with duct tape.

A spectrum of commercially made dry bag sizes is handy for storing different kinds of items. The smallest size makes a good day bag, which can be placed between the knees to hold things that might be wanted while paddling—sunglasses, compass, small binoculars or camera, sunscreen, snacks. Intermediate sizes are handy for sleeping bags, spare clothes, or food. The largest sizes are not very handy for stowage except in larger K-2s. In general, the larger the bags you use, the less you can get into your boat because you cannot fill all the spaces effectively. I do carry a large, empty dry bag with shoulder straps for transporting and storing gear on shore. (For more on stowage, see "Cruising.")

Unless you carry a waterproof diver's camera or (less expensive) a water-resistant one, your camera should be carried in a waterproof bag or box when not in use. A stowage unit small enough to be accessible while paddling yet large enough for additional lenses is a problem. You also will want to be able to get your feet in and out of the boat while the camera bag or box stays in place. Waterproof camera bags fit most compactly and can hold a camera with a zoom lens, but they are a bit slow and cumbersome to open and close. A variety of plastic waterproof boxes are suitable, as well as either plastic or traditional steel ammunition cans, and all have the advantage of easy opening and closure. Bigger ones may take too much space in cockpits of the average K-1 for foot and leg access.

Visual Distress Signals

Though kayakers are required to carry distress signals only while paddling at night, carrying them at any time is prudent. There are many options, which vary in price and effectiveness under different circumstances. These and their use are discussed in "Emergency Signaling."

VHF Radio

Handheld radios are generally the most effective emergency signaling device (and have other important uses, too). Marine VHF radios (radios that use Very High Frequency channels dedicated to marine users) have a range of 5 to 10 miles at sea level; Citizens Band radios (CBs) have a bit more. Once the Coast Guard has received your call for help (either directly via their own powerful antennas or indirectly through another vessel), their rescue helicopters can home in on your signal as long as you keep pushing the transmit button periodically.

The big question, of course, is who is listening, and VHFs offer a greater likelihood than CBs. Both the U.S. and the Canadian Coast Guard monitor VHF frequencies and may monitor CB channels, too, though with a lower priority. Many vessels, particularly commercial ones, monitor VHF, but few use CBs consistently. Though a CB is cheaper, a VHF is probably more effective and useful for more than dire emergencies.

Almost all marine VHF transceivers (radios that both transmit and receive) also have at least four weather channels, which receive forecasts and local condition reports broadcast continuously by either the Canadian Coast Guard or the National Oceanic and Atmospheric Administration (NOAA) in the United States. These radios will pick up these channels in marginal conditions when the cheaper weather radios will not. Also, the weather radios usually do not include WX4, also called Channel 21B (161.65 MHz), which is used for weather broadcasts in many locations in Canada. (See "Tides, Currents, and Weather" for use of marine weather radio reports.)

Marine VHF radios can be used to make telephone calls to anywhere in the world via marine operators. In British Columbia, the system of radio repeater stations is so extensive that even hand-held radios can reach a marine operator from almost anywhere! Technically, marine VHFs are to be used only from boats, so calling from camp is not legal. Monitoring your VHF radio puts you in touch with the surrounding marine world. There are separate channels for commercial fishing boats, pleasures boats, towboats, marine traffic management, telephone calls, and many others.

A few accessories are important for your VHF. The most important is a special plastic "baggie" that will keep splashes off your radio and will keep it afloat. This allows use even after a capsize. The bags include an internal finger glove for operating the controls without compromising waterproofness. The seams of these baggies, however, are prone to split, particularly in cold weather.

For long trips, a special battery pack for AA batteries is a good replacement for the standard rechargeable one. I often go through three sets or so in a month's cruising, though it depends on the amount of transmitting I do. Batteries will receive for many hours, but transmit for less than half an hour.

A telescoping "five-eighths-wave" (technical description of the best length for marine frequencies) antenna will about double the range over the short, flexible "rubber duckie" antenna that comes with the set (though this big antenna will not fit inside the plastic bag). Changing your position may be the most effective way to get through. If you must make contact, climbing a few feet above the water and then walking around to find the right spot can make an amazing difference.

In the United States, handheld VHF radios to be used in kayaks must be licensed with the Federal Communications Commission. You will need to get a station license, specified for use as a portable ship station. This is good for five years and requires an application fee. If you are going to be paddling in Canada or other foreign waters, you must also get a restricted operator license, which also carries a fee but lasts your lifetime. No tests are involved. For residents of Canada, licenses are obtained from the Department of Communications and require both a fee and a test.

Emergency Position Indicating Radio Beacon (EPIRB)

The advantage of EPIRBs over VHF radios for emergency signaling is that they transmit a special beep continuously and automatically for up to twenty-four hours once activated; they are waterproof, and they cost less. They can do only that, however; they will not receive nor transmit voice. (EPIRBs are discussed further in "Emergency Signaling.") As with VHF radios, EPIRBs must be licensed.

Roof Racks

Though a boat can be tied directly to a vehicle with padding from life vests and carpet scraps, neither the boat nor car will benefit from it, and the time required to tie it securely will probably send you shopping for a rack. Straight bar racks, which work well for canoes and skiffs that are carried upside down on their gunwales, need customized padding to secure kayaks tightly but without caving in the hull over the rack (called "oil canning"). Racks designed specifically for kayaks provide excellent support but may be expensive. Types and use are described further in "Transporting, Storing, and Maintaining."

Kites and Sails

You certainly do not need a kite or a sail, but they are nice for traveling and just having fun on breezy days. Both kites and sails have advantages and disadvantages depending on the circumstances. Kinds and uses of sails and kites are included in "Cruising."

Carts

Sometimes called "dollies," these little devices are handy whenever you need to transport a kayak any distance by hand, especially with a load of gear inside. These are not suitable for towing behind a car, though they might be used behind a bicycle. In the Pacific Northwest—Washington, British Columbia, Alaska— carts are almost indispensable for the kayaker traveling as a foot passenger on a ferry. With a cart the kayaker can use this extensive sea route network without dependence on cars. Also, carts are handy if you live within walking distance of a paddling launch site, particularly if parking is limited. And sometimes the parking is a long way from the water.

End-mounted carts (see fig. 9–1), which usually attach to the stern about a foot from the end, are lighter, simpler, and cheaper than center-mounted ones on which the boat is roughly balanced. They are small and light enough to carry in your boat without disassembly and are handy for wide beaches at low tide or whenever you cannot park near your launch point. They require, however, that you carry about half the weight of the boat and whatever gear is in it. Center-mounted carts make carrying a heavy boat and load easy. Most carts disassemble or collapse for storage in the boat or on deck. The wheels are the bulkiest item to store, so the trade off in size is between bulk and the ability to traverse rough or soft ground. Wheels with bearings roll more easily but cannot be submerged in salt water (nice to be able to do when launching a loaded boat). Pneumatic tires are very helpful on rocky shores or corrugated sand flats but require that you carry a pump. The less expensive carts use plastic-hub semipneumatic wheels.

7

Clothing

Clothing's primary role is to keep you comfortably warm and dry as you paddle along. It should also adjust for varying weather conditions. And, because the water is much colder than the air (sometimes by as much as thirty degrees) in all but tropical situations, clothing that has insulative value in the water, should you capsize, could be equally important.

In warm-weather cold-water environments, finding a suit of clothes that provides reasonable immersion protection without cooking you while you paddle is an almost impossible task, and a decision has to be made about the acceptable degree of discomfort while paddling versus the degree of risk of capsize, which might force you to swim. If your brace and roll are very strong, you may judge this risk as minimal and dress more for the air than for the water. Or, as has happened to a few paddlers, one dunking in cold water may convince you always to wear full immersion protection, no matter how hot the weather. As a compromise, you might adjust your clothes toward immersion protection during times of more significant risk, such as exposed crossings.

The task of choosing comfortable clothes for paddling is difficult enough. Kayaks are warm, as you are covered from upper torso downward. If you feel comfortable standing around before you get in, chances are you will be too hot when you get into your boat.

The presence or absence of wind greatly affects the comfort level of kayaking clothes, and you must take off or add garments accordingly in the cockpit (they must be ones that can be changed easily in conjunction with sprayskirt and life jacket). Taking off clothing when winds die is as important as adding when it breezes up, because too much clothing usually results in perspiration and damp inner layers. And, clothes are likely to get damp or wet in one place or another during an outing due to splashes, spray, drips, slips while wading in the shallows, or perspiration. Sleeves are particularly susceptible to repeated wetting.

Just as for other active outdoor sports, layering clothes provides the best way to adapt to changing conditions.

The Inner Layer

Depending on the weather, the inner layer may be long or short underwear. One of the functions of this layer is to transport moisture away from the skin (driven by body heat) to the next clothing layer. There it can evaporate without making you feel cold because of the inner layer's insulation or, if an outer vapor barrier (such as a paddle jacket or dry suit) prevents evaporation, at least condense moisture on garments not in contact with your skin. Cotton performs the inner layer function poorly because its absorbent fibers hold large amounts of moisture next to the skin, giving that lingering cold and clammy feeling from the evaporation that occurs in direct proximity to the body.

Synthetics with impermeable fibers—polypropylene or polyester—are the best choice. These feel warmer than cotton when damp because they transport moisture away from the body. Because they do not absorb moisture, they dry much faster. Polyester is somewhat safer for hot washing and dryers.

Long underwear made from synthetics under nylon shorts is all that some paddlers wear on the lower body in moderate weather. Protected by the boat's dead air space, the lower body is least susceptible to changes from wind and air temperature. One consideration for long underwear bottoms is what happens to them when you wade. Options are to slide them up your leg (if loose enough), wear footgear (see page 60) that keeps them dry, or live with them wet to midcalf. The synthetics will not feel as damp and will dry quickly.

The Intermediate Layer

If you decide (perhaps for reasons of fashion) that long underwear bottoms are not appropriate outer wear, replace them or augment them with ordinary pants. Again cotton is a poor choice because it absorbs so much and dries so slowly. Instead, use a blend of polyester and cotton (most work pants are). Unless you wear rubber knee boots (see Footwear, page 60) that you can tuck the pants into, they should be loose enough to roll to knee level for wading. Unless you take the time to roll the pants back down again after you board, you also paddle with bare legs. Whether this is a problem for you depends on the weather and even more on your temperament. Some waterproof paddling pants have tight dry-suit–type cuffs that keep water out while wading (but keep in mind that they could be difficult in an immersion situation by trapping in water that got in through the waist unless they can be loosened to let it out).

In warm weather, a light-colored shirt with long sleeves will be needed for sun protection, especially in sunny places such as Baja. The fabrics made for solar protection are much more effective than cotton. In warm climates where clothing dries quickly, a cotton shirt may be fine. If it is worn as the outer layer in windy weather, however, it will soon become amazingly stiff with accumulated salts from absorbed and evaporated spray. (This happens to some degree with any garment repeatedly exposed to salt spray or drips.) Rinsing in fresh water will relieve the problem, as will laundering in sea soap and salt water (and wringing well) if you are short on fresh water.

Either wool or pile are good choices for shirts in cool weather. If you wear long underwear under an outer shell, the underwear sleeves may provide enough arm warmth, and a short-sleeve shirt or pile vest may be a sufficient intermediate layer. In cold weather, another insulating intermediate layer may be needed—probably a pile jacket and pants. These also will be very welcome in camp on shore. Looser weaves are best, as they hold less water and dry more quickly. But they also pass air more readily, so outer shell clothing becomes more important for retaining dead air space within the pile.

The Outer Shell Layer

The paddle jacket is the primary defense against both wind and water. It is worn often, even in warm and sunny but windy conditions, to prevent spray accumulating in the inner layers. Being impervious to both wind and water, this shell layer also leads to excess heat and moisture buildup, particularly when you are paddling hard. Some paddling jackets have fairly effective ventilation via zippers or flaps. Paddling action pumps air through the arms and upper trunk. Underarm zippers further improve air circulation.

Until recently, breathable fabrics, such as Gore-Tex, have not proven effective in the saltwater environment, as salt seemed to clog the pores, preventing ventilation and also reducing waterproofness. Newer fabrics do work if they are washed periodically to restore breathability.

Jackets or rain gear with open cuffs are horrible in waves—the lower arm of the paddling stroke can easily catch a wave crest, turning the open cuff into a scoop that quickly transfers a cupful to the elbow (where it remains until you do a draw stroke and drain it to the underarm).

The ideal paddling jacket should also resist seepage as much as possible during immersion. Unfortunately, the better the jacket's ventilation potential (particularly underarm zippers), the less the watertightness, even if buttoned up. The waist should have a toggled drawstring. Neoprene cuffs with an adjustable flap seal quite well if you pay attention to adjusting them tightly. Neoprene at the neck does not do quite as well as it will strangle you before sealing completely. Fabric closures at either neck or cuffs are not as effective. The worst jacket is one that lets water in and then traps it. I once bailed out after a practice capsize wearing a paddle jacket. By the time I had my paddle float rigged and was ready to reboard, my jacket had collected so much water that I had to open the bottom and cuffs to let it out; the weight made re-entry very difficult. The more effective garment for rolling or swimming is a dry top, designed like a dry suit (see "Immersion Protection" below). Ventilation is zero in these suits, and you will find it quite uncomfortable in hot weather unless you periodically immerse yourself to cool off.

Pay special attention to fit in purchasing a paddling jacket. It should be no looser than needed to accommodate whatever you wear under it (to trap as little water as possible), yet roomy enough to easily get on and off in the cockpit and to prevent binding and chafing, particularly under the arms. Too much bulk or constriction under the arms becomes *very* uncomfortable. Jackets will wear out first under the arms and at the contact point with the seat back.

Many paddling jackets have a hood—nice for short rain showers and wonderful in a cold following wind. A few have tight neoprene seals around the face for head immersion protection. The hood must not restrict visibility and must move freely when you turn your head.

Hats and Gloves

The head is a very important part of the body's temperature control system, and it is an easy one to adjust simply by putting on

Fig. 7–1. Neoprene pogies.

or taking off hats. Brimmed hats are very important for sun protection. Unless the hat fits tightly, add a chin string and toggle to keep it on in wind. Many paddlers in the Northwest like the Gore-Tex rain hats made in this area for use on cooler sunny or rainy days. The fisherman's sou'wester hat is perfect for foul weather (especially if you dislike hoods), and it can be turned long-brim-forward as a sun hat. For possible capsizes (or practice rolls) in cold water, a neoprene hood offers vital hypothermia protection (half of the heat loss in water occurs through your head), whether you wear a wet or dry suit or not.

Your hands may need protection from the elements, too. Several specialized paddling gloves are on the market, offering either abrasion or thermal protection. Dishwashing or cannery-workers' gloves may also serve. Pogies (see fig. 7–1) are mitts that seal over the paddle shaft and allow direct hand contact with the paddle, yet provide all the wetting and wind protection that you probably will need. I prefer the stiff neoprene ones as you can shove your hands into the cuffs without binding them. If your hands are really prone to cold, accessory pile liners are available for the fabric pogies.

Immersion Protection

In addition to general paddling safety, wet and dry suits allow practice in real conditions. In the Pacific Northwest, water warm enough to risk a dump is found only in lakes during the summer, where conditions with sufficient challenge are rare during that season. A wet suit or dry suit lets you do saltwater wave, surf, or tiderace paddling at almost any time of year.

I have met a few sea kayakers who carry *survival suits*—thick neoprene "body bags" with integral mitts, boots, and hoods designed for commercial vessel crews. Though cold-water survival time in these is almost indefinite, they are impossible to paddle in, very difficult to don in the water, bulky to stow, and quite expensive. And if you do get back into your boat following a capsize, taking it off again in order to paddle may cause another one. A few other paddlers wear *Mustang suits*—synthetic, fleece-filled suits that provide both flotation and hypothermia protection. These are also expensive, hot, and bulky to paddle in.

Many sea kayakers choose light wet suits as a compromise between paddling and in-the-water comfort. A ⅛- to ³⁄₁₆-inch-thick farmer John suit (lacks arms) worn over polypropylene underwear and under pile clothing or a shell provides good weather protection and fairly good immersion insulation. Heavier wet suits (¼-inch thick) are probably too stiff for paddling comfort, and full suits (with sleeves) are just too restrictive (though suits that combine fabric and neoprene on arms and shoulders have been introduced for paddling). Wet suits depend on a good fit to control water circulation within them (too many clothes underneath add to circulation), and by themselves they are chilly out of the water. Wet suits may be worn with a synthetic shirt under for chafe protection and usually a paddling jacket or (better) a dry top over.

The trend is toward dry suits, with dozens of suitable models now on the market, including separate dry tops and full suits (see fig. 7–2). Dry suits are comfortable, usually warmer than wet suits, and let you wear most of your usual clothing under them. (I once wore my street clothes under a borrowed dry suit for a pool rolling practice session that I had intended to simply observe, and then went off to a meeting afterward.) Dry suits depend on internal clothing for insulation, though the neoprene suits provide some of their own.

Dry is a relative description; most suits leak a little and perspiration will dampen your clothes in time as there is no ventilation in dry suits. Seals at the neck, ankles, and wrists depend on latex cuffs, which are quite fragile (they can be replaced). Lubricating the gasket seals can greatly extend their life. Avoid jewelry and watches, and spread the cuff with the hands before pulling it on. For men, small leaks at the neck are usually inevitable between the tendons in the Adam's apple area. The potential danger of dry suits is a large (though unlikely) leak that lets the suit

Fig. 7–2. Dry suit.

fill. Hence, never wear a suit with a broken zipper or ripped cuff. Large leaks definitely present problems, though my own experiments with holed dry suits showed that they do not totally fill with water and that kayak re-entries can still be done if you open or break the ankle seals to let the water out as you reboard the boat.

Entry to dry suits is via a zipper on the chest or back. Rear-entry zippers usually require an assistant to open or close them, and solo paddlers choose a front-entry suit. Most suits use waterproof zippers (probably the most expensive element of the suit, so take care of it with an occasional waxing). One uses a standard zipper covered with a roll-down flap for a seal (these are more apt to leak). Two-piece suits have a complex seal system at the waist, which usually is effective, and are less expensive (the waterproof zippers of one-piece suits are the most expensive element).

Semidry suits have nonwaterproof zippers and can be opened at the neck and the cuffs for ventilation while paddling. These are less expensive than dry suits. Though they do not keep the water out, semidry suits offer minimal immersion protection by limiting the exchange of body-warmed water within the suit. Ankle cuffs that can be loosened enable you to drain the water while reboarding following a capsize.

The latest development in paddling outerwear garments is made from a "thermal stretch" fabric that has a waterproof coating outside and soft, lightweight fleece inside. These flexible jackets can be worn with nothing underneath, since the fleece is against your skin.

Footwear

If you have loyal paddling friends who will launch you and retrieve you at your destination, you can wear almost anything on your feet. Running shoes are very comfortable; one friend paddles in the off season in down booties. But more typically, you will need to wade, sometimes in smelly mud, over sharp barnacles or sea urchins or even human detritus such as broken bottles.

Neoprene booties are the most popular footwear for cold water wading. (See fig. 7–3.) These are made in a variety of weights, some with light soles and others with thicker soles and side stiffening. Though the thermal protection of most booties is excellent, the lighter ones have inadequate soles and side protection for pebbles, barnacles, or feet jammed between beach boulders. The heavier ones are much better but still uncomfortable on occasion, particularly when carrying a heavy load over uneven ground.

While paddling, you may not care for the soggy feel of booties and bare lower legs. Though the soles of most models are adequate for pressure on the foot pedals, the heels in light booties may get sore from pressing against the hull; some padding may be desirable if you wear this sort of footgear.

Another option is neoprene socks worn with sandals. This combination gives better sole protection and a bit more to the sides due to the overhang of the sandals. I like their paddling comfort too, as the rear strap of the sandal keeps my heel off the hull surface. They are versatile, too—wear them in camp with wool socks or without on warmer days. The sandals should have a thick sole, a forward strap that goes all the way over the toes (rather than between the big toe and the others), and heel straps, all closed by either buckles or Velcro.

A small but annoying problem of sandals is that they pick up gravel and sand while you wade, which must be cleared before boarding to avoid transferring it to the bilge. One friend partial to sandals embarks by removing each sandal before the foot goes into the boat, setting it on the deck, and then putting it on again once settled in the cockpit.

Knee-high rubber boots (alias, Wellingtons, gumboots, or Sitka slippers) are my favorite whenever the weather is cool. I find

Fig. 7–3. Alternative footgear *(left to right):* neoprene socks, sandals, light and heavier neoprene booties, rubber knee boots.

them clear winners for warmth, foot protection, and paddling comfort. Fitted to wear with felt inner soles (have a spare dry pair of soles on hand) and wool socks, they allow me to wade and walk ashore with impunity. I also like being able to tuck my pants into them, wear long underwear, and (except for the occasional "going in over the top") keep them dry.

Rubber boots, particularly larger men's sizes, will not fit in many single kayaks. The test is whether the heels can touch together without the toes rubbing on the hull when you move the foot pedals (this can be adjusted somewhat by lengthening the footbraces and extending your toes a bit). The footroom problem is worst for tall people as most hulls tend to taper forward. Fortunately, my high-volume kayak has plenty of room for my size-ten boots without too much leg torquing or constriction, and though my heels do get sore after a few hours, my feet are more comfortable in knee boots than booties or sandals while paddling.

Some paddlers shun rubber boots for fear of having to swim in them and not being able to get them off. To find out, I tried it and had no trouble staying afloat in them either with or without a life jacket. Knee boots, however, do dramatically reduce kicking effectiveness, making it hard to swim even a short distance. Also, I found it very difficult to hoist myself onto my inverted boat, which depends on a strong kick to help you up. The clunkiness and weight of waterlogged boots do make a solo or assisted re-entry more difficult, but not impossible.

I had no difficulty removing rubber boots in the water (though the suction of wet socks makes them difficult to remove on land). Audrey Sutherland, who performed a successful self-rescue amidst icebergs in Alaska, claims that her problem was *keeping them on* in the water. She tucked her legs up under her until she righted her boat, and then tossed the boots in before reboarding. (Keep in mind that the thermal protection of submerged boots is poor, and zero when removed!)

Some paddlers claim that athlete's foot is unavoidable in either rubber boots or neoprene booties. Whether you get it depends on the climate, your personal habits, and your constitution. A daily change of socks, fresh felt inner soles for my rubber boots when the others get damp, and a can of medicated foot powder keep mine under control. If athlete's foot does persist for you, the bared foot alternatives (sandals or really bare) are probably your best recourse.

Many Baja paddlers wear sandals. There, as elsewhere in

more tropical waters, foot protection from sea urchins and coral is important (in northern Pacific Northwest waters urchins are deep enough to be a problem for wading only at extreme low tides). With sandals, heel straps are important to ensure that the heels do not slip off on uneven footing.

If cold water is not a problem, you might prefer paddling barefoot or in wool socks. This style is probably best suited to more "civilized" launch sites where clean, short wades lack natural or man-made hazards to your feet. You will also want to add some pads in your boat. Heel pads can be made from 2-inch foam with cavities scooped out for your heels (a Surform rasp works well) and permanently stuck in place. One aficionado also claims that the security of such heel pads will greatly help your Eskimo roll. You might also want to pad the footbraces and sides of the hull to protect your bare feet.

8

Transporting, Storing, and Maintaining Equipment

Fig. 8–1. Two ways to car-top kayaks: *right,* edge stacked; *left,* in saddles.

Racks

More kayaks are damaged during car-top transportation than during paddling. Poorly tied boats fly off, sometimes with the racks, with disastrous consequences to the kayak and worse, to other vehicles. Boats tightly tied but improperly supported on the rack are cracked or distorted. Hence, the right transportation equipment and techniques for securing your boat are equally important.

Roof racks for car-top transportation may be designed exclusively for kayaks, designed as a system for canoes, bicycles, or skis, or adapted from general purpose "bar" racks. The rack must fit your car's doors: either guttered doors or gutterless "aircraft" doors. A number of racks are now made for pickup trucks, with a superstructure that assembles over the bed of the truck and is often easily collapsible.

Boats may be carried flat in saddles or stacked on their sides using a vertical stacking bar (see fig. 8–1), which can be added to racks. If carried flat, the saddles support the hull and allow it to be tied tightly without damage. Edge stackers are popular with white-water kayakers because a half-dozen boats can be carried on one vehicle. Because sea K-1s are about 24 inches wide and 15 inches deep, three can be stacked on edge on most cars, compared to two carried flat. Weight capacity of the rack usually prohibits carrying more. Boats carried in saddles are easier to load and tie unassisted.

Unmodified straight bar or board racks are inadequate for transporting kayaks. Unlike canoes or skiffs, which can be carried upside down on their gunwales, kayak hulls or decks are almost certain to "oil can" (cave in flat) when tied securely over the bar. Stacking on edge is less stressful because the shape and seaming material in the sides of the kayak give it much more strength. Thus, if you want to use your bar or board rack, you must modify it with a do-it-yourself saddle or stacking bar.

Board racks are the least expensive if you are willing to do some work yourself. Purchase them as brackets to mount to guttered car tops and use standard two-by-four lumber as the crossbar. Construct saddles using foam or from plywood edged with carpet or foam pipe insulation. Ethafoam blocks, 3 or 4 inches thick, are probably the easiest to carve into saddles using a bread knife. Secure them to the rack with contact cement backed up by a deeply countersunk screw (use a large washer to prevent the foam from pulling out). However you build the saddle, aim for as even support around the hull as possible.

Loading

The fear of not being able to load and unload a kayak from a car alone discourages some independent-minded would-be sea kayakers from buying a boat. There are ways to do it by yourself, depending on the design of your car and the racks. The "over-the-back" method is easiest—sliding the boat onto the car from the

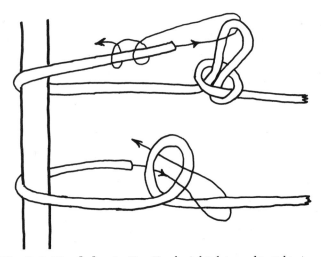

Fig. 8–2. Handy knots. *Top:* Trucker's hitch is used to tighten and secure a line. Tie loop in line, pass free end around attachment point, and back through loop. Pull down to tension line and tie off with half hitches. *Bottom:* The bowline is useful for tying decklines to grab loops or wherever a secure, slip-free loop is needed.

rear. This requires secure racks that can take the forward force of the sliding boat and a sliding or rolling surface on the rear rack (special pads are available as an accessory for some racks) for the boat to move on. Carpet taped or sewn onto the rack tube between the saddles works well. You may need to loosen the rear saddles so that they can be rotated forward and down out of the way during the loading and unloading operation.

To load, place the boat on the ground behind the car, bow next to the car and far enough forward to reach the rack securely when that end is lifted up. Be sure that the rudder is cocked and clear of obstructions. A piece of carpet will protect the end on the ground from abrasion. Next, lift the bow onto the rack. Then move to the stern, lift and slide forward.

The "over-the-side" approach works best with cars that have a square back (such as a pickup canopy) with the rack too far forward for the boat to touch it when one end is on the ground behind the car. This approach needs enough space beside the car to position the boat about 6 to 8 feet away. Lift the bow on to the front saddle (rotating the outer saddle forward and down may be helpful). The distance between boat and car prevents the boat from resting on the car rather than the rack in this half-up position. Now raise the stern and put it in the rear saddle. The boat will probably need to be slid forward to its proper position.

If you lack the space next to your car to position the boat a distance from the car, a rack extension may help. This is a 2-foot piece of tubing (1¼-inch Schedule 40 PVC plastic plumbing pipe works well on many racks) that fits on the end of the forward rack bar and is tied on to prevent slipping off during loading.

Securing the kayak should include tying it to the rack and to the bumpers. Though rubber bungees with hooks are convenient for the boat-to-rack connection, they are not as secure as rope or webbing ties. Tie off the end toward the center of the car to the rack with a bowline before loading. Lead the line over the boat and secure it to the outer end of the rack with the simplified trucker's hitch (see fig. 8–2); pull tightly, but avoid stressing the hull from too much tension.

Tie both bow and stern to the bumpers, leading the line to the bumper on the opposite side of the vehicle to prevent lateral movement should the rack or your central tie-down points fail. Use strong but light line with as few doublings as possible to retain good driving visibility (you can be cited for ropes that obscure your vision). Watch for chafe points at the bumpers, and avoid tying around sharp corners that could wear through the rope as it vibrates in the wind. Special bumper hooks are available for just this purpose. The same trucker's hitch works well for tying off. Again, avoid too much downward tension, which could overload the rack and even change a plastic kayak's rocker!

On a stack-loading rack, lines are tied off to the rack just behind the post (on the opposite side from the boat's position), led over the hull, looped around the post above the hull, and back around the boat to the rack where it is finished off with half hitches or a trucker's hitch. Placing the hull against the post is preferable to leaning the generally weaker deck against it. This position also allows access to hatches and cockpits of the outer boats on the vehicle. Watch for oil-canning against the post from too much tension.

Stacking posts usually are positioned to make room for one boat on one side and two on the other. On the two-boat side, secure the inner boat as above and then lead another line from the top of the post over both boats and down to a point on the rack between the two boats so as to generate inward pull on the outer boat. Be sure to secure the ends of *all* boats to the bumpers. Be careful to avoid overtightening the inward-pulling bumper lines, which can crush the deck of the middle boat. Also be watchful for peaked coamings and deck-mounted compasses that are easily damaged from pressing against other boats.

The accumulation of rainwater in boats may cause them to come loose from vehicles, or it may damage the hulls and bulkheads during braking, so use a cockpit cover. Also, avoid carrying anything other than light gear (paddles, PFDs, etc.) in the boat.

To secure your kayak from theft, lock it to the rack with a bicycle lock cable (also available specially for kayak racks). Secure the lock around the side of the seat (if the seat is hung from the cockpit coaming) and around the rack, if the latter is locked to the car. Otherwise, use a cable with swaged loops at both ends (available as a rack accessory or made up at a marine rigging shop) a bit longer than needed to reach from stern to rear bumper. Feed one end through the stern grab-loop fastening (the metal part not the rope), if it allows, otherwise consider installing a stainless U-bolt through the deck just forward of the stern end-pour (the solid material in the bow and the stern of fiberglass boats). Loop the cable through its own loop to make it fast to the deck fastening. Lock the other end to the bumper.

Home Storage

Long-term home storage should provide security, weathering protection, and support against hull distortion. The security system for the roof rack should be adaptable to a storage location if the boat cannot be locked up.

All kinds of kayaks suffer to varying degrees from prolonged exposure to ultraviolet light, moisture, and temperature changes. This is most severe for the fabric of folding and inflatable kayaks; hence, they should not be stored outdoors.

Fiberglass degrades, too, though slowly. Moisture that penetrates into seams and air bubbles or fibers within the laminate may cause damage in repeated freezing and thawing. Though gelcoat is designed to protect the laminate from ultraviolet light, it does oxidize from prolonged exposure to sunlight and weather. This is particularly true for dark colors, which have a high pigment content in relation to resin and weather more easily. If you store your boat outdoors, protect it from sun and precipitation with a cover.

Boats should be supported to prevent dents in the hull and gradual changes in hull shape due to weight distribution. Both folding and plastic boats are particularly vulnerable to the latter (though folding hulls always flex to some extent). Plastic boats should *never* be hung by their grab loops for long periods of time, as they may take on significantly increased rocker. Heat buildup in the storage area is particularly dangerous for plastic boats, as it increases the chances of distortion.

Hardshell boats are best supported where they have sharp corners, such as the V toward the ends of the keel, or in saddles conforming to the hull shape. One or more middle supports also help to relieve the stress on the ends and prevent hull sag, particularly for plastic boats. I prefer a box pattern, with two longitudinal two-by-fours attached to the end supports and set far enough apart to just contact the edges of the bilge in the middle of the boat.

Maintenance

Salt water can degrade boats and fabric gear, and both benefit from a fresh water rinse after each sea outing. The metal parts of your kayak are vulnerable to corrosion, though most manufacturers are careful not to mix metals that result in electrolysis corrosion (such as aluminum in contact with brass) and use materials that are least corrosible (stainless steel and 6061 aluminum stand up very well). Removing the accumulated salt by rinsing with a garden hose retards the corrosion process during storage.

Wax protects the fiberglass hull and deck from the elements and from abrasion and ultraviolet light. Use any wax designed for fiberglass cars or boats. Some cleaner waxes have a fine abrasive additive to remove surface dirt and oxidization simultaneously. Severely oxidized gelcoats can be restored with fiberglass rubbing compound. Do not use this more frequently than absolutely necessary, as it removes some of the gelcoat layer.

Folding boat hulls may require special surface protection, and regular car waxes may make some hull fabrics brittle and susceptible to cracking. Use what the manufacturer recommends.

Fabrics, particularly coated ones, degrade in salt water and can be severely damaged by mildew. Though synthetic fabrics do not rot, the coatings are attacked by fungi and may separate from the fabric, allowing water to pass though. Rinse the insides of dry suits and paddle jackets carefully to remove body salts. All such garments, sprayskirts, sea socks, and life vests last longest if stored hanging in a cool, dry place where they can ventilate. Dry suit latex cuffs should be treated with compound sold for that use to preserve their elasticity and strength. Lubricate the waterproof zipper with a special wax available at dive shops, and avoid storing with a fold across the zipper.

Repairs

On all but the shortest outings, carry a repair kit that can deal with various damage to your craft and gear in at least a temporary fashion (long enough to get back to the launch site safely). For a day trip in fairly civilized waters, the kit can be quite rudimentary. For an expedition in wild or remote country, the kit must repair most conceivable damage permanently enough to complete the trip. In the checklist at the end of the book, I have suggested component items to consider, depending on your outings.

Duct tape is the first line of defense for leaks, cracks, or breaks in your boat and most equipment. It is strong, watertight, and sticks well if applied to a warm, dry surface. It can splint a broken paddle joint or patch almost any hull damage well enough to last the day. It will not survive grounding or scraping. Duct tapes vary greatly in adhesive qualities and strength. Many kayak retailers carry conveniently small rolls of the good-quality tape.

In cloudy, cold, or rainy conditions, you may have to innovate to get duct tape to stick well. Drying the surface can be done by careful application of heat from a lighter, candle, camp stove, nearby fire, or even clean, warmed pebbles covered loosely with a cloth.

A good second line of defense for fiberglass boats is epoxy putty. It bonds fairly well (even to wet surfaces), cures in cool temperatures (though slowly), and resists abrasion quite well. It is useful for patching holes and short cracks as long as the two edges do not flex independently. Epoxy putty is excellent for field repair of fiberglass keel ends that have worn through and are leaking from repeated grounding. It can secure a cockpit coaming that has broken loose from the hull of a fiberglass boat or repair a delaminating paddle blade tip. Using it is easy; just be sure to get the right proportions before mixing. Be sure to use disposable rubber gloves when applying the epoxy.

Avoid using silicone sealer for repairs or for bedding fittings. Silicone may penetrate into the laminate and prevent a sound fiberglass repair in the area later.

On a long trip, fairly permanent fiberglass hull or deck repairs may be necessary. These can be done in the field from a small repair kit, but the procedure is tedious and difficult in cool weather. If possible, use other temporary remedies until you get home.

A fiberglass laminate repair kit consists of resin, catalyst, fabric, sandpaper, a disposable container for mixing (or count on finding something on the beach), a brush, and acetone for clean up (optional if you use a disposable brush and keep excess resin off things). Either polyester, vinylester, or epoxy resin can be used (if the boat is epoxy, the repair resin must be also). Vinylester may adhere better to a repair then polyester, but either is quite strong if the surface is prepared well. Half a pint should be sufficient. Resin has a shelf life of up to one year. Discard any that is crystallized or lumpy.

For fabric, use either light cloth or unwoven mat. Most mat is not compatible with epoxy resin, which lacks the styrene needed to dissolve the bonding agent in the mat and let it "relax." Cloth is marginally stronger than mat, but also develops pinholes as the resin cures (this can be overcome by spreading plastic wrap over the repaired surface and pressing all of the air out before the resin cures).

To repair a hole or crack in your hull, first dry the area well using some of the options described earlier. If you can reach it, do your repair on the inside to avoid the difficulty of fairing the surface and replacing the gelcoat on the outside. For major damage, do both inside and outside. Sand the surface thoroughly to a radius at least an inch beyond the damage. For an outside repair, the patch will adhere best if the gelcoat is completely sanded through. Clean the area with a little acetone if you have it.

Mix the resin and catalyst carefully and thoroughly: use a ratio of one part catalyst to fifty parts polyester or vinylester resin in weather below sixty degrees, or one to one hundred or less in warmer weather (epoxies have their own proportions). Catalyst in your eye can blind you, so pour and mix carefully, tilting the mixing container away from you slightly as you mix. (Should the worst happen, flush the eye copiously with water *immediately*.)

Both cloth and mat are best cut with scissors (the ones on a Swiss army knife work fine). Cut three pieces: one slightly bigger than the damage, another about one inch larger in all dimensions, and yet another about two inches larger. Next, paint the area with resin, stick on the smallest piece, and tap more resin into it with the tip of the brush until all of the air bubbles are out. Repeat with the successively larger pieces of fabric.

To aid curing in cool weather, you might try external heat.

First tape plastic wrap smoothly over the repair to protect it and retain heat, then apply warm (not hot) pebbles in a plastic bag; or use a small clear plastic "tent" taped over a repair to provide a greenhouse effect to trap sunlight or heat from a campfire. I have used a zip-lock bag in this way for paddle blade and joint repairs in cool sunlight several times.

In the field, there is little to be done for damage to a plastic boat beyond duct tape. When you return from your trip, take it to a *skilled* plastic welder. Many recreational vehicle shops, who do plastic welding for holding tanks, may be able to fix your boat. Check with boat retailers or manufacturers for a local reference. Both linear and cross-linked polyethylene can be hot-air welded, but the latter requires special adaptations to the equipment and more skill.

The most common breakage occurs in rudder cables, which usually fray and break at the connection to the rudder. (This may be preventable by ensuring that the connector is lubricated and swivels freely to prevent the cable from bending back and forth each time the rudder moves.) Carry a spare cable in your repair kit. If you lack a spare, you may be able to fix it by shortening and reattaching the cable at the rudder. Good cutters are needed to make a clean end on the cable, and you must have sufficient adjustment at the footbrace to compensate for the reduced cable length.

9

Launching and Landing

Kayaks are the least demanding of boats when it comes to choosing a launch site; almost anything short of a vertical seawall will work. Public access to water is usually plentiful though sometimes obscure. In urbanized waterways, look under bridges or at public street ends where roadways dead-end at the water's edge. Tidelands at these locations often also are public. Parking may be more difficult.

A public launching ramp, where there is a large parking lot, is often a good place to start a trip (see fig.9–1), but avoid stalls

Fig. 9–1. Public boat ramps often provide the easiest access to the water and the closest parking.

reserved for cars and trailers. To reduce congestion at the ramp and conflicts with other boaters, carry your kayak well out onto the dock (if any) alongside the ramp before launching or use the center of wide ramps since trailered boats prefer the areas next to the dock. If you have equipment to load, do it in an out-of-the-way spot.

Ironically, sea kayakers' activities *on shore* produce the most complaints, primarily from private landowners whose property is used for launching without permission. Though some may not mind an occasional request when there are no nearby alternatives, shoreline dwellers in popular kayaking destinations get overloaded and fed up with people who want to use their beach as a launch site. First check marinas or waterfront businesses and be willing to pay a fee to launch and park at them.

Carrying a kayak from a vehicle to the water's edge is easy with a helper—just use the grab hooks that every boat should have on both ends. Some have toggles on the grab loops, which make the grip much more comfortable. If not, pick up a short length of stick to make a temporary one if you have any distance to carry .

Carrying a boat alone is a more difficult task. Start by lightening the boat by removing everything possible. Even a few small items, such as a marine compass, will make a difference. You want the boat balanced at the cockpit when it is picked up by the coam-

Fig. 9–2. Shoulder carry. The hand inside the cockpit helps to balance by grasping the coaming and pushing up inside. The device on the forward deck is a removable folding mast step for my sail. (*Audrey Sutherland*)

ing. Carrying the boat at waist level is usually easiest for short distances, gripping the coaming with both hands and holding the boat across your front, at waist level, if there is enough space to the sides. Because you cannot see your feet, the footing must be easy.

The shoulder carry (see fig. 9–2) is more effective for longer distances. It allows you to see where to plant your feet, and it frees one arm for balancing as long as there is little wind to blow the boat around. Not every paddler, however, can handle boats in this position. The hardest part is getting the kayak from waist level to carrying position, which requires hoisting it up and ducking under to catch it on the shoulder in a single motion. The coaming rests on your shoulder just behind the boat's balance point, giving it a little positive weight in the bow. Counteract this with the same arm and hand by holding the coaming or pushing up inside the boat forward of the cockpit. This two-point contact gives good balance and directional stability. The other hand can help support and control the kayak or be used for balance if the terrain is difficult.

Fitting Yourself to the Kayak

If you are using a boat for the first time, the foot pedals must be adjusted to fit you, a job best done on dry land. Whether the boat has a rudder or not, the pedals need to be positioned so that both of your knees are lightly touching the underside of the deck, while the balls of your feet are resting at a relaxed ankle angle on the pedals. If there is a rudder, it must be pointing straight back when your legs feel evenly positioned.

Some foot pedals can be adjusted while seated in the cockpit; others require getting out to see what needs to be done down there. If there is a rudder, start before you get in by sliding the pedals to move the rudder to centered position. Adjust the pedals to the right length without moving the rudder cables, and the rudder will be centered when your feet are even with each other. Rudder cables usually are cut to the same length on both sides, which makes centering the rudder easier by matching the adjustment position on both footbraces. Then seat yourself to verify the pedal length and that the rudder is tracking straight when your feet are in a neutral position.

Next, put on your sprayskirt followed by the life vest. The sprayskirt should be worn so that the bottom of the tunnel (the tube that fits your torso) is even with your lowest ribs, and the top is just under your armpits. Adjust the shoulder straps, if any, to hold it at that height. The tunnel of a sprayskirt that has no shoulder straps should be snug around your torso. If unfamiliar with the boat or new at sea kayaking, make a dry run at putting the sprayskirt on the cockpit before launching.

To fit the sprayskirt to the boat when seated in it, start by putting the skirt over the coaming *behind you,* beginning at the middle and working out to the sides until about even with your back. Next, lean forward and hook the front of the skirt over the point of the coaming. If the rear slips off, then it was not attached for a sufficient distance around your sides, and it needs to be done again before attaching the front. Finally, make sure that the skirt is hooked over the coaming along both sides.

Entry and Exit at Calm Beaches

The paddle-brace entry is suited for any low or gently sloping shoreline where waves are not large enough to splash into the cockpit while you board. It involves entering the boat in shallow water, so be prepared to wade in water about 6 inches deep.

Set the boat in the shallows parallel to the water's edge. To avoid a spill during boarding, all but the widest kayaks will need to be steadied, using a paddle support, during the boarding process. The paddle bridges between the back of the cockpit coaming and the beach (rock or low dock), stabilizing the boat and anchoring it in position while you get in. (See fig. 9–3.)

Lay the paddle just behind the back of the cockpit coaming, with the offshore blade just clear of the cockpit and the other blade lying flat on some dry land or slightly submerged feature that it is not likely to slip off. Stand facing forward between the boat and shore just ahead of the paddle. Squat down and reach behind you with both hands. The hand over the boat should grip the *coaming and paddle shaft* firmly at the center of the boat, with the thumb to the rear and gripping the paddle. The other hand should grip the paddle shaft slightly more than hip-width distance toward shore.

You must keep your weight *equally distributed between both hands* until you finish boarding. With your attention on this weight distribution, sit carefully on the paddle shaft just inside of the hand that grips the coaming, though some weight also should stay on your feet until you are ready to sit in the seat.

Put one foot into the boat as far forward as is comfortable in this position. Put some weight on it and lift the remaining foot. (If you are maintaining your grip on both shaft and coaming, your

Fig. 9–3. Paddle-brace entry. Note the hand grasping the coaming and the paddle shaft and how the weight is centered between the two hands. (*Audrey Sutherland*)

weight distribution, and the paddle blade's position on shore or bottom, the paddle will now be doing an excellent job of providing all the stability you need at this precarious point!) Last, slide down into the seat. If the cockpit is small, you will have to walk and slide both feet forward inside until your legs are straightened enough for your knees to clear the coaming before dropping into the seat.

If you are a particularly husky person, be careful about the weight you place on the hand between boat and shore; more than a few paddles are broken this way. Jointed two-piece paddles are particularly vulnerable. They best survive this ordeal if the joint is positioned near the center of the boat, giving less support on shore but minimizing stress on the joint.

To get out, first remove your sprayskirt and then set up the paddle support (make sure the skirt is not entangled in your grip behind you). After your hands are in position, and your upper body weight is distributed between them, slide up and back until your buttocks are over the paddle shaft, and then step out. If the cockpit is large enough for you to raise your knees while seated, you may prefer to bring your feet back to just ahead of the seat before sliding up and back.

With practice, you will be able to eliminate the paddle brace for entry and exit, particularly in double kayaks, wider singles, or most laden kayaks (the brace is difficult in folding and inflatable

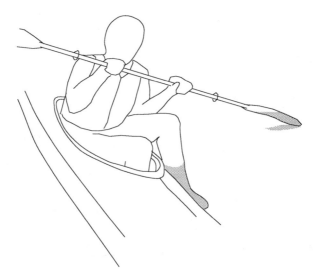

Fig. 9–4. The high-brace entry. The tip of the blade resting in
the shallows provides support while you board.

boats). Laying your paddle aside, grip both sides of the coaming
behind you, keep your weight distributed evenly between them,
and step in as above, quickly and smoothly. This entry is more stable if the boat is gently grounded in the shallows.

I most frequently use a high-brace entry: a quick procedure
that offers ample stability once you have established good balance
in your boat and a solid bracing reflex (see fig. 9–4). It also requires
a cockpit long enough to clear your knees.

Place the boat in enough water to float it with you aboard, and
stand in the shallows next to it. Put one foot in the cockpit, as far
forward as possible. Next, squat down and sit in the seat, retaining
a good proportion of your weight on the foot still in the water to
keep you stable. Hold your paddle in the high brace position and
gently ground one blade on shore or in the shallows. Last, lean
firmly on your brace, using it for stability while you swing your
other leg aboard. With practice, the high-brace entry can be done
in deeper water with the blade supported on the surface, as long as
the last step is done quickly and smoothly.

Entry and Exit from Low Docks

The paddle-brace support (laying the shaft across the back of
your coaming) also works for any surface no higher than the top of

the cockpit coaming, including low floats or docks, swimming pool edges, or swim steps on large powerboats as long as the blade on "shore" makes firm contact. It does not work well on floats with a raised wooden rail used to tie lines (another method is suggested for that situation).

To board your boat from a low dock, the hand position on the paddle and the coaming behind you is the same as before, except that you start by sitting on the dock or pool side just ahead of your paddle with your legs ahead. Again, check for a firm paddle/coaming grip and weight distribution before stepping in with one foot, shifting your rear over to inside the hand that grips the coaming, and continuing as before.

If the dock is a little higher than the top of the kayak or has a raised rail, put your paddle aside and use the following method. This method may be more secure on powerboat swim steps that are too slippery for a secure paddle support.

Sit on the edge and place both feet in the cockpit as far forward as you can reach and centered along the boat's midline. Twist your upper body toward the bow until you face toward the dock, and grip the edge (or rail if there is one) on both sides of you. Ease your buttocks off the edge, keeping the majority of your weight over your hands. Too much weight on your feet at this point will result in the boat moving away and will make a spill likely. While in this suspended position, walk your feet forward until your knees

Fig. 9–5. For the dock entry, keep your weight primarily on your arms until ready to drop into seat.

clear inside the coaming. When your buttocks are in position, drop quickly and smoothly into the seat. (See fig. 9–5.)

This launch is not as difficult as it might seem. To start, have someone hold the boat in position for you. To exit, start with a firm grip on the edge, hands far enough apart for your buttocks to fit between them, and shift your weight to your arms as you raise yourself from the seat.

Entry and Exit from High Docks

Docks more than a few feet high, the sides of larger sail or powerboats, or ladders from very high wharfs make the most precarious launches of all, but it can be done. Some of my most challenging moments have been attempts at a dignified departure from anchored fishing boats where I was invited on board for coffee. Descending their smooth 5-foot-high sides into my tiny, rocking cockpit in cold Alaskan waters took all the adrenaline I could muster.

You will need fairly good arm strength to do it (the ability to do at least one chin-up), as you must suspend yourself from your arms at various heights and pull yourself up by your arms to get out at these places. The key is concentrating your weight on your arms, not your legs, during the transition from dock to seat or vice versa. Relax your arms, and the boat will move off, leaving you hanging in a dire position.

Before starting to get in, place your paddle where it will be within reach from your kayak seat, perhaps with one blade extending over the dock. Grip the edge of the dock, facing toward it as before, and lower yourself until your feet are centered in the bottom of the cockpit. If your cockpit is large enough to allow you to raise and lower your knees while seated, you can now drop straight down into the seat before letting go. If not, you will have to sit on the back deck and work your legs forward while hanging from your arms (probably requiring a lower grip position).

A cockpit large enough to raise your knees is even more helpful for getting out at a high dock. Pull your knees up and place your feet just ahead of your seat. If you can reach the dock's surface, grab it with both hands. If not, put both hands on the sides of the cockpit. Now lean forward, gather yourself, and *spring* upward into a standing position, transferring your weight to the dock via your arms before the boat has a chance to react. If the cockpit is too small for knee withdrawal, you will have to hang from whatever you can reach while working your way out and then pull yourself upright.

Entry and Exit from Rough Water

Launching in breaking waves at a beach is sometimes unavoidable. Unlike real ocean surf (discussed in "Paddling the Outer Coast"), shore break from choppy inland waters usually produces no hazard other than getting doused or, at worst, a capsize alongshore. Beyond the shore break, the choppy waters may be quite manageable, but getting out there without getting soaked can be a challenge.

Usually, it is best to start with the boat perpendicular to the shore—the bow in the water, the cockpit at the water's edge. If the waves are coming onto the beach from one side, aim the boat that way. Get in (no paddle support should be needed here because the boat is grounded) and attach the sprayskirt. In a group, one person should launch the others by pushing them out, bow first, into the waves. Each person should paddle strongly to get out through the shore break as quickly as possible. The last individual uses the procedure below, as would a solo paddler.

After you enter your boat, you will need to "walk" yourself forward using your hands and probably the paddle. If the surface under you is firm, hold the paddle just above the blade and push with the end of the blade while you use your hand on the other

Fig. 9–6. A kayaker in a white-water boat waits for the surge. Here the sand is too soft to allow pushing with a paddle.

side. If the surface is soft sand or mud, the paddle will sink too much; stow it across your lap or with one blade under the deck bungies and push with both hands. Try to time your entry just ahead of a wave's breaking, so that you can catch its surge and backwash and perhaps miss the worst of the next one. (See fig. 9–6.)

On a steep beach, the most difficult part is when you are mostly afloat but the stern is still supported on the beach. This *bridging* situation is very unstable, so watch your balance and keep pushing with both hands (or if the water has become too deep, with just the paddle).

If the slide-in method will not work for you, then the alternative for shore break is to put the boat into the water at the front edge of the wave area (facing into the waves), get in fast (using the high-brace entry), and paddle to get out of the breakers without delay. You are sure to get some water into your open cockpit, but unless the waves are quite big or you delayed too long, this amount should not be too much to bail or sponge out.

Double kayaks usually are easier to launch on rough-water beaches. First, the front paddler gets in and seals up. The stern paddler then pushes the boat out to the point where his cockpit is just clear of getting splashed and puts on the sprayskirt while the front paddler holds the boat's position. Pushing off usually is easy enough, while the front paddler strokes ahead. Landing is the reverse. The front paddler should be able to get ashore without getting wet before pulling the boat up.

To land on a rough-water beach, the choices are to chance getting wet or to mistreat your boat a bit. You could paddle into the shore break and then leap out quickly, though you will probably get wet. Or, you can paddle full speed onto the beach in the hope of sliding high enough to allow a leisurely exit.

A full-speed slide onto a beach makes a dramatic landing, but surely shortens your boat's life. Use this landing judiciously. Sliding onto coarse sand or rough pebbles is very abrasive to gelcoats and folding boat skins. Smooth pebbles are less likely to damage your craft, but impact with hidden rocks can crack the hull, particularly on steep beaches. Cutting obliquely into steep beaches will help reduce the impact. On a steep, smooth-pebble beach, you will probably slide back into the water anyhow.

The Slide-in Launch

Occasionally one encounters waves breaking on a beach of smooth pebbles with a steep slope above the water (size depending on the tide and wave magnitude). Waves at different tidal stages create one or more level plateaus just above the slope. For this situation, gravity will do the launching for you!

Set the boat pointing down the slope, but on a spot level enough to hold it in place. Sit down and seal up. When ready, push off hard. The more speed you can build up on the way to the water, the better. The problem comes when the front half enters the water while the stern is still supported on the gravel slope, resulting in a very unstable position. Enough speed will get you through this stage in a flash; too little may leave you teetering in a position that is difficult to push off from. On the way down I usually lean to one side slightly and use a skimming low brace for stability as soon as my paddle blade crosses the water's edge.

10

Paddling

Speed is just one of the many criteria in an effective sea kayaker's paddling stroke. For covering distance, an efficient and sustainable paddling stroke must deliver power evenly from many muscle groups to avoid fatigue, strain, or tendonitis—a common ailment resulting from paddling style. In rough, windy conditions, the stroke must be tailored for least interference from wind and also be readily convertible to a brace support stroke. And for your own comfort, it should minimize drips, splashes, or spray blown from the paddle.

Incorporating all of these into your technique at once is a tall order. Instead, begin with the basics and then add refinements, using exercises to help you master particular steps before going on to others. If you are already somewhat experienced, skip to the step that is appropriate for you.

Blade Control and the Basic Stroke Cycle

You should already be familiar with your paddle's features and the feathered/unfeathered paddle controversy (see "Basic Gear"). Since most people prefer to use feathered paddles, I recommend starting with that. If later you opt for unfeathered, it is easy to change.

First, decide which will be the *control hand*—the hand that stays fixed on the paddle shaft and does the twisting. The other hand slides on the shaft as it rotates. Right-hand control is natural for most people whether they are right- or left-handed. Others find lefthand-control more comfortable, and still others can switch from one to the other with ease. I suggest beginning with right-hand control as described below.

The paddle's blade setting will dictate which hand is the control hand; a one-piece feathered paddle is permanently set for either right- or left-hand control. A breakdown paddle can be set to either, or it can be left unfeathered.

If you have a breakdown paddle, set it for right-hand control as follows. Put it together and stand it on end with the front (the *power face*) of the lower blade on the ground facing you. Now release the catch in the joint and adjust the upper blade so that it is edge toward you, power face to your right. For left-hand control, set the upper blade power face to your left. (See fig. 10–1.)

Some shore exercises will familiarize you with important elements of the paddle stroke, beginning with the grip. Stand where there is plenty of room to swing the paddle. Hold the paddle overhead, thumbs to the inside, hands far enough apart so that your

Fig. 10–1. Setting up the breakdown paddle for right-hand control. The lower power face is toward me, and the upper one is to my right. (*Audrey Sutherland*)

forearms are vertical as shown in figure 10–2. (Some paddlers prefer closer hand spacing, particularly with shorter paddles, placing the hands with thumbs about shoulder width apart.)

Look at your control hand. Your grip on the paddle shaft with this hand will be your link to your blade angles in the water. Align your knuckles with the top of the blade on that side (see fig. 10–3). Throughout *every* stroke, maneuver, and brace, your control hand should stay where it is on the shaft, with this knuckle-to-blade alignment. This allows you to sense the position of your blades through your hands.

Holding the paddle in front of you with control-hand wrist in a neutral position, the blade on the control-hand side should be vertical with the power face toward you. The other blade should be horizontal with the power face up. You are ready for a stroke on the control-hand side. To shift blade position for a stroke on the side opposite the control hand, raise the control-hand to about nose level, roll that wrist back slightly, and let the shaft slide around inside the other (non-control) hand, keeping that wrist straight. The blade opposite the control hand should have rotated toward you into vertical position. Note that simply raising your control hand from waist to nose level rotates your shaft quite a bit in itself, so that only a few more degrees need to come from wrist rotation (even less for paddles set to seventy or eighty degrees feather instead of ninety).

The paddle stroke should generate power from as many mus-

Fig. 10–2. Hand placement on the paddle showing possible range.

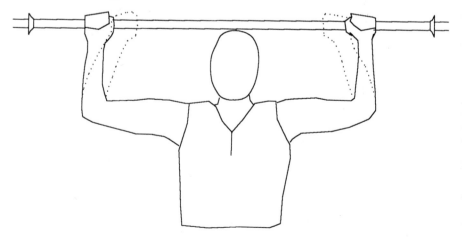

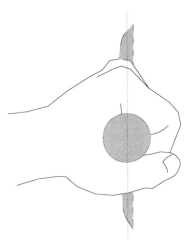

Fig. 10-3. Control hand knuckle alignment with paddle blade.

cles through the body as possible, beginning with those in the trunk and shoulders. For a dry-land demonstration of torso and shoulder rotation, hold the paddle as indicated, extending your arms straight from the shoulder (see fig. 10-4A). Now rotate the paddle around you without bending your arms. It is entirely possible to paddle like this—arms acting as largely rigid struts that support the paddle—deriving all of the power from the rotation of the trunk and shoulders. With some changes to be described, you should try this technique once on the water.

In contrast, one could paddle exclusively with arm motion. Least effective is a stroke style common among many paddlers, deriving power from pulling with the stroke-side arm, while the other arm provides a rigid fulcrum (see fig. 10-4C). This certainly works, but it leads to fatigue of the few muscles doing all of the work.

A vast improvement is made by pulling on one arm while simultaneously pushing with the other, as though there were an invisible fulcrum at the middle of the shaft (see fig. 10-4B). To try it, start with the stroking arm extended and the other bent with the hand near your chin. As you push and pull through the stroke, watch the center point of your paddle shaft to see that it remains stationary about eight inches in front of your chest.

Two styles—shoulder rotation and push-pull arm opposition—are the key ingredients to a strong and sustainable paddle stroke. They can be used in varying proportions depending on conditions and mood. Before going on to apply them in the boat, practice the

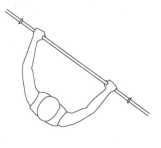

A

B

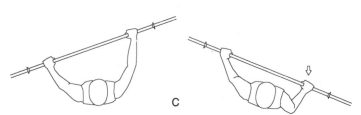

C

Fig. 10–4. *A,* power derived from shoulder rotation alone. *B,* power derived from arm push and pull. *C,* power derived from arm pull only (least desirable).

shoulder-rotation style, adding up-and-down paddling motion and some refinements. Pay attention to the following:

—The arms can be slightly bent, but hold that position throughout the stroke. The paddle should be held well in front of you, with the center staying at least a foot from your chest (depending on arm length). Think of your shoulders, arms, and paddle as a box being rotated at one edge. Much of the strength of the stroke comes from the pushing arm. Visualize the trunk pushing the shoulder forward, which pushes the upper arm, finally transmitted forward to the hand.

—Take long, smooth strokes. Viewed from overhead, each stroke should swing the paddle shaft almost ninety degrees.

—Ensure that neither hand rises above nose level. The object is to keep your paddle shaft as nearly horizontal and low as possible (though shorter paddles require a more vertical shaft). If the upper blade goes too high, it will catch more wind and will drip water on you. And, your upper arm cannot provide as much power if that hand is over your head.

—Pay attention to how your hands control the changing blade angles. Both wrists should remain as straight as possible, with the control hand rolling back a few degrees to present the opposite blade to the water.

—Most important now and later: *watch your blade angles* when they are in the "water," keeping them vertical. Turn your head as the blade passes if you wish. If you allow the top edge of the blade to rotate forward (as by rolling your wrist forward), a stroke on that side will cause the blade to dive, and you will likely capsize!

Seating Position and Basic Forward Propulsion

The next step is to try this basic stroke in the boat. Be sure that you are correctly fitted to the boat for effective paddling. (See "Launching and Landing" for more details about getting fitted.) Once seated, check your posture. Your buttocks should be well back in the seat, and your back should be straight and upright—no slouching or leaning back. The footbraces should be adjusted so that your knees are lightly touching the underside of the deck next to the cockpit when the balls of your feet are resting on the footbraces and your ankles are in a neutral, relaxed position. Good contact at feet and knees (or thighs if your boat has thigh braces) is important for transmitting propulsive forces, for balance, and for controlling your boat during maneuvering, bracing, or Eskimo rolling.

To begin, I suggest using the trunk-shoulder rotation style exclusively until you have a feel for that, keeping both arms nearly straight to form the rigid box of arms, shoulders, and paddle shaft. It is important to experience rotation at the start, since many individuals have trouble integrating it after learning to paddle. This exercise will seem a bit awkward, since the elbow on the stroking side will want to bend toward the end of the stroke. Try to minimize that for now until you have a good feel for your trunk doing the work rather than your arms. Arm push and pull will be added shortly. Start slowly and *watch each stroking blade* for proper vertical angle.

Rotate to bring your stroking blade as far forward as possible, but do not lean forward. The blade should go only deep enough to cover it. Now rotate smoothly to bring the blade back past your body. Most of its work is done by the time it passes you, and the blade will begin to exit the water soon after.

Once you are comfortable with paddling primarily from shoulder rotation, add some arm flexing, but without diminishing the shoulder rotation (see fig. 10–5). Try to prevent either elbow from bending more than ninety degrees. The center of your paddle shaft should stay away from your torso throughout the cycle.

Begin the stroke with the elbow opposite the stroke partly bent, which will allow you to place the stroking blade farther ahead and closer to the hull. During the stroke, concentrate on extending this elbow smoothly through the entire stroke, thinking about pushing with the shoulder, which pushes the elbow, which in turn adds to the force driving the hand forward. This hand should appear to arc

Fig. 10–5. Feathered stroke on right side. *A,* right blade is ready to enter water; right arm is extended. *B,* midstroke: right arm is pulling from shoulder; left arm is pushing from shoulder with added push from elbow extension. *C,* last third of stroke: right arm is pulling from shoulder with added pull from bending elbow; left arm is almost extended. *D,* right blade has exited water; with raised and rotated right arm and wrist, twist the shaft to present left blade for next stroke.

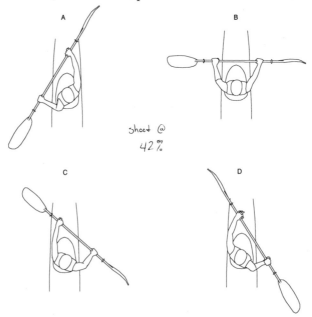

shoot @
42%

Fig. 10–6. A course correction with an edged turn. This turn to the paddler's left is initiated by lifting the left knee and making a combination sweep-and-propulsion stroke on the right.

forward and gently down along the horizon toward your midline (see fig. 10–6). Let the fingers relax during the push, and they may be opened at the end of the stroke to reduce the need to bend the wrist sideways as the shaft becomes more fore-and-aft.

The arm on the stroking side should remain almost straight for the first half of the stroke. Think of pulling from the shoulder. The elbow begins to bend as the blade passes your body, adding more pull and leaving you in position to begin the next stroke as arms switch roles.

Try for a complete cycle about every four seconds at this point, though this cadence will depend on your paddle length, your speed through the water, and conditions. Upwind paddling has a slower cadence because of the lower speed.

Is your paddle getting you wet? Watch for blades going too high and launching drops from overhead. Since most drips leave the paddles at the drip rings (that is their purpose), check their adjustment. Properly located rings should stop drips far enough out to miss your cockpit and arms while you paddle. They should be as far out on the shaft as possible without submerging them (if that happens it simply pumps water down the shaft and onto your hands).

Finding and Refining Your Own Style

The stroke style emphasized so far—derived from trunk rotation with minimal arm movement—is powerful and durable. But many paddlers (myself included) use variations relying more heavily on arm motion with less rotation to fit mood and changing sea and wind conditions. Though I encourage you to try making rotation a major component of your stroke, you should settle on a personal style that works best for you. Pay attention to the elements of your stroke and experiment.

For instance, you may find that increasing the range of your push and pull may feel more natural or that too much trunk rotation leads to chafing under the sprayskirt at times. Starting with the pushing elbow more completely bent will allow you to hold the paddle closer to you if the rotation style's more extended arm position proves tiring. I intentionally vary the components of rotation and push-pull for variety in a day's paddling, and I find that my rotation fades considerably when I am feeling tired or just lazy. But I always use a good amount of push. The two used vigorously together provide a strong but slow cadence that, though not natural enough for me to use frequently, I find very fast and sustainable with a heavily laden boat in calm water.

Staying on Course without a Rudder

Using the rudder or paddling harder or more frequently on one side may seem the obvious way to stay on course. But rudders do break, and one should be able to paddle a desired course without a rudder in difficult conditions (one instructor thinks too many sea kayakers become excellent "rudderers" but poor paddlers). Without a rudder, there are better ways to hold a course than simply paddling more times on one side. If you have a rudder, pull it up for now!

Carved turns, as discussed in the chapter on boat designs, are possible in some boats (edge the hull one way and the boat turns toward the other direction). At this writing, there are few boats that initiate carved turns when edged. But almost all boats become easier to turn when they are edged, and the technique is very helpful for effective course control. Edging increases a boat's turning ability by raising the ends out of the water slightly as one of the rounded sides at midhull goes deeper into the water; a stroke on the edged side can have more turning effect. (See fig. 10–6.)

Rather than simply leaning your upper body over the side, edging must tilt the boat. To do this, lift with the knee on the opposite side from the lean direction. Lifting hard with the opposite knee gives the hull maximum angle without shifting your center of balance beyond the critical point.

Edged turns can be made more radically by leaning: edging the hull so far that you must also shift your torso to or beyond the capsize point. Performing a leaned turn depends on a sense of balance: knowing exactly how far you can shift your weight without capsizing, and sensing where you are relative to that point. Bracing extends your weight-shifting limits well beyond the boat's point of capsizing, and it significantly increases your ability to use leans. (Leaned turns are in return an excellent way to practice the bracing reflex.) But until you have a good brace (see "Bracing"), use gentle edged turns that keep you well within your boat's stability limits. In time you will also learn to use leans to counteract a force such as an approaching wave or change in current direction.

A sweep is a variation in the paddling stroke, which is designed to turn the boat while also contributing to its forward progress. Your hands and the paddle shift to the side so that the nonstroke-side hand is at the midline (as in all strokes, *do not change your grip position on the paddle*). The result is torquing leverage that turns the boat much more than a normal stroke.

If one sweep is not enough, follow it with a normal stroke on the opposite side and then another sweep. For small course corrections, use a stroke halfway between the normal and sweep strokes with gentle edging.

While paddling along, a sweep stroke accompanying edging easily can take the place of a normal stroke in order to make a course correction, with no interruption to the cadence.

Staying on Course with a Rudder

Rudders are often overused by new paddlers. The more the turning angle of the rudder, the more the drag in the water. So, a little rudder applied over time will hold you back less than a radical turn. And, the less you use the rudder (keeping it in the water but straight), the less the drag.

If you are new to "ruddering," remember to *push with the foot on the side toward the turn*. A rudder requires forward speed to work—it has no effect standing still and little at slow speed. In fact, maneuvering in close quarters is best done using the maneuver strokes (described in "Maneuvering") and with the rudder cocked out of the water. The boat will spin faster with the rudder out of the water, and there will be less risk of damage to it by backing into an underwater obstruction.

Since most sea kayaks are a bit slow to respond to their rudders (particularly small rudder blades), course corrections are most easily made by anticipating the need for them. Use your rudder sparingly as soon as you detect course wandering and reduce the rudder angle just before you come back on course.

Here is an example. You find that you are aimed to the right of where you should be heading (marked by a particular landmark you can watch). Gently push on the left foot and allow time for the boat to swing to the left. As the bow approaches your aiming mark, reduce the amount of left rudder before you come back on course, so that your rudder is straight by the time you are aimed where you want to be. This is far more effective than pushing hard on the left pedal, letting up as your bow *passes* the aiming mark, and then probably using some right rudder to get onto course.

As a practical exercise for staying on course (either with or without a rudder), pick a landmark and try to keep your bow right under it as you paddle toward it over some distance. Concentrate on noticing deviations immediately and correcting them while they are small. The result will be a straighter course, fewer paddle strokes, and less rudder drag.

Fine-Tuning Your Paddle Stroke

Most of these pointers come from Olympic flat-water competition style, where the concern is getting every millimeter of forward propulsion from every calorie expended. Whether you are competitive or not, these pointers may help you get a bit farther for an hour's worth of strokes and with fewer aches and pains.

Avoid Rocking

When you reach forward to start your stroke, be sure that the torso rotates rather than leans forward to achieve reach. Leaning with each stroke produces a bobbing, rocking motion that slows the kayak.

Simultaneous Push, Pull, and Torso Rotation

Keeping all three power sources working at once greatly increases efficiency. A common problem is in the exertion of most of one arm's push before the other arm starts to pull, which results in lost force and a paddle that arcs away from the kayak. The pushing arm should be nearly extended as it finishes the stroke and prepares for the next to allow relaxation and to avoid cramps.

Both the push and the pull should stay close to the body,

where the muscle groups are strongest. Be especially watchful that the elbow of the pulling arm stays in close to the body. The pushing arm should follow a straight line forward from the shoulder toward the midline, hand at eye level.

Try for a split-second rest during the transition from the end of one stroke and the beginning of the opposite one, but only after the stroking blade has exited by an upward snap of the upper arm and wrist on that side. Muscles should be loose during the paddle's vertical swing to its position for the next stroke.

Preventing Physical Problems from Paddling

Sore spots and blisters are the most common problem for anyone who does not paddle regularly. They usually form at the base of the thumb. Conditioning the hand by practice usually takes care of the problem; but in the meanwhile, some adhesive tape or a Band-Aid on emerging "hot spots" may head it off. Zinc oxide is an excellent lubricant and healer for blister-prone areas. Gloves are another solution for some paddlers. Specialized paddling gloves are available. One friend uses spandex driving gloves; others use bicycling or sailing gloves.

Attention to your paddling style will also help reduce hand sores. Keep your hands dry (no easy task in wind) by keeping the drip rings out of the water. Also watch your grip—too much tension aggravates the skin. And finally, check your paddle shaft for roughness, particularly wooden ones that need refinishing; sand if necessary. For fiberglass shafts, wet-sanding with 300-grit or finer paper may help rough spots.

Tendonitis is a catchall kayaker's malady that includes muscle strain, tenosynovitis (inflammation of tendon linings), or nerve injury in the forearm or wrist. Much of the blame for such forearm problems has been placed unfairly on feathered paddles. The repeated blade angle changes in feathered paddling need not cause tendonitis problems if attention is paid to paddling style.

The stressful power-exertion phase of the stroke, when the muscles are working, is the most likely setting for injuries. But the switching movement of feathered blade rotation occurs in the most relaxed phase during the transitional swing. Little wrist movement is needed for this blade switch if the proper hand positions, discussed previously, are maintained. Note that the control hand (in this case, the right hand) does not need to roll back more than a few degrees for the stroke on the opposite side. Most of this rotation is taken care of by changing arm position as the nonstroke-side hand is raised to eye level.

Problems commonly develop from *wrist extension*—the wrist bending back beyond the neutral position. Symptoms of extension include pain and swelling of the muscles on the outside and back (side opposite the palm of the hand) of the forearm and/or the tendons at the back of the wrist. These occur most commonly during the pull stroke. If you begin to experience extension symptoms, concentrate on keeping your wrist as neutral as possible as you pull. Also do not let the pushing arm cross over the midline, which can cause similar problems as the wrist is forced to bend sideways by the fore-and-aft paddle shaft.

Wrist flexion—bending forward—has its own symptoms and typical causes. Pain and swelling associated with flexion occur on the inner forearm and at the palm side of the wrist. Numb fingers also are associated with flexion; the tendons compress the nerves and vessels in the wrist in the flexed position. Too much flexion is common in sweep strokes.

A third problem is the "death grip"—holding the paddle too tightly. When the grip is tight, force from the trunk and back is transmitted to the paddle mostly through the forearm muscles, which places undue stress on those muscles. Instead, relax as much as conditions allow (hardest in wind and rough water). The pushing hand can open to allow the hand to relax and to let the fingers flex occasionally for circulation. (This will also reduce sideways bending of the wrist as it follows the shaft at the end of the stroke.) Force on the pull stroke is important too; use only what pressure is needed to keep a secure grip and proper blade angle.

Either bent wrists or excess grip tension can lead to pinched nerves in the wrist, called carpal tunnel syndrome, which is evidenced by prickling fingers followed by numbness. This can become a chronic and serious problem because the tendons' pressure on the nerves may scar them and ultimately require special medication or even surgery.

Aside from eliminating the causes, application of heat, rest, and nonprescription pain relievers or anti-inflammatory medications may assist in controlling moderate problems. Aspirin and ibuprofen are popular because they control inflammation as well as pain. However, they also cause stomach and intestinal irritation and may inhibit blood clotting. Tylenol works well for pain but has no anti-inflammation effects.

Changing the distance of the hands on the paddle to suit conditions may also help prevent muscle strain. If you think of the paddle as a lever like an oar, with the fulcrum (or oarlock) at the pulling hand, then increasing the hand distance is like moving the fulcrum or oarlock outward to give you more leverage—in effect, a low gear. This is what you need for upwind paddling; your push-pull movement will result in fewer strokes but more powerful blade movement through the water.

Part of the problem of upwind paddling is that the cadence becomes too slow to be comfortable due to the slower boat movement. "Gearing down," by increasing the spacing of the strokes, will help to maintain the cadence. Reversing the blades (revolving the shaft 180 degrees) to increase the "slip" in the water has been suggested to produce the same effect.

11

Maneuvering

In addition to paddling forward, there are occasions when you need to stop suddenly, back up, move sideways, or turn in place. Maneuvering skills will pay dividends in countless little events: avoiding a rock spied at the last second, getting to a dropped glove quickly before it sinks, or turning around in a crowded boat basin cul-de-sac without scraping the pristine side of some yacht.

Stopping

Emergency stops are done with the back of the paddle by freezing the normal paddle stroke with the vertical blade held firmly in the water just aft of the body (so that the blade is angled back relative to the boat's axis). Pull your elbows in close to your sides and bring the shaft back against your torso for firm support. Hold this for a second on one side, then shift to the other to keep the braking force even. Keeping the brakes on one side is appropriate if the braking swings your boat away from whatever you are about to bump into. At full speed, an emergency stop takes a good effort, and your stability in the process depends on proper blade angle. A few such practice stops are worthwhile.

Backing Up (Backpaddling)

Backpaddling consists of short strokes in reverse direction. Since the grip on the paddle should not be shifted between types of strokes, backing strokes are done with the reverse side of the blade.

Backward directional control is somewhat tricky. Pull the rudder up. It will do you little good and could be harmed by striking an obstruction. Keep looking back over one shoulder; switching is disorienting and has caused capsizes. Most kayaks tend to veer in one direction or the other in reverse because they are trimmed for forward steering, so proceed slowly and use braking strokes and sweeps if you are heading off in the wrong way.

Spinning in Place with Sweep Strokes

In tight quarters, there may be a need to turn the boat in its own length, sometimes with little room to spare at bow or stern. This is easy with paired sweep strokes.

The sweep stroke was introduced in the chapter on paddling as a variation on forward propulsion, used to make course corrections. The sweep used here for stationary maneuvering is similar, but a little more pronounced (see fig. 11–1).

The main difference between a sweep and a normal stroke is that the paddle moves out to the sweeping side, moving arms and paddle sideways *without shifting your hand position on the shaft*. In position for the sweep, the hand opposite the sweeping side should be at your midline.

The hand on the opposite side from the stroke should stay stationary against the chest on the midline until the last third of the stroke. Then, a push with that arm as the blade is pulled in toward the stern will add extra turning force to the stroke.

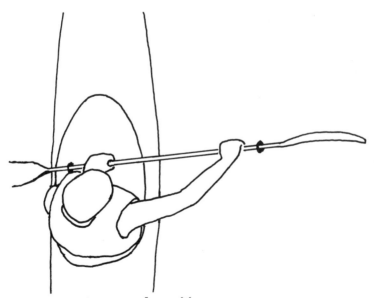

Fig. 11–1. Sweep-stroke position.

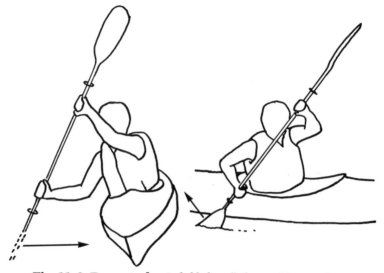

Fig. 11–2. Draw stroke. *Left,* blade pulled toward boat; *right,* blade exits to rear.

To execute a right sweep, shift the hands and paddle right until the left hand is on center. Reach forward (rocking forward with the torso is fine in this case) and immerse the blade next to the boat. Now pry away from the boat, letting the blade circle out and away, the left hand staying against your chest. Continue back until the blade approaches the boat behind you. Near the end of the sweep, push with the left hand to give the blade a final drive toward the boat.

Sweeps can be either forward or reverse strokes. Alternated forward and reverse strokes on opposite sides will spin the boat in place for turning in tight quarters. Like backpaddling, the reverse sweep is done with the back of the blade. Offset the paddle sideways as before, reach back close to the boat, and begin a strong outward arc that continues toward the front of the boat. The first portion of the stroke, during which the force is outward and then forward, will have the most effect on turning the boat.

As described in the chapter on paddling, sweeps used with edging and leans are more effective for turning, because edging lifts the ends from the water slightly as the middle pushes deeper. (Edging is tipping the boat while keeping well within stability limits; leaning is edging taken to extremes near or even beyond the capsize point.) This also applies for stationary turns: edge in the direction of the sweep, lifting with the opposite knee to tilt the boat.

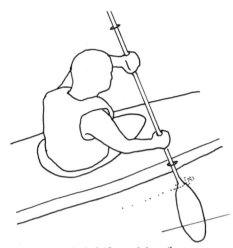

Fig. 11–3. The parallel shift position (here to move the boat
to the paddler's right). The left forearm is anchored against the forehead for stability.

Much more radical leans can be used with a sweep that is also
a supporting brace, allowing you to reach out farther and tip the
boat more on its side to spin it even faster. These leans are introduced in the Bracing chapter.

Moving Sideways with the Draw Stroke

Few other boats can perform this sideways maneuver. For the
kayaker, it comes in very handy at times: you might be parallel to but
just out of reach of a dock, a few feet from a dropped object, or—
most critical—not close enough to a capsized companion's boat. A
draw stroke will get you there quickly and easily. (See fig. 11–2.)

The draw stroke is one of the few strokes that calls for holding
the paddle shaft nearly vertical, and it is ineffective unless in this
position. Consequently, a properly executed draw stroke will get
you wet from drips and water running down the shaft.

To perform a draw stroke on your right side, raise the left
hand over the right to bring the shaft into an almost vertical position, then reach out about 3 feet from the side of the boat with the
blade (reaching with the left arm too to keep the shaft vertical). As
with all strokes, *do not change hand position on the shaft*. Later,
bracing will allow you to reach farther for more powerful draws by
incorporating a high brace for support; for now stay well within
your limits of balance.

Be sure that the power face of the blade is squarely toward you (i.e., blade edge parallel to the boat). Submerge it to cover the blade but not to the drip ring (otherwise, you get wetter). Now pull straight toward you. As the boat moves sideways, the end of the draw stroke becomes important because the moving hull can "trip" over the blade and produce a capsize. Hence, the stroke must be ended in one of two ways. You can end the stroke by withdrawing the blade by slicing the blade toward your stern and out of the water. Or you can rotate the shaft to feather the blade perpendicular to the boat's axis at the end of the stroke and then slice outward through the water to the position to start another draw stroke (this ending requires a bit more finesse).

Commonly, new paddlers find that their draw strokes unintentionally move them forward, aft, or turn their boats. Blade angle and start positions of the draw are usually at fault. Check that your blade is really parallel to the boat, and that the stroke originates from a spot straight out to the side from the cockpit. Then be sure that your draw is straight toward your body. (The boat can be turned intentionally by starting and finishing your draw to either the front or the rear.)

Avoiding Obstacles with the Parallel Shift

The parallel shift allows you to move to the side to avoid an obstacle and still retain your forward momentum. This maneuver requires forward motion to work. (See fig. 11–3.)

To move to the right, hold the paddle shaft vertical with the right blade just beyond the boat and about opposite your knee. Steady the paddle by putting your left forearm against your forehead. Now rotate the shaft so that the right blade is about twenty degrees from the direction of travel, front face forward, and put it into the water vertically. The water moving past your blade will push it and the boat to the right while keeping it roughly on the same heading. Always insert the blade on the side you wish to move toward, as rotating the blade's forward edge toward the boat to move the other way invites a capsize.

Those learning parallel shifts commonly use too much angle, which results in blade drag and little of the desired result. Practice carefully at slower speeds on both sides.

Maneuvering Double Kayaks

All of these strokes work for K-2s. Because they are bigger, doubles are more cumbersome to maneuver, but teamwork strokes by the two paddlers can achieve a particular movement quite rapidly. For instance, to spin in place, one paddler can do a forward sweep on one side while the other does a reverse sweep on the opposite side. The forward paddler is usually the first to see an obstruction and is also in the best place to apply a parallel shift—which in that position is really a bow rudder—while the stern paddler either does the same or a forward sweep on the other side.

12

Stability, Capsizing, and Righting

This chapter's focus is the capsize: preventing it, practicing it, and recovering *without getting out of your boat.* Some of the skills you will find here are elemental for the first-time kayaker, others should be learned after you have become comfortable with paddling, and still others might be tried once you have mastered bracing.

Since you cannot progress far in learning bracing if fearful about getting out of your capsized kayak, the act of capsizing and bailing out of the inverted boat is something that every new kayaker needs to experience. With that source of anxiety removed, you can go on to some exercises to help you test your stability limits (with the chance that you may exceed them and spill again) and to use your hips to angle the boat. Then, you can try some methods of recovering from capsizes *without* exiting. Unlike the Eskimo roll, these are primarily used in practice sessions rather than real emergencies at sea. They are very useful during bracing practice, when bailing out after each missed brace is counterproductive. These exercises depend on mastering the "hip snap"—rotation of the hull with the hips independently from the upper body. The chapter concludes with comments about the Eskimo roll, which depends on the same skills.

The Capsize and Wet Exit

The act of capsizing is an important experience for every kayaker. The purpose is to prove to yourself that you will not become trapped in the cockpit, and in the process, to become comfortable with hanging upside down underwater for a short time (essential for the Eskimo rescue and Eskimo roll). During practice, a nose plug is desirable for keeping water out of your sinuses, and a mask is helpful to see what you are doing.

First check that the grab loop on your sprayskirt is readily at hand (not caught under the skirt), and that you can pull the skirt off easily. On skirts with a loop that is really a strap across the forward part, a pull to one side is needed. For others, pulling up and back will release the skirt. Be sure that you can do it with your eyes closed.

Try to develop the reflex of holding onto the paddle throughout the capsize to prevent it from becoming separated from you

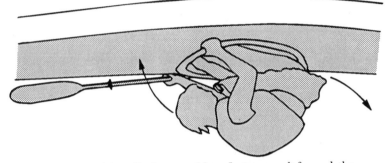

Fig. 12–1. Exiting the inverted kayak. Somersault forward; the hand holding the paddle can assist by pushing upward against the deck.

and your boat. You cannot afford to swim around collecting things, and a paddle even a short distance away becomes impossible to see in choppy seas. The cockpit-exiting maneuver can be done entirely with one hand, and you might try establishing a habit of holding the paddle in your left hand and pulling the skirt and exiting with the other, or vice versa.

Get ready for your tip-over by holding the paddle alongside the boat. Be sure that your feet are placed securely on the braces, and that your knees and/or thighs are securely braced to hold you in place as you capsize. Part of the exercise is to experience what it is like to hold yourself in place while inverted, yet be able to exit easily when you are ready to.

Now lean and let yourself go over. Once down, try to keep yourself locked in position for a few seconds before exiting. (At first, you may not be able to do that until you have convinced yourself that you can get out and back to the surface.) Next, pull off the front of the skirt (the back will take care of itself) and somersault forward, allowing your legs to slide backward out of the cockpit, and using your free hand for a little assist against the coaming as you go while the other hand continues gripping the paddle shaft (see fig. 12–1). This forward roll is much easier than scrambling backward and upward toward the surface, which is liable to give you the sensation of becoming trapped (although you should have no difficulty getting out this way either).

Back at the surface (and still gripping your paddle), *immediately* grab your boat. In windy conditions, an empty kayak can blow downwind faster than you can swim. In cold water, if you are not beginning the recovery procedure immediately (for instance, if you are waiting for your paddling partner to approach), pull your upper body over your inverted hull to reduce heat loss. Keep the boat inverted to trap air in it and keep seas from washing into the cockpit until you are ready to begin the recovery. Getting onto the hull may be easiest if you begin at one end of the boat and then slide toward the center.

Balance, Edging, and Leaning

Having found that capsizing is not a problem, you can go on to extending your balancing skills in the boat. Learning the limits of stability—which depend on *both* the boat's hull and your body size and arrangement—is primarily a matter of practice. Start slowly, and lean carefully to one side with some firm support such as a dock to catch if you should go too far. If your boat is one with low initial stability, it may seem tippy within a few degrees of level, but you will find that it has more resistance when it is leaned a bit more. You will soon get used to the initial tippiness (and start to appreciate its uses in time). While you have something solid to hang on to, experiment with just how much leaning it takes to make it capsize. You should have a feel for the "comfort range" within which you can shift your weight in a particular boat before going far from your launch point.

Next, work on twisting the hull using your hips and trunk. (Be sure that you are well secured in the kayak as discussed in the Paddling chapter.) Start by lifting with your right thigh and knee, rolling the hull to the left, while keeping your upper body centered over your hips. Hold this for a second, and then do the other side. Move on to a rocking motion, gradually increasing the amount that you roll the hull. Concentrate on keeping your torso centered in your balance zone (see edging in fig. 12–2). This independent movement of hips within hull and upper body will become very important to you.

Try experimenting with this in waves by letting the boat adjust to changing surfaces while you stay centered. For instance, turn side-on to a non-breaking boat wake, and let the boat roll with the waves as your torso flexes over them. If you are loose at the hips, this should not feel threatening to your stability.

What you have been doing is *edging* the hull—tilting it while keeping the upper body centered. As shown in the Paddling chapter, this is very useful for turning the kayak because the underwater portion of the hull changes shape as the boat is tipped. In contrast, gently try *leaning*—inclining both hull and upper body such that your balance is shifted toward the capsize point. Note the difference between the two in figure 12–2.

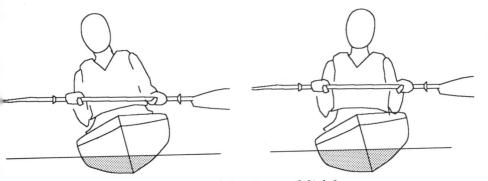

Fig. 12–2. Leaning and edging. Leaning *(left)* shifts your center of balance toward the capsize point. Edging *(right)* seeks to keep it centered.

Obviously, leaning puts you closer to a capsize than edging. But leaning is often used together with bracing to prevent a tip-over in rough water, strong winds, and currents. For instance, steep waves usually cause capsizes away from the wave face, so leaning (and bracing if necessary) into the wave is the best way to maintain stability. And, crossing from an eddy into a strong current mandates leaning downstream to avoid being unbalanced on the upstream side. Both situations are described in subsequent chapters.

Thus, stability depends on flexing at the hips—allowing the boat to adjust under you while keeping your body weight centered—and on shifting your weight as needed to compensate for potentially upsetting factors. Usually you will strive to stay in the middle of your stability "comfort zone," but there will be times when you will need to move toward its edges.

In-Cockpit Capsize Recoveries and the Hip Snap

Now we move on to uses of body flexibility to recover from tip-overs while staying seated in your boat. If you are new to sea kayaks, you may wish to spend some time paddling, maneuvering, and getting a taste of bracing before trying these. The key concept for all of the methods described here is the *hip snap*. It is also vital for "deep" bracing, in which you recover from being well past the point of capsize. The same principles are also critical for successful Eskimo rolling.

These recovery techniques involve righting yourself with some external object you can push down on—a pool edge, another kayaker's bow, a foam or inflated float—or by pushing off the bottom with either hands or paddle. The key is this: it must be done in two coordinated stages by first righting the hull with your hips and then righting your upper body. These two stages are the hip snap.

Start by grasping a firm object next to your kayak with both hands, such as a low dock or the edge of a swimming pool. After

Fig. 12–3. The hip snap. A–C, rotation of the hull with the hips precedes recovery of the upper body. Head must exit the water last. D, trying to raise the torso before righting the hull is usually not succesful.

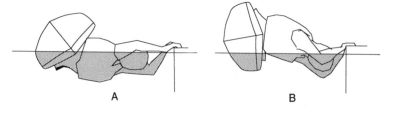

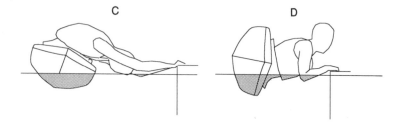

ensuring that you are firmly braced in the cockpit, slowly lower yourself into the water. Stop when your torso is at the surface, turning your face to the side so that you can breathe. Use your hips to rotate the hull so that it is on its edges (tipped ninety degrees), and then rotate it as far toward level as you can while keeping your upper body stationary in the water. Repeat this several times, being sure that you maintain your seat in the cockpit and that your head and upper body stay at the surface. Next, try a full recovery: start with the hull tipped on its side, rotate it toward level, and then push yourself up and toward the boat with your arms. Your head should leave the water surface last (try looking down as you come up). Repeat this as many times as necessary, striving for a one-two sequence of hull rotation followed by upper body recovery. This should require little strength from your arms; if it does, you are probably trying to come up too early or are raising your head prematurely. (See fig. 12–3.)

Now extend the technique to a more complete capsize. Take a deep breath and lower your torso under water while maintaining your handhold near the surface as before. A stronger hip snap will be needed now, starting with a windup: rotate the hips and hull *away* from the direction of capsize so that the hull is fully inverted, and then use a continuous twist of your hips to bring the hull toward upright, beginning to recover your upper body as the hull passes the halfway point. Think of the motion as a windup window shade: the inertia of the rotating roller (your hips and the hull) winds on the shade (your upper body as it is pulled toward the upright position). And think of your torso as being pulled in toward the hull along the surface for the last part of the recovery, rather than pulling itself upright. Again, your head *must* be the last to leave the water.

The Eskimo Rescue

The Eskimo rescue is a practical extension of the same techniques. It is simple: capsized, you wait in your cockpit for a companion to approach and then use his bow to right yourself (see fig. 12–4). Hence, the reliability of this maneuver depends on your ability to wait confidently for your rescuer and on the rescuer's proximity to you and ability to maneuver into position in time. The Eskimo rescue is used frequently in the beginner river kayaking classes before students have mastered the roll. Sea kayakers are less likely to use it because the distance between paddlers is usually

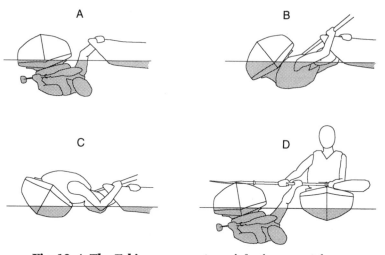

Fig. 12–4. The Eskimo rescue. *A,* reach for the rescuer's bow. *B,* hook hand with paddle over bow and get breath. *C,* use hip-snap sequence to right hull before raising head and torso. *D,* alternative set-up with hulls parallel.

greater, and the boats are slower to position. Nonetheless, it is an easy-to-learn and efficient technique that is excellent for recovering from missed rolls and braces in practice sessions.

If you capsize, first call attention to yourself. Trap your paddle between your upper arm and the hull, reach upward, and pound loudly on the bottom of your boat. Then start to "search" for your companion's bow by moving your arms back and forth along both sides of the boat. (The disorientation of inversion may confuse you about which side he will approach from.)

Once you contact the rescuer's bow, grab it with one hand and pull your face to the surface for a breath. Next grab your paddle with the other hand and place both on top of the rescuer's bow so that you can get some support from both arms to right yourself. As before, it is important to right your boat with your hips before trying to raise your head and torso above the surface.

Figure 12–4 also shows an alternative arrangement for the rescue—with the boats parallel and the rescuer's paddle laid across the hulls. This has some advantages over the perpendicular approach already described. In the latter, the approaching rescuer must be careful to avoid ramming the other hull or, worse, the victim's head if he or she has exited and surfaced at the wrong moment. And, the victim must grope above the surface for the rescuer's bow, while the rescuer cannot move his bow quickly enough to help make contact. With the parallel approach, the paddle can be placed in the victim's hand. Furthermore, keeping two perpendicular boats properly positioned in rough water is much more difficult than coming alongside.

Float Practice

Holding a small floating object in place of a fixed object can be very helpful for practicing hip-snap recoveries (see fig. 12–5A). The small self-rescue float that I use taught me quickly the importance of a good hip snap. Starting from a full capsize, I found that simply pulling myself to the surface and then pushing down on the little float did nothing to get my torso out of the water—it just sank. Then I concentrated on a good windup and hip snap with my head down, and the float hardly seemed to leave the surface as I righted easily! I practiced until it seemed easy and then began letting a bit of air out of the float. I still had little difficulty.

After you practice using a float with your hands, try using it on the paddle blade, which can give you a good feeling for the Eskimo roll. (In fact, a small, flat piece of foam slit to accept the paddle blade is a common assist for learning to roll.) This should be easier to use for recovery than the hand-held float because of the leverage on the paddle.

Fig. 12–5. Float and bottom rolls. *A*, using the paddle float. *B*, bottom roll with paddle.

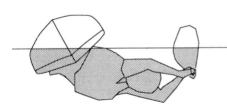
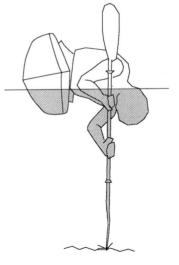

Bottom Rolls

Pushing off the bottom is also a practical way to recover from capsizes in shallow-water practice sessions. Bracing can be practiced in as little as 2 feet of water (best to avoid rocky bottoms at that depth). Unless the bottom is soft mud, you should have little difficulty righting yourself in water as deep as the length of your arm if you have developed a strong hip snap. But you will likely be unable to right yourself in water as shallow as a foot deep if you do not follow the one-two sequence of hull and hips followed by torso. Hold your paddle in one hand and push off with the other, remembering to face down and let your head and arms come up last.

Use of your paddle extends the bottom-rolling depth to the length of your paddle. It is easiest to do in water shallow enough to reach bottom while gripping the paddle normally. (See fig. 12–5B.) Start and finish your recovery promptly after you contact bottom, as the boat will tend to move off to one side as you push. One note of caution: avoid soft bottoms that could grip your paddle, causing you to leave it behind in the interest of making the surface.

Fig. 12–6. Some Eskimo rolls do not require changing grip position: *left,* the screw roll; *right,* the high brace or "C-to-C" roll, so called because of the reversed body bends at the beginning and end.

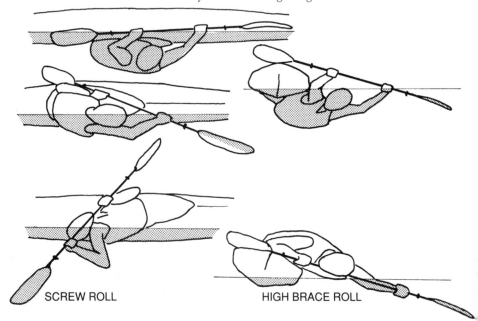

SCREW ROLL   HIGH BRACE ROLL

The Eskimo Roll

For the average sea kayaker, the Eskimo roll is a paradox: it is the most effective capsize-recovery technique, yet it may be the least reliable. It is effective because it is quick, results in less exposure to cold water and less expenditure of energy, and it is the most feasible in very rough and windy conditions (particularly if you can roll up from either side). It is probably the only method for heavy breaking seas.

But the roll needs frequent practice to make it reliable for the average paddler. White-water kayakers who paddle in water that tests their limits use the roll on most outings. But accidental capsizes are rare for sea kayakers, and unless practiced regularly, the roll cannot be counted on to work when it is needed. Though I do practice my roll, it is not regular enough nor are my skills consistent enough to make me confident that it will always work when I really need it.

Whether you should learn to roll depends on your nature. If you enjoy learning and refining that sort of skill (and are comfortable hanging upside down underwater), then you are likely to spend enough time practicing to make it reliable. But if learning to roll seems like an ordeal, you are not likely to become proficient at it, and your energies are best applied to other elements in your rings of defense (particularly bracing and the other capsize-recovery methods).

There is a wide variety of Eskimo roll styles. Learning them from a book is difficult. For this reason I will not describe how to do them here. The easiest ways to learn the roll are through classes or with the assistance of a skilled friend. Some videos are helpful, as are some manuals on the subject. I would suggest concentrating on rolls that do not require a change in hand position from ordinary paddling such as the screw rolls or the high-brace roll—also called the "C-to-C" roll (see fig. 12–6). These will be fastest to set up and also lead naturally into braces for a little assist or some stability at the end of the roll.

Though I have not yet mustered the nerve to risk my gear with it, rolling a fully laden kayak is said to be as easy or even easier than an empty boat because of the momentum, which helps at the end. Be sure that you pack your cargo to avoid shifting in inverted position.

13

Bracing

Braces are paddle strokes that prevent a capsize. When combined with a good sense of balance, they can make the otherwise tippy kayak an extraordinarily seaworthy craft. *Preventing* a capsize is worth a dozen Eskimo rolls and ten times as many wet-exit recoveries. Braces are fundamental skills for the river kayaker, and they should be for the sea kayaker, too. (See fig. 13–1.)

Braces are used in two different ways. The first is to recover your balance, applying the brace after you sense a loss of balance just as you would move your foot to recover your balance while

Fig. 13–1. Bracing can offer extraordinary stability and control in difficult conditions, such as this leaned turn while surfing small waves.

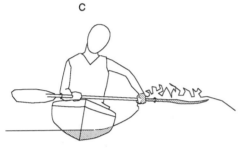

Fig. 13–2. Uses of braces. *A,* reactive "slap brace" to restore balance. *B,* anticipative coasting low brace for stability while looking back. *C,* anticipative low brace into breaking wave.

standing. This is called a *reactive* brace. The other kind of brace is *anticipative:* you see some imminent situation that will likely jeopardize your stability and use the brace together with a shift in balance to forestall it. Figure 13–2 illustrates both types of situations.

Reactive bracing must be a reflex. If teetering at the point of capsize, the new paddler commonly releases the paddle and reaches for the water. This futile reflex must be replaced with an equally automatic brace, accomplished only through practice. Anticipative bracing allows a bit more time to think, but you must know when and how to brace for particular circumstances. Both types of bracing are described in this chapter, beginning with the reactive brace.

Effective bracing comes with the repetition and regular practice that makes bracing automatic. Some suggestions are included here for building braces into your outings. You will get more from them than just keeping upright: bracing lets you lean your boat for more effective use of direction-controlling sweep strokes (described in "Maneuvering"), and leaned sweeps help reinforce the bracing reflex, because you depend on the brace for support in an otherwise unstable position.

Before beginning, check that you are firmly secured in your kayak as described in "Paddling." Bracing requires solid connection to your boat at hips, lower back, knees and/or thighs, and feet. You should be able to twist the kayak with your hips and knees and not slip in any direction when the boat is on its side.

To learn effective bracing, you must be willing to *commit* to your braces—to risk a capsize unless the brace prevents it. Hence, either warm water or a wet suit or dry suit for comfort in cold water is important for learning. At first tip-overs are inevitable, so practice in water shallow enough for someone to stand nearby to pull you back up (rather than bailing out each time). Also see "Stability, Capsizing, and Righting" for other methods of recovery from missed braces, such as the Eskimo rescue (if you have a partner standing by) or bottom rolls.

A paddle float also is helpful in practice to prevent capsizes until your brace becomes reliable. The inflatable floats for self-rescues work for this, but a flat rigid float slipped over the blade will allow you to practice sweeping braces with additional back-up support. About one-quarter cubic foot of ethafoam suffices. Cut it to 12 by 18 by 2 inches and slit it with a bread knife or keyhole saw to receive the blade.

Start with some dry-land exercises, sitting in your boat. These steps require that you already be comfortable with paddling movements described in "Paddling" and that you have settled on either feathered or unfeathered paddle blades. Make sure you have each step well in hand before going on to the next.

As you practice all of your bracing, *watch your blades!* Blade angle and position are vital to the successful brace. New paddlers tend to watch the horizon as they try braces; instead they need to focus on their blades until able to sense their position through the control hand, which comes in time.

The Low Brace

The low brace is the most commonly used reactive brace, though it is used frequently in anticipative situations too. This brace is easy to apply from the rest position (paddle held across your lap) and allows you to brace quickly to either side—handy in choppy water when balance could be lost to either side. The reactive low brace is frequently called a *slap brace,* since it involves vigorously striking the water surface with the flat of the blade, giving a strong but short-lived base for recovering your balance.

Step One. Position the paddle blades for the low brace. As has been stressed for paddling strokes, the position of one hand is always constant in relation to the blade on that side. For a feathered paddle, your control-hand knuckles (the hand that does not slide) remain aligned with the blade edge of that side (see fig. 13–3A). If you paddle unfeathered, both knuckles should be in line with the edges of the blades.

The low brace uses the *back* of the blade (the nonpower face) flat on the water. Hold the paddle perpendicular to the boat and as level as possible just above your spraydeck. For the back-of-blade-down low brace position, the paddle shaft must rotate forward (see fig. 13–3B) to brace either blade of an unfeathered paddle or to

Fig. 13–3. Components of the low brace on the control-hand side (here, the paddler's right hand). *A*, normal hand position, knuckles of the control hand aligned with the blade edge. *B*, rotate; *C*, offset; *D*, slap; *E*, rotate and retrieve.

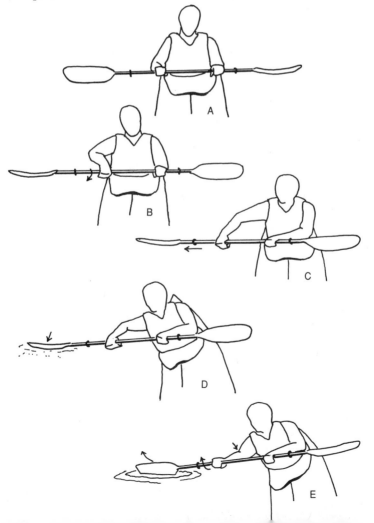

brace with the control-hand-side blade of a feathered paddle. Since the blade opposite the control hand of a feathered paddle starts out in back-down position, that side requires no rotation for bracing. During the brace, neither wrist should be bent; this is a weak position that may result in losing your grip on the paddle. Instead, rotate the paddle forward by lifting the elbow somewhat and moving the hand and shaft to the rear, close to your stomach. Practice moving rapidly between normal paddling and low brace positions on both sides (no rotation needed on one side for feathered paddles).

Step Two. Shift the paddle outward to the bracing side (see fig. 13–3C). This gives more leverage for the brace than keeping it centered. *Do not change your grip.* Move both arms and paddle far enough to put the hand on your bracing side about 2 feet from your hip and the other in front of your stomach. Incline your head toward the bracing side. Repeat steps one and two on both sides, returning to normal paddling position in between.

Step Three. Slap the water surface with the back of the blade (see fig. 13–3D). Concentrate on keeping the opposite blade low and your paddle shaft nearly horizontal, so that the blade will be almost flat on the water surface. Strike the surface opposite your buttocks. The force should be a downward and slightly forward punch transmitted along the line of your forearm.

Step Four. Rotate your bracing blade back to vertical, raise the blade, and return to a normal centered position (see fig. 13-3E). In the water, the motion will be a short arc as you push forward while dropping the elbow to increase the blade angle to vertical. Make sure that your blade clears the surface at the end of the brace so that you are ready for another one should it be needed. Ending with the blade deep and horizontal may result in a capsize as you try to pull it up!

Practice this dry-land, four-step sequence to both sides: rotate to horizontal blade (if needed); shift laterally; slap; and rotate to vertical blade and retrieve. Watch your blades. Repeat until it works as an integrated automatic motion on either side. When you feel you have it, close your eyes and do it some more. You want the motions for each side engraved in your brain.

So far we have the reaction. Now for the stimulus to trigger it—the beginning of a capsize. In general, I suggest that bracing be practiced as preventing a capsize in order to establish the automatic stimulus-response reaction.

Step Five. *Gently* lean your boat to the beginning of a capsize and recover with a brace. For this step, delay using the brace until you sense you need it to keep balanced.

Start in the bracing position, as at the end of step two, with your blade held flat just above the water. Lean the boat by lifting with the knee on the opposite side. Lean both boat and body together (as opposed to leaning over the upright boat's side or tipping the boat while you stay upright). Proceed gently; find the point where the boat is about to go over and hang there, still in bracing position just over the surface. Now go a bit farther.

When you feel you are capsizing, slap firmly with your paddle blade, pushing down with both arms, and bring yourself back to stability. Repeat on both sides, and you will learn a great deal about balance, your boat's stability characteristics, and a bracing reflex, too.

After more practice allow yourself to fall into a capsize so that a hard slap and push are required to recover. Also, start your lean in a normal paddling position, going through all the steps *after* you lose your balance. But be sure the brace is a reaction; do not use it until you sense losing stability.

Notice that this "slap" brace supports you only briefly. You must recover quickly, before the paddle pushes deep into the water. In a more severe recovery, a "hip snap" (described in the last chapter) needs to be added—righting your boat with a twist of your hips before you bring your upper body upright during the brace.

Here are a few errors commonly made in learning the low brace.

No offset. Be sure to move your paddle outward on the bracing side so that your opposite hand lies near or even beyond your midline, as in figure 13–3C. Leverage from the extended blade is important.

Blade and shaft too vertical. Keep the hand on the non-bracing side low so that your shaft stays as horizontal as possible. A more vertical blade lacks horizontal support and dives easily.

Blade too far back. Keep the bracing blade about opposite your hip. You lose leverage as it moves back and in toward your boat. Though you may use the low brace in that rear sector for some situations, keeping it opposite your body will make bracing easier to learn.

Locked elbow on bracing side. This could leave you vulnerable to injury when your paddle strikes the water or (worse) rocks. A locked elbow also limits the mobility that you need for the brace and recovery.

The low brace is most useful at times when your paddle is

held in the low at-rest position or whenever the blade on the appropriate side is behind or even with your body (for instance, at the end of a paddle stroke). In a potentially unstable situation like tide rip waves or waves rebounding from a wall, being ready to low brace on either side is the best way to be prepared whenever you are not paddling.

The low brace also provides very powerful support whenever the boat has forward speed—done by skimming the blade on the surface. Try this *coasting low brace:* paddle ahead at normal speed and then lay the back of the blade on the surface with the leading edge slightly raised. Brace gently on this planing blade and notice how much support it gives you until the boat slows down. The flat-

Fig. 13–4. Sweeping low brace. Here the paddle moves forward, turning the boat clockwise.

ter the blade on the surface, the less the drag on your boat. The coasting low brace is often used for stability while looking behind you (brace on the side you turn toward). I frequently use it when sailing my kayak, particularly during gusts.

If your boat is not moving, you can get the same support with a *sweeping low brace* (see fig. 13–4). which develops the lift by moving the blade forward on the surface. Using the same blade angle as for skimming, start with the blade behind your body and move it forward until the paddle shaft is perpendicular to the boat. Avoid doing it too fast. Plenty of support can be developed without splashing or making white water.

To get a feel for the support from the sweeping low brace, first try it without leaning. Start by turning to place your blade on the surface in low brace position to the rear near your hull. Sweep the blade forward on the surface until it has passed your seat. Push down gently as you sweep, but stay within your stability limits until you have a sense of the support from blades swept at different speeds. Watch your blade, seeking an angle almost flat on the surface. Too much angle will drag and loses lift. Then try leaning to (and, later, beyond) the capsize point, being sure to recover as the sweep passes your hip.

You can lean quite hard on the brace as long as the blade is moving; just be sure to return to centered balance with a hip snap and a firm push at the end of the brace. Later, we will see how to use this sweeping low brace with a lean for maneuvering. And, if you learn to Eskimo roll, the sweeping low brace is an excellent way to finish up your roll, especially for one that did not have quite enough energy to get you upright.

The High Brace

The high brace is a very powerful capsize preventer with both reactive and anticipative uses. It is done with the *front* (power face)

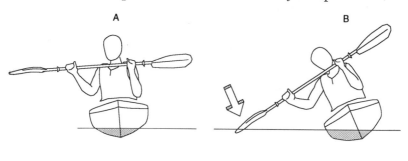

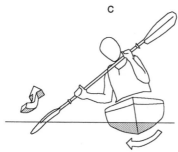

Fig. 13–5. The high brace. *A,* shift paddle outward. *B,* pull downward and back. *C,* hip snap and rotate blade back and up to recover.

of the blade with the paddle held in a position similar to normal paddling. In fact, the reactive use of the high brace is really a modification of the forward stroke used to head off a mid-stroke capsize. The power of the high brace allows "deep recoveries"—righting yourself even when the torso is totally submerged (in fact, some Eskimo roll styles are essentially high braces).

While the low brace is used in the aft sector of the paddle's arc, the high brace is most effective in the forward sector and back to just aft of your body. As with the low brace, you should practice to develop a reflex sequence for both sides.

Step One. Proper position for the high brace is similar to a knuckles-out, chin-up exercise. Hold the paddle level at about chin level and about 6 inches from your face, with the nonbracing-side elbow tucked into your body. Shift the paddle laterally to bring the hand opposite the brace next to your face, as for the low brace. Lean your head toward the bracing side (see fig. 13–5A) .

Fig. 13–6. The high brace on the side opposite the control hand (here, the right) requires flipping the shaft almost 180 degrees by pushing the right elbow forward and bringing that hand back against the chest. (*Audrey Sutherland*)

As with the low brace, wrists should be straight during the brace to prevent buckling or loss of grip. The paddle can be rotated by swinging the elbow forward so that the forearm is vertical, giving a horizontal blade on the control-hand side of feathered paddles, or both blades on unfeathered ones. For a high brace on the noncontrol-hand side with a feathered paddle, you need to flip that blade over 180 degrees from the normal at-rest position. (See fig. 13–6.) Let that hand slide while you rotate the paddle to achieve more rotation than needed for normal paddling by moving the control-hand-side elbow forward and that hand back close to the shoulder (a little wrist extension will be needed too).

Keep the elbows in and the hands below eye level throughout the high brace. There are two reasons for this. First, the shoulders become very vulnerable to dislocation in the elbows-out, arm-over-the-head position. Second, the paddle blade should be kept as level as possible at the beginning of the brace by keeping the opposite hand below eye level.

Start in a normal paddling position and practice the shift for bracing on both sides—forearms vertical to chin-up position, non-control hand sliding as needed for blade positions.

Step Two. Slap the surface, with the blade about opposite your thigh. (See fig. 13–5B.) The power will be a downward pull of your bracing arm with the other arm stationary. This will bring the bracing blade down into the water and toward you. Start the blade in the water about 3 feet from your hull. The closer the paddle blade comes to the boat, the less lift you derive from it. However, the end of the high brace can be used to pull the boat under you (with the hip snap) to recover your balance. (See fig. 13–5C.) While you are getting started, try to recover your balance before the blade goes deep and close to the boat.

Step Three. Retrieve the blade. As with the low brace, retrieving the blade should be automatic in order to be ready for a follow-up brace. Retrieve the blade by rotating the shaft (by moving the bracing-side elbow back), which gives an arcing slice ending with a vertical blade (see fig. 13–5C). Or, if the blade is deep and close to the boat, you can pull the shaft straight out of the water. Or, you can switch to a sweeping low brace (a forward movement) to continue the support and get the blade to the surface (this is how a low brace is integrated into the end of an Eskimo roll). The first two alternatives are used most often.

Spend some time practicing steps one through three on both sides on dry land. Then try the high brace in the water, beginning gently, as with the low brace.

The high brace is quite powerful and provides support throughout the time the blade is pulled down and toward you (though the deeper and closer to the boat it goes, the less effective the support). As you gain more confidence, lean farther and throw more weight onto the brace, even to the point of putting your upper body at water level as you start. Add the hip snap and pull the boat under you at the end of these more extreme braces. Keeping your head down against your brace-side shoulder is very helpful (it is vital for successful Eskimo rolls that are an extension of the high brace).

A *sweeping high brace* generates even firmer and longer support. It is very similar to a forward paddling stroke. Start the brace with the blade ahead of you close to the hull. Keep the rear edge of the bracing blade slightly higher and skim the blade on the surface as with the low brace (except that the direction is now toward the rear). Again, go slowly; the blade need not plane like a water ski. Start by pushing down gently to feel the lift until you get the paddle angle right, then gradually lean as you start the sweep, being sure to end with a strong downward pull on your brace-side hand to restore balance at the end of the stroke.

This becomes a *sculling high brace* by adding a forward sweeping component. Sculling alternately forward and back can give you indefinite support with your high brace. The forward sweeping component is done with the front of the blade and in a high brace position (in contrast to the low brace sweep, which is done with the back of the blade). Proper blade angle for the forward sweep is attained by rolling the wrists back a bit and pushing the elbow forward to raise the front edge of the blade.

A forward paddling stroke can easily be changed into a sweeping high brace by rolling your wrists back slightly to give a blade position halfway between vertical and horizontal. The stroke can be any degree of combination between forward propulsion and support, depending on the blade angle. It is most effective with the paddle shaft kept as horizontal as possible. Once you are comfortable with using the high brace to recover during the forward stroke, you can reinforce this reflex every so often by alternately falling toward each stroke and recovering with the combined stroke and high brace—a bizarre way to paddle but good practice.

This high brace forward stroke is particularly useful for paddling diagonally into waves as described in "Paddling in Wind and Waves." (High and low braces used in following seas are also described in that chapter.) Techniques for bracing in surf are described in "Paddling the Outer Coast."

When practicing your reactive braces to a surprise loss of balance, it is helpful to have an assistant standing in waist-deep water knocking you off balance. That person can stand out of your sight at your stern and shove the hull to one side or the other, giving it a twist in the process.

Leaned Sweeps for Turning

In the paddling chapter I described how edging the boat can aid turning by changing the underwater shape as the boat is tipped. Much more tipping edging allows sharper turning but requires you to lean as well—shifting your torso sideways to or even beyond the point of capsize. Combined leaning and edging can put the hull nearly on its side, pushing the center deep into the water while raising the ends and making it much easier to turn. Doing this without tipping over requires a brace combined with the turning sweep.

I strongly advocate practicing these leaned sweeps on normal outings. It will allow you to reinforce your bracing reactions regu-

Fig. 13–7. A sweeping high brace is used here to turn the kayak counterclockwise. Note how the extreme lean lifts the bow from the water and aids turning by shortening the waterline.

larly and secondarily extend your ability to maneuver in tight quarters. Without this sort of regular exercise, opportunities to develop bracing are limited to pool or similar practice sessions. With regular repetition, properly executed braces can allow you to pass the point of capsize with little chance of taking a dip. Obviously, you should limit your leaned turns to places where a capsize would be merely inconvenient until you feel confident about your braces.

The sweep stroke easily blends into a brace to give you stability during the maneuver. First, review the forward sweep stroke as described in "Maneuvering"; then make it more radical with a high brace. In short, the forward sweep is distinguished from the normal propulsion stroke by the following: arms and paddle offset to the side, opposite hand largely stationary at your midline, and a longer arc stroke farther from the hull and sweeping from bow to stern.

The high brace is used to support a forward sweep by angling the blade back to add a sweeping high brace element. The strongest lean is at midstroke; begin to straighten up to center your balance with a hip snap by the end of the stroke. The difference between a pure forward sweep and sweeping high brace is the degree of lean and blade position. Any degree of combination is possible, depending on how sharply you need to turn. The greater the lean and sweeping arc, the tighter the turn (see fig. 13–7).

A reverse sweep, done with the back of the blade, easily converts to a sweeping low brace for the same kind of lean support. Alternated forward and reverse leaned sweep braces will turn you in place very quickly.

To refresh your bracing reflexes each time you go paddling, try a few high and low braces to each side. If you have a rudder, pull it up and spend some time paddling with leaned sweeps for course control. This practice will keep your bracing reflexes well tuned. And, a deep, sweeping high brace is a great way to cool off on hot days!

14

Paddling in Wind and Waves

Rough-water paddling is difficult to teach, partly because the right conditions for practice are rarely available on demand. Additionally, when conditions do get rough, more experienced paddlers in a party may be too busy taking care of themselves to teach others. Your own experiences may well be your instructor, but you should try to develop your technique in controlled conditions (some suggestions follow) and take advantage of paddling with more experienced people to see how they handle waves. There is no substitute for experience, but the information below may help when you are on your own and challenged by sea conditions.

This chapter is concerned with waves caused by wind (or sometimes boats and ships) in fairly deep water. Techniques for handling beach surf are found in "Paddling the Outer Coast" (though surf is an excellent spot to practice general wave handling).

Wind above about fifteen knots usually will produce whitecaps (waves that are beginning to break). Under the same conditions, whitecaps will appear sooner on salt water than fresh water. The longer it blows and the larger the *fetch* (the distance of open water upwind), the bigger the waves become and the more frequently they break. Waves persist for some time after the wind dies, but they quickly become rounded and less challenging. As discussed in "Tides, Currents, and Weather," a current running counter to the wind direction will produce steeper waves that are more likely to break.

Larger, steeper, and more frequent breaking waves—and the stronger winds that cause them—bring the challenge of boat control and require that you focus some of your attention on staying upright. Your direction of travel relative to the waves is especially important in how they affect you.

Paddling into Wind and Waves
(Head Seas)

Head seas—wind waves coming from ahead of your bow—are generally the least threatening, though big and steep ones may get you wet because your boat's bow does not have time to lift over the rapidly oncoming waves (particularly if the boat is laden with gear). (See fig. 14–1.) Seas from this direction are least likely to cause a capsize because the forces are parallel to the hull's axis. Because of the combined speed of the boat and the oncoming waves, you are more likely to punch through big waves rather than be surfed back with them (with consequences to be described later). And, because it is important to keep your attention on what is coming your way from upwind, paddling into head seas is a psychologically more comfortable position than trying to keep track of oncoming seas to the side or behind. If you suddenly find yourself in very bad seas, paddling gently into the waves is usually the best way to last out a squall (fishing boats and towboats often choose to "jog to weather"— motor into the waves under low power—in the same situation).

Paddling into wind is always drudgery. (My temper wears pretty thin after successive days of paddling windward.) Progress through the water is slow (and probably approaching zero in winds

Fig. 14–1. Head seas.

above twenty knots), and the slow, hard paddling cadence may strain the arms.

If you carry a narrow-blade or a shorter spare paddle, windward paddling is a good time to use either one. Try for a steady cadence with long strokes, bending forward for more reach and less body windage. Because the early part of the stroke provides a bit of lift, some paddlers advocate trying to time the strokes just ahead of the waves to help the boat's bow lift over them. In gusts, I ease up a bit, letting adversity become a bit of a break, and then try to progress each time the gusts subside.

Quartering into head seas—attacking them at an angle—is probably the most common traveling direction in sea kayaking. Upwind travel seems to occupy about half of all windy paddling time, and much of this is quartering into the wind to get to a destination across the wind without being blown downwind.

Quartering into seas is fairly comfortable, and though still arduous, it can be more fun than slogging straight into moderate seas. Most boats are at their best here, and with a little help from the paddler, come as close to dancing as sea kayaks can in all but heavily breaking waves (these and beach surf are best taken head on).

Attack waves and always lean into them, never away. This is a physical and mental attitude that should be applied regardless of the direction of travel, as capsizes almost always occur on the down-wave side. When quartering into waves, I try to time my strokes, beginning with a downwind-side stroke in the trough to help me climb over the wave. Simultaneously, I rudder slightly upwind and start my upwind lean. I gently lean over the wave's crest and plant my upwind stroke just behind it as the boat passes over the crest. This stroke helps the boat to accelerate down the back side of the wave and is easily converted into a high brace for some support as described in "Bracing." (The ability to turn a stroke into a high brace allows you to chance overleaning into steep or breaking waves.) My favorite point is that at which the boat poises at the crest of the wave, seemingly (and to some extent actually) able to turn on a dime, before plunging down the back side pushed along by the up-wave stroke.

Less of a favorite is the grumbling approach of a breaking wave. Then, getting wet is a certainty. Leaning into it to accept a chestful of white water becomes even more important, perhaps with the paddle raised a little higher before planting the stroke brace behind the wave. Then I intone to myself, "Watch out for his brother": big waves often travel in pairs, and the next one can be expected to be similar. (This occurs because the energy in waves travels at half the speed of the waves themselves; large-wave energy gets passed back from one wave to the next.)

Paddling Across the Winds and Waves (Beam Seas)

Lacking the up-wave inertia of head-seas paddling, the boat is much more vulnerable to the forces of bigger and steeper *beam seas*. A capsize is likely if you do not anticipate these seas enough to counter them. As with upwind quartering, lean into the wind and waves. Leaning to windward will balance the wind's force and reduce your windage slightly. It also may reduce *weathercocking* (turning into the wind), which sometimes occurs in boats without rudders. If weathercocking is a problem you may also try offsetting your grip on the paddle to move it to windward. This will give you something of a sweep stroke on the windward side to help counteract weathercocking.

In strong beam winds the wind lifts the horizontal upwind blade of the feathered paddle during the downwind stroke. I once encountered a sudden gust of wind whose lift was so strong that I had to let go of the windward hand and let the paddle flip over to the lee side—not pleasant. Some remedies are: use a narrow-blade paddle, paddle unfeathered (makes the upper blade vertical), or simply keep your upwind blades as low as possible. If you have a rudder, you might eliminate the downwind strokes entirely during gusts. If the accompanying seas are not too big (as when the fetch is limited or the wind only recently arrived), try shifting your grip to windward on the paddle to move it to leeward in order to reduce the leverage and angle of the upwind blade. This is not a good practice, however, when the seas are developed enough that an upwind brace may be required.

The major factor in beam-sea paddling is the tendency to capsize on the downwind side. Though this is a possibility for other directions of travel, you are especially vulnerable in beam seas because your boat has no inertia up- or downwind. Three forces could be working against you as a wave crosses your path. As a wave approaches, the trough movement toward the wave may "pull the rug out" by moving your boat sideways, leaving you leaning precariously away from the wave. This occurs because water in a wave moves *with* the wave direction in the upper portion and the crest, but *contrary* to the wave direction in the lower portion and trough. Or, your boat attempts to float at the angle of the sloping face of the approaching wave, tipped on its side (the greater the initial stability of the hull, the greater this tendency). Or, if the wave is breaking, the white water carried along in its top striking your body may simply bowl you over.

Because of these factors (primarily slope and cyclical water movement), develop the habit of leaning toward a beam wave as it approaches. In more rounded waves, a gentle lean will be plenty. The steeper the wave and stronger the wind, the more lean needed. In severe breaking waves, you may also need to brace toward the wave to allow enough weight shift and to help you recover as the wave passes (remembering that the water now moves with the wave direction on and just behind the crest).

When you see an especially large, breaking beam wave coming, you have two choices: get ready to lean, brace, and take it side-on; or turn into it and punch through it.

In most deep-water breakers taken from the side, only a brief bracing support is needed just before and as the crest arrives, and then the wave passes under you. But a very steep wave or surf in shallow water could surf you sideways on the forward face. If so, the brace must be sustained until the wave loosens its grip on you—usually a short interval in irregular deep-water waves. The fact that the wave and your boat move faster than the water within the wave work to your advantage; a paddle blade placed flat on top of the wave will plane on the water. Just lean on your brace on top of the wave, and the movement of the wave will support your paddle as long as you stay with it. Be sure to recover your balance before the wave passes under you.

The practicality of turning up into waves to take them as head seas depends on your boat's agility, which in turn depends on its loading and design (ruddered turns usually are too slow). If you see a particularly big wave in time, using an intervening wave crest can help by turning when the center of the boat is on the crest and the ends are relatively free of the water. A reverse (backward) sweep on the up-wave side will help make the turn, done primarily in the aft quarter because of your forward momentum. It will rob you of forward momentum, however, and increase your likelihood of being surfed backward. The reverse sweep also puts you in a good position for a supporting low brace on the wave if you need it. A forward sweep on the upwind side will turn you back to the beam-on course again once the threat is past.

Downwind Running (Following Seas)

Running downwind is the least comfortable direction of travel and is the worst way to be going when seas get really bad. One problem is disorientation—you cannot watch your boat's action and pay attention to what vengeful demon is roaring after your stern. Repeatedly swiveling your eyes and head between front and back leads to gaps of attention and vertigo.

Though downwind paddling is faster, it can be stressful because of the constant acceleration and deceleration associated with each wave's passage. But the most persistent problem is the boat's tendency to turn sideways, known as *broaching*, across bigger waves.

The broaching problem is most chronic for boats with slim bows and sterns and little rocker, and it is worst in waves a little farther apart than your boat's length. The faster you go, as when you surf with a wave, the greater its directional instability and vulnerability to broaching forces.

When you are running down the face of waves that are about a boat length long, the bow buries into the trough or into the lower back of the preceeding wave, while the stern digs into the crest. The water in the crest of the wave is moving forward with the wave, but the water in the trough is moving backward toward it. Hence, the bow is meeting more water resistance than the stern. Because you cannot keep running exactly straight down wave, these forces are applied at an angle to the boat's travel. The bow begins to veer off to one side while the stern tries to overtake it to the other side, and a broach begins. Once it starts, there is little that can be done to correct it in most sea kayaks, and like it or not, you end up side-on to the wave, still moving sideways. Unless you are ready for the consequences as discussed for beam seas, a down-wave capsize becomes likely.

In smaller and more closely spaced waves or larger and longer ones, the broaching tendency is less severe, although most boats will try to yaw off course to one side or the other to some extent. Often, this will result in an oscillating course, with some broaching action to one side of the front of a wave, followed by a compensating straightening while you are on the back side of a wave (there, the water directions within the wave at bow and stern are reversed from the combination responsible for broaching). If these course oscillations do seem to cancel out, and you seem to be able to hold your overall desired direction, just let them happen. If not, try to anticipate such wandering by heading it off with sweep strokes, stern rudder strokes, and the boat's rudder. For instance, if you are not traveling exactly down the waves, you can head off the broaching tendency by steering the rudder toward the down-wave side just as a wave lifts the stern and/or by making a sweep stroke on the up-wave side at the same time.

But in bigger and steeper seas, these simply may not be enough to prevent frequent broaches. Slowing down, particularly on the front of waves when you tend to surf ahead, will reduce directional instability. Paddle slowly, letting the wind do most of the work, and even use braking strokes to prevent surfing. But if none of these is working to prevent a broach, give up on trying to go straight and shift to the up-wave lean and brace.

Riding particularly big and steep seas can also result in *pitch-poling*—the bow digs into the trough so deeply that the stern is carried up and over for an end-over-end loop and capsize. This happened to a friend of mine halfway across a 17-mile crossing in the Sea of Cortez. His folding K-1 pitch-poled while surfing big following waves. Fortunately his partner was able to help him re-enter, and no gear was lost. They finished the crossing more slowly and without catching rides on the big waves.

Traveling downwind in conditions that produce unavoidable broaches is nerve-wracking and, if you have to devote a lot of time and energy to dealing with broaches, slow and fatiguing. Instead, look for another way to get to your destination or simply go somewhere else.

If you must get downwind, other ways to get there include quartering *upwind* with just enough paddling effort to keep your heading and prevent backward surfing while letting the wind blow you down there. Or, if there is a shore that you can divert to and then follow downwind, try quartering into and across the waves toward it to minimize your time in open water, and then seek a more quiet shore route to your destination. I frequently choose such circuitous routes rather than take a long and exposed downwind run.

Surfing for Distance

Occasionally the waves are just right for catching a fast ride without the broaching hassles. Longer waves work best, even ocean swells (surf skis use the swells to race across Moloka'i Channel in Hawaii at speeds averaging ten knots). Where there is current, wind waves running in the same direction as the current can produce excellent distance-surfing waves.

My favorite surfing experience occurred when I was traveling down the Inside Passage behind Vancouver Island, British Columbia. In the channel between Whirlpool and Green Point Rapids we picked up a south-flowing two-knot current pushed along by a twenty-knot northerly wind. The long waves produced glorious and almost effortless rides that lasted for hundreds of yards. We were going so fast with our heavily laden kayaks during these rides that for short distances we outran a forty-foot sailboat motoring along.

Catching a wave takes power applied just at the end of the time when the boat seems to wallow between waves, seemingly making little progress (usually the time to lighten up your paddling effort). The bow usually will be digging deeply at this time; watch for the moment it begins to rise to apply the power. As the wave behind you lifts your stern and begins to pass under you, throw your weight forward and push hard on your strokes to get the boat moving with the forward wave face. You will know when that has happened, as your speed increases dramatically. Ease off on the paddle effort, as you may actually outrun your wave.

Boat wakes can produce excellent surfing rides, too. Generally I find it takes a large pleasure boat or smaller commercial vessels (tugs often make good ones) to get the right wave length, and you need to be fairly close to the origin to get a good ride (not the safest or most welcome place to be). Some wakes will give rides only if you quarter across them to achieve the right wave length, but then the broaching tendency may require that you put too much effort into steering to keep your speed up.

Practice for Rough-Water Paddling

Finding a place with challenging waves and wind but without the risks is rarely easy. Sometimes boat wakes can give you the broaching experience that requires a brace, but they are rarely steep enough to do so. Heavy boat traffic in a channel with sea walls can produce confused, conflicting, and patternless waves, which can challenge your balance.

In Seattle, Washington, we sometimes put on dry suits to practice in southerly winter gales on the city's Lake Union, where a 1-mile fetch produces big enough waves to make interesting paddling along the windward shore at Gasworks Park. The cement bulkheads produce reflected waves crossing the oncoming ones (called *clapotis*), which require quick braces to keep your balance.

In general, look for windward shores where you and your boat will be washed onto a hospitable shore such as a beach. Long offshore shallows produce good breaking seas and are convenient for wading ashore, if need be. Low summer surf on a gently shoaling beach also presents excellent wave practice.

15

"Wet-Exit" Capsize Recoveries

In the smoothest sea conditions, a loss of balance or a paddle blade pulled through the water at the wrong angle can produce a capsize. But more likely, a tip-over will result from water rough enough to overcome your capsize-prevention abilities, and a successful recovery in these trying conditions will require all the skill and confidence you can muster. *Practice* is the key; understanding how to do the procedures is not enough to make them work in real conditions. The familiarity of actually having done them makes all the difference, especially when waves, cold, and exhaustion dim your recollections.

I recommend that you try all of the procedures described here at least once; the more you can repeat and master, the better. Take roles of both rescuer and victim and wear what you normally paddle in. If you can do it safely, practicing in rough water is infinitely more valuable (gentle surf on a beach is excellent).

The following recovery methods work for a paddler who has capsized and bailed out of his boat either when alone or when other paddlers, still in their boats, are there to assist. There are many more variations for special situations not described here, such as "all in" recoveries used when an entire party has come out of their boats. These are used rarely but are worth learning after you have mastered the more common ones. (See Derek Hutchinson's *Guide to Expedition Kayaking on Sea & Open Water.*)

To do any of these, your boat *must* have sufficient flotation at *both* ends to support your weight when you are seated in the swamped boat, and the cockpit coaming must be well above water level to allow bailing or pumping. In other words, you must be able to empty your swamped boat while seated in it. Bulkheads at both ends will suffice (backed up with air bags if there is the chance of hatch or bulkhead failure). Air bags alone are fine if they are secured so that they cannot slide out of position. A sea sock will increase the buoyancy and limit the amount of water to be bailed or pumped out. Sea socks are very desirable in large-volume K-2s or in heavily laden K-1s.

These procedures may appear straightforward and simple, but the movements will not come naturally or smoothly when you actually try them in rough, cold water, so practice each as the rescuer and the victim. Knowing exactly what to do in each role is critical, particularly for the rescuer who may need to direct the movements of an inexperienced or hypothermic victim.

Learn these procedures in a pool or still water where you will not need to be concerned about drifting or boat traffic. You may appreciate more clothing than a bathing suit for protection against abrasion, such as a long-sleeve T-shirt and light synthetic pants, long underwear bottoms, or exercise tights. Footgear with a firm sole is particularly important for comfort and protection (the sling rescue described below is too uncomfortable for bare feet).

Simple Assisted Recovery

This frequently used recovery requires only one rescuer, and it is usually effective unless the person capsized (henceforth, the victim) is extremely tired, weak, or hypothermic (in which case the *H-I* maneuver, described later, may be better). The sling variations also described here usually are needed only if the victim is similarly incapacitated or is substantially heavier than the rescuer.

The recovery may begin by inverting and emptying the capsized kayak. Alternately, it can be bailed or pumped out after getting back aboard, probably the best choice in extremely rough seas when the inverted-emptying maneuver is difficult, and water may re-enter while you reboard anyhow. The latter is the only choice with a gear-laden kayak.

The victim can partially empty the inverted boat by pushing down on one end until the other end is raised from the water to the point that the cockpit is exposed (this will not work with poor flotation). The hardest point may be breaking the suction of the cockpit, which holds the water inside it and prevents raising it from the water. Slightly twisting the boat on its side may help. Once the water is drained from the cockpit for a few seconds, the boat must be flipped to right-side-up just before releasing the depressed end.

Fig. 15–1. The assisted recovery. The rescuer's arms grip both sides of the cockpit, allowing the victim room to re-enter. The paddles can be locked under the arms for added rigidity.

Avoid cuts and scratches from the rudder by using the bow. Obviously, neither this nor the next method will work if much gear is in the boat.

The rescuer may also dump the boat by lifting the inverted boat's bow over his lap and holding it until the water drains from the cockpit, then spinning the kayak upright while releasing it. Or, he may pull the boat across his deck to balance at the midpoint while it drains. Be careful, as this procedure could crack the deck of either boat (and is very likely to leave a few scratches).

After righting the kayak (emptied or not), the rescuer pulls alongside, with the victim on the far side of his own boat. Both kayaks can face in the same or opposite directions. The victim passes his paddle to the rescuer, who lays both paddles across the decks of the two boats.

The rescuer's primary job is to steady the victim's kayak as he reboards, which is not difficult unless the victim is much heavier or is very clumsy with fatigue or cold. The grip on the victim's cockpit is the key: one hand firmly on each side at the widest point, yet still allowing the victim clear access to the rear and center of the cockpit for reboarding. To minimize the obstruction from his arms, the rescuer should reach to the far coaming with whichever arm is toward the victim's bow. The two paddles should be positioned across both cockpits and trapped under the rescuer's forearms to aid stability. He pulls both boats tightly together and leans across to distribute his weight equally over the two kayaks, elbows in tightly for a rigid, strong position. (See fig. 15–1.)

The victim pulls his upper body onto his rear deck just aft of the cockpit and faces toward his boat's stern. (As with climbing onto the inverted hull, this may be easiest to do near the stern; then slide forward.) Lying face down, he can put one arm across the rescuer's deck for added stability. Next, the victim puts his inside leg in the cockpit, but keeps the outer leg in the water for stability until the last moment. *Keeping low with his torso on the deck,* the victim slides backward, keeping his leg straight as it moves into the cockpit. The other leg can enter the cockpit when his hips cross the rear coaming. At this point, a low center of balance is essential. The victim should keep the torso on the deck and avoid kneeling.

The critical stage is the turnover to a sitting position, as both paddlers are now vulnerable to a capsize should the rescuer lose his grip or the victim lose his balance. The victim should turn toward the rescuer, keeping one arm on the rescuer's deck (or on the rescuer himself) for balance as long as possible. When about halfway over, it should be possible to drop quickly into the seat.

The rescuer should retain his tight grip on the victim's coaming, as many paddlers capsize again after this point. That boat may be quite unstable from the water in it, and the victim's balance may be impaired. The rescuer should stay in position until the victim has reattached his sprayskirt, pumped out if needed, and had a chance to rest before taking control of his kayak again.

If the seas are rough, pumping is best done through the sprayskirt; slip the pump in next to the forward edge of the coaming or, if the skirt's tunnel is loose enough, next to the body.

The Sling Stirrup Rescue

This rescue variation offers two advantages: it provides a stirrup to assist in getting out of the water and aboard the kayak, and the victim's weight in the stirrup securely stabilizes his boat so that the rescuer is free to aid the victim. The sling takes more time to set up, but it may be necessary for some victim-rescuer pairs. A hundred-pound woman will probably need the sling to rescue her two-hundred-pound husband. A person lacking the upper body strength to pull himself onto his deck also may need the sling.

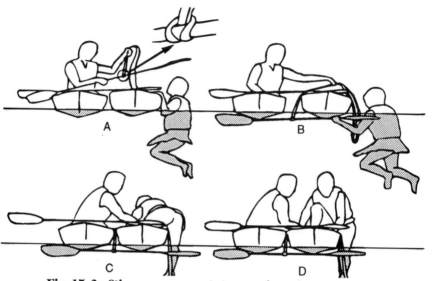

Fig. 15–2. Stirrup recovery. *A,* A rescuer loops sling onto victim's paddle; *B,* victim feeds paddle under boats and rescuer picks up sling; *C,* entry facing to rear; *D,* alternative "horse mounting" entry.

The basic requirement is a 15-foot length of either webbing or rope (½-inch polypropylene is good, and it floats). This rope is tied into a loop to fit the boat it will be used with (see the procedure below for sizing). The sling should be prepared in advance and stowed in an accessible spot on the boat.

The rescue starts as before, with the optional emptying of the boat and then righting it next to the rescuer's kayak, facing either way. The rescuer takes the victim's paddle and attaches the sling to the middle of the shaft by passing one end of the sling through the other to form a loop around the shaft that will not slip easily (see fig. 15–2A). The victim then feeds the paddle under both boats, and the rescuer picks up the sling between the boats and passes it over the victim's cockpit (each side of the loop to front and rear of the coaming) and into the water next to the victim (see fig. 15–2B). The paddle should *not* go through the loop on the victim's side.

When the victim steps into the loop in the water, his weight pulls on the paddle beneath both boats. When stepped into, the loop should be long enough (sized in advance of the capsize, of course) to place the victim's knee at the surface. He will have difficulty getting his foot into a loop that is too short and will not be raised high enough for reboarding by one that is too long.

When facing his cockpit, either foot can be placed in the loop.

If the foot toward the stern is placed in the stirrup (see fig. 15–2C), reboarding is similar to the previous method: he lies on the rear deck and starts into the cockpit with the other leg. If the forward foot is placed in the loop, reboarding is like mounting a horse (see fig. 15–2D); a much more upright and quicker but less stable alternative. For the latter, the key is to swing the leg in and then immediately sit in the seat, bringing the second leg in last. (This will be difficult if the cockpit is too short for the knees to pass under it while seated; use the stern-side foot in the stirrup in that case.)

The stabilizing effect of the sling ends abruptly as soon as the victim's weight comes off it. The victim must watch his weight distribution at that point, and the rescuer should grip his coaming or steady the victim's body. Be particularly wary of a loss of balance toward the rescuer just as the victim steps out of the sling.

A simplified variation on the sling rescue is faster but offers less stability. The rescuer puts a much shorter loop onto his paddle near one blade and lays the shaft over both cockpits so that this loop hangs into the water just in front of the victim. This method requires the rescuer to bear down hard on his paddle as the victim reboards. It does not stabilize the victim's boat as well as the standard procedure. However, the short loop can be used universally on all boats, sized long enough to hang from deck level.

H-I Rescue

The H-I recovery involves rescuers in two boats. They form an "H" with their kayaks and all three paddles across their cockpits. The inverted victim's boat (the "I" component) is pulled over the

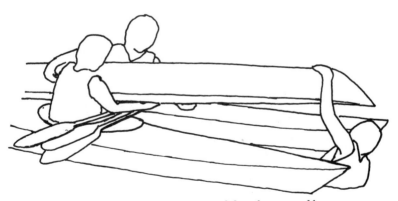

Fig. 15–3. The H-I recovery requires sliding the inverted boat across all three paddles.

paddles and "see-sawed" to empty it. (This is not possible with gear in the boat, and paddles have been broken during the maneuver.) Then the boat is flipped upright, and the victim is assisted aboard between the other boats. (See fig. 15–3.) The rescuers' teamwork provides a more secure recovery than the one-on-one methods and is the best alternative if the victim is having difficulty.

Paddle-Wing Self-Rescue

The self-rescue with a paddle wing has been used successfully by many solo kayakers in rough seas and surf, and it is an important ring of defense for anyone who paddles alone. Because no help can be expected, practice for proficiency in this somewhat tricky maneuver is all the more important (see fig. 15–4).

The critical elements are a float securely attached to the paddle blade and a means to fix the paddle firmly to the deck to stabilize the boat. Many sea kayaks are designed with a flat deck between the cockpit and a pattern of strong bungees arranged to hold the paddle outrigger. Boats with a rounded rear deck are more difficult to stabilize with the paddle, and they may require customized rigging to limit the hull's rotation under the paddle (such as loops of webbing with quick-release buckles near the sides of the deck).

The float can be anything that can be quickly and securely

Fig. 15–4. Paddle-wing recovery.

attached to the blade. It should provide at least a half-cubic foot of flotation. This might be one of a few inflatable float bags specifically designed for the use, rigid foam blocks (slit to receive the blade), empty water jugs, dry-storage bags, or even a PFD. Some paddlers prefer a rigid or permanently inflated float (to avoid having to inflate it), which can be carried just aft of the cockpit where it adds little resistance to head winds.

The solo paddler may drain an unladen kayak as described earlier by pushing down on the end and flipping the boat. But in rough seas it is probably best to keep the boat inverted and to lie over it while securing the float to the paddle, thus making the work easier and minimizing heat loss from cold sea. (If righted earlier, the cockpit would fill as waves splash in while you prepare the float.) The commercially designed paddle floats must be pushed onto the blade before full inflation. Air pressure keeps them from slipping off, but a short line clipped around the shaft above the blade is a good backup.

Once the paddle outrigger is attached, reboard as in the simple assisted rescue described earlier. Start on the side of the outrigger and just forward from it, sliding onto the rear deck facing aft. As before, stay low on your stomach (no elbows or knees) and keep the outside leg in the water for stability until you are ready to slide into the seat. The critical point is the turn-over; avoid shifting your weight away from the outrigger, as there is nothing to prevent a flip in that direction. (If you use a water jug as a float, a few quarts of water in it will provide a counterweight. A small open-ended sock attached to other floats could do the same.) Keep the outrigger in place while you attach your sprayskirt and pump out, then be sure that your balance is as secure as possible for the precarious step of removing it.

Inverted Re-entry and Float Roll

This maneuver (see fig. 15–5) requires that you first re-enter the cockpit of the inverted kayak and then right yourself using the paddle with the float attached to it. The inverted re-entry is a good alternative to the Eskimo roll (I often use it during deep-water roll practice whenever my roll fades). The inverted re-entry and float roll is probably more feasible than the *paddle-wing* recovery in really rough seas. Immersing the head, however, greatly increases the rate of heat loss in cold water and hastens hypothermia. Few of us have the breath capacity to reattach the sprayskirt before rolling back up, so you will be obliged to do that and then pump or bail after righting (using the paddle and float for stability).

First attach the float to the paddle, preferably while lying over the inverted hull. Then slide into the water and face the cockpit. Lay the paddle next to the cockpit coaming with the shaft fore and aft and grip both shaft and coaming with the hand on the side toward the bow.

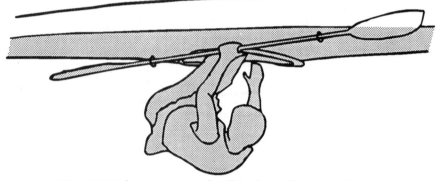

Fig. 15–5. The re-enter and roll (or float roll): somersaulting into position.

Now do a sideways somersault, ending upside down in position to slide your legs into the cockpit. Grasp the far side of the coaming with your free hand partway through the somersault to help pull you into position. Your life vest hinders the maneuver at the start but helps at the end by floating you up into the seat. Initial practice with a mask in warm clear water is almost mandatory.

Once seated (upside down), be sure that your feet contact the footbraces, and that your knees and thighs are firmly braced. Swing the paddle perpendicular to the boat, hands in normal position, and you are ready to roll up to the surface. Ease in doing that depends on body movements that also are critical for the Eskimo roll as discussed in Chapter 12: "Stability, Capsize, and Righting." Essentially, you must right the boat with your hips before you raise your upper body from the water. If you try to push yourself up from your paddle, the float will simply sink. Instead, concentrate on keeping your head on the surface until the boat is nearly righted; then the rest will be easy. With the float on the paddle, you can pull yourself to the surface and take a few breaths if you need them before finishing the recovery.

16

Emergency Signaling

Employ this last line of defense when you are incapable of saving yourself or one of your companions. There are numerous devices that you might carry, all with different effectiveness in varying situations. The key is having more than one type of *backup* on hand or plenty of single-use devices.

Though U.S. and Canadian laws mandate that most boaters carry distress signals, requirements for kayaks and other hand-powered vessels are minimal. They must carry signals only while

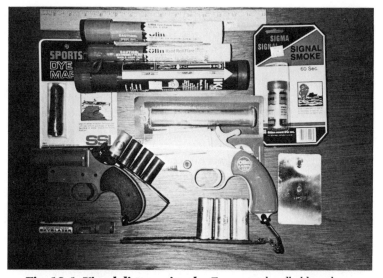

Fig. 16–1. Visual distress signals. *Top center:* handheld smoke signal, hand-held flare, 40,000-candela parachute flare. *Upper right:* smoke canister. *Lower right:* signal mirror. *Center:* 25-mm pistol with meteors and parachute flare. *Lower left:* Skyblazer and 12-gauge pistol with meteors. *Upper left:* dye marker.

traveling at night (not a requirement in Canada at this writing). Such devices must be rated for night use, either an approved distress light or flares (three of the latter must be carried). Also, you must have a flashlight to identify yourself and to prevent collisions (though most flashlights will not qualify as a night distress signal unless they have a built-in automatic SOS sequence).

Attracting help is a twofold effort. First you must *alert* others that you are out there and in trouble. Devices designed for this purpose generally expend themselves brilliantly (and some with a loud bang) but quickly, and some go so fast that they are easily missed. But since a considerable delay might occur while whoever saw your signal summons the Coast Guard helicopter or comes to investigate for himself, you also need signals with a *locate* function—bright enough to be seen (though perhaps not as eye-catching) and long-lasting enough to pinpoint your position.

Most signaling choices do either the alert or the locate function best, and a few do both well. Below is a summary of your options. (See fig. 16–1.)

Flares and Smoke Devices

Flares burn with an intense light. All marine flares are waterproof and should fire when wet by scratching a cap on the other end or by pulling a chain or trigger. *Meteors* use a rocket to propel the light hundreds of feet into the air, where it burns while falling back toward the surface. *Parachute flares* do the same except that the light burns much longer aloft, suspended under a little parachute. Both meteors and parachute flares are primarily alerting devices; meteors are quite short-lived, and parachute flares may drift a considerable distance from your position. *Handheld* flares, which last about two minutes, are good locators but have limited visibility at distances because they are surface lights.

The most popular meteor for sea kayakers is a pencil-type flare called the Skyblazer. They are small (will fit in a pocket), inexpensive, and come in packages of three. They ascend to about 500 feet and burn with a fairly bright light for six to eight seconds. But because they are brief, and because they can fail to ignite, carry at least six of them. Firing them sequentially in pairs, when you see a potential rescuer, will increase your chances of being spotted and responded to. Be sure to grip the body of the flare firmly to prevent it from being pulled downward through your hand as you pull the igniter chain.

Meteors can also be fired from special pistols. The smaller 12-gauge gun fires a meteor that, at least for one popular model, is dim, low, and short-lived in comparison to the Skyblazer. The bigger 25-mm pistol sends up a much more effective meteor and can also fire a fairly dim parachute flare. Both guns are somewhat expensive, but the cartridges are inexpensive to replace.

Self-contained parachute flares also can be bought singly and are quite expensive. But they are major attention getters: 40,000 candela of brightness at 1,000 feet altitude for forty seconds (compared to 20,000 at 500 feet for eight seconds for the Skyblazer). Remember that one is not enough. Since parachute flares drift a considerable distance with wind, fire it up to forty-five degrees from vertical into the wind so that it will drift over you and mark your position more accurately.

Handheld flares should be held as high as possible to increase their range of visibility. However, the more popular ones will drip hot slag that will burn you or your boat (particularly folding or inflatable boats), so hold the flare on the downside and with the tube horizontal.

Meteors and handheld flares are least effective in bright sunlight. The smoke device emits a large cloud of bright orange smoke that is more visible on sunny days, though wind may dissipate the cloud and keep it low on the water where it is hard to see at a distance. Smoke devices may be handheld or in a canister to be ignited and tossed into the water. Both last about a minute.

Though supposedly waterproof, all flares and smoke devices should be kept in a tight container in your boat and stored in the open in a cool, dry place at home. Flares kept in a life jacket pocket when you practice the Eskimo roll or ones allowed to roll around in the boat's bilge stand a poor chance of working. Your "day bag" (a dry bag kept handy in the cockpit with essentials that you use during a day's paddling) is a good place for them. Skyblazers carried on your person might be stored in a knotted condom.

Flares and smoke devices have expiration dates, which are three and a half years (United States) or four years (Canada) after manufacture. Expired flares do not fulfill any legal requirements, and older flares have higher failure rates.

Strobe Lights

These little devices are probably the most effective approved nighttime signal, and they are also quite visible during the day. The main advantages are that they have a long life if the batteries are maintained, are reliable (and testable, which flares are not), and can be switched on or off depending on whether a potential rescuer is visible. Strobes, however, are not a distress signal in International Waters (navigation zones that are primarily offshore) though both the Canadian Coast Guard and U.S. Coast Guard will investigate them when they are displayed without other navigation lights. But since most kayaking occurs in areas where Inland Waters rules apply (primarily lakes and coastal approaches to ports), strobes are fully appropriate for emergency signaling.

Signal Mirrors

Though mirrors carry no official approval, search-and-rescue pilots think highly of them for alerting and locating victims in sunny weather, even from long distances. A signal mirror should be made of noncorrosive stainless steel. It should also have a lanyard that will attach it to you.

In the center is a hole. To use the mirror, sight through the hole and hold your thumb at arm's length so that its tip covers your target. Then adjust the mirror so that you can see the flash on your thumbnail. Keep moving the mirror back and forth to flash across your thumb, giving a strobelike flash visible to the target. Stop flashing when an aircraft is approaching, as it blinds the pilot.

Flags and Dye Markers

Neither flags nor dye markers are popular with kayakers, and they have limited effectiveness. Approved distress flags are orange, 3 feet on each side, and have a black ball and black square on them. They are fairly compact to carry, and if you use one, be sure that it is fitted with a quick way to attach it to a paddle. Dye markers are spread on the water to produce a yellow or green patch that is most visible from the air. They are effective primarily for locating victims. Dye markers are less useful in poor light or when there are extensive breaking seas.

Emergency Position Indicating Radio Beacons (EPIRBs)

Though EPIRBs cost several hundred dollars, they are reliable and attract attention from a huge radius. They are also waterproof and float. They must be licensed, as with VHF radios.

The type B EPIRB sends a signal on aviation distress frequencies that is picked up by an international network of search-and-rescue (SAR) satellites anywhere in the world. Their signal can pinpoint your position within five miles. (The type A is identical except that it turns on automatically when immersed). Class B EPIRBs are the most effective device when you are paddling in remote areas. The disadvantage to this system is its huge false alarm rate (over 90 percent, primarily from aircraft automatically activating their EPIRBs during hard landings). Signals are not investigated until confirmed by a second satellite pass or other evidence (such as an overdue notice). For these reasons the type B probably will not provide a quick enough response to save you if you are swimming in cold water.

The type C EPIRB emits signals on the marine VHF radio frequencies—series of beeps on channels 16 and 15—used by VHF radios. As for all hand-held VHF transmitters at sea level, range is only about 5 to 10 miles, depending on the antenna of the receiver. These EPIRBs could be heard by any boater or shore station within range and monitoring these channels. Unfortunately, many boaters may not recognize distress calls from an EPIRB, and the likelihood of a response is uncertain. If someone does understand it, however, response would be much quicker than to a class A or B EPIRB and quite possibly fast enough to save capsized kayakers from hypothermia.

VHF Radios

Most everyone agrees that a VHF radio is the best way to signal distress, assuming that you have a means to keep the radio dry while it is in use even when swimming. At sea level the average handheld radio has a range of between 5 and 10 miles, depending on the antenna height of the receiver (the Coast Guards have powerful receiving stations in many places). A few feet of elevation on shore greatly increases your calling range. Emergency calls should be made on channel 16; be sure to use the word *"mayday"* and state your position and situation.

Make Yourself Visible

In recent years there have been a number of searches for kayakers in trouble. Lacking distress signals, several were not found in time to save their lives. These sad outcomes underscore some lessons about making your boat and person visible to search-and-rescue craft. First, stay with your boat. Kayaks are far easier to spot than swimmers. Second, use shades of white, yellow, international orange, or neon colors (which convert nonvisible light to visible) on boat decks and hulls as well as clothing and PFDs. Blues, greens, grays, and reds have poor visibility against the sea (red fabrics darken considerably when wet), especially in poor light. Third, reflective tape on paddle blades, deck, or PFD shoulders is very effective at night with searchlights. Of course, carrying *any* light source is better yet.

17

Hypothermia

Extended immersion in cold water cools the body to the extent that it is unable to maintain its heat, even after leaving the water if the process is sufficiently advanced. Death is eventual if the temperature continues to drop. Sea kayakers who have drowned probably did so because of hypothermic incapacitation. Drowning and hypothermia are medically related, and new findings about each has affected how near-drownings and hypothermia are medically treated.

This brief discussion of hypothermia is written with a layman's understanding of a complex medical problem. Misreading the severity of hypothermia and mistreatment of it may result in death. Read as much as you can about it (see suggestions at the end of the chapter), know how to head it off, and be conservative if you must treat it.

Hypothermia becomes critical when the body core—brain, heart, and lungs—begins to cool, which may be ten to fifteen minutes after the skin and tissue begin to cool. As the core cools, certain symptoms usually appear. The first are the sensations of cold and shivering. When the body temperature goes below about ninety-three degrees Fahrenheit, signs are loss of manual dexterity, clumsiness, slurred speech, and rigid muscles. Confusion and impaired judgment are also likely, and one may cease to feel cold and may even feel euphoric. A temperature below eighty-six degrees will render the person unconscious, and the heartbeat will become erratic. Death usually occurs at temperatures below eighty degrees. The symptoms above may not be reliable indicators of the state of hypothermia. The best indicator is a rectal thermometer (oral or armpit temperatures may be quite different from the critical core temperature).

Though hypothermia easily can occur from cooling in the air, especially with inadequate or wet clothing, immersion in water robs body heat twenty-five times faster. The colder the water, the faster the progress of hypothermia. Yet it can even happen in the warmer waters of Hawaii, though it takes much longer. There is no sure way to predict how long an individual can survive in water of a given temperature; it depends on body mass and fat, clothing, and the person's activities in the water.

Of course, a wet suit or dry suit may protect you from hypothermia indefinitely. Multiple layers of loose clothing that can trap and warm water will help (the semidry suit works this way). In fifty-degree water, a person wearing a life vest may survive up to three hours by holding still, and wearing a life vest will extend your margin by keeping you from drowning if hypothermia makes you unconscious. Swimming reduces survival time by up to one quarter, so striking out for shore should only be attempted if shore is very close. Because blood circulation increases heat loss, keep the heart rate down by avoiding unnecessary exercise in the water. A huddled position—drawing legs up and arms in to protect the critical heat loss areas at armpits, sides, and groin—can almost double survival time. A group should huddle in a circle.

At least 50 percent of heat loss happens through the head and neck, so keeping them out of the water is critical (and may be a good reason to avoid capsize recovery techniques like the re-enter and roll). "Drown-proofing"—a technique for extending survival without flotation in warm water by lying for periods face down with the head submerged—should *not* be used in cold water as it can cut survival time in half.

A lack of ready energy reserves greatly increases vulnerability to hypothermia, in or out of the water. An individual who skips breakfast before an outing is a prime candidate. Eating quick-energy snacks such as candy or dried fruits throughout the day is important to maintain reserves. Dehydration can enhance hypothermia so be sure to drink fluids regularly.

In diagnosing hypothermia, the earlier symptoms—shivering, impaired coordination, or slurred speech—may not always be reliable indicators. Some people do not shiver, and some victims may deny that they have hypothermia or insist that they can recover on their own. As indicated earlier, the rectal temperature gives the most reliable diagnosis. If in doubt, treat for it anyway; letting hypothermia progress to a more advanced stage reduces the chances of recovery in less than ideal conditions.

Treatments for early hypothermia when the core temperature

is above ninety degrees Fahrenheit should *not* be used for more advanced cases. Shivering, which is the body's effort to rewarm itself, occurs in the early stages of hypothermia but may continue into more advanced stages and therefore is not a reliable measure. Exercise is suitable only in the early stage and as long as the person is protected from any further heat loss. Likewise, hot showers, baths, and drinks (the last actually do little good) are fine for persons that are clearly in the early stage (again consult the thermometer) but should be avoided for more severe cases.

After removing wet clothes, insulate the victim to prevent further heat loss. In all but early cases, an external heat source also will be required when the body is unable to generate enough heat on its own. Rewarming treatment during the advanced stages can be very dangerous, so evacuation with protection against further heat loss should have priority. If help is not available, the keys to treatment are *slow, gentle,* and *long.* Body temperature continues to drop during treatment, so care must be sustained, perhaps for days. Avoid moving or jarring the victim, which could bring on a heart attack. Most important, apply *moderate warmth,* not heat. (What might be considered common-sense and traditional treatments can be fatal in the case of advanced hypothermia.)

A drop in body temperature triggers a defense mechanism, which reduces the flow of blood to the extremities to protect the temperature of the core. A rapid or massive application of heat to a hypothermic victim signals the core to restore circulation to the extremities, a condition called *after drop.* Cold blood returning from these areas can cause an unusual heartbeat—it shivers rather than pumps—and a heart attack may follow. Hence, avoid hot showers or tubs and drinking hot liquids. In fact, any liquid may be dangerous for a victim in shock (usually the case in moderate or advanced stages) as the liquid could be vomited and taken into the lungs, resulting in pneumonia. Never give alcohol, as this can "fool" the body into believing it is warm and produce after drop. Nor should you rub the limbs to encourage circulation.

External heat sources can be anything warm (what feels warm to the person doing the treatment—do not trust the victim's opinion): chemical heat packs, warm rocks, lukewarm water bottles, or towels soaked in warm water. About 105 degrees is ideal. Insulate the victim well and apply heat to the head, neck, and sides, but *not* to the arms and legs. Lukewarm baths may be used, but keep the limbs out of the water.

Body-to-body external heat is often the most effective source in difficult conditions. Chest-to-chest, skin-to-skin contact in a sleeping bag is best, with one or two heat donors, who should exercise to increase heat levels before getting in with the victim. But avoid moving or exercising the victim.

Treatment should be continued for at least one hour. If breathing or pulse ceases, begin artificial respiration (which does little to warm the victim) and CPR (heart massage). Note that CPR can *cause* damage to the heart if the victim's temperature is very low, so undertake it only if no pulse is found. A weak pulse may be sufficient for life under those conditions.

For the solo paddler, treating one's own advanced hypothermia is difficult. You will have to make an external heat source while avoiding exertion and additional heat loss and while working with impaired motor control and possibly befuddled judgment. If you get ashore in settled areas, do not be bashful about seeking help from strangers immediately.

In the wilds, chemical heat packs (at least three), a sleeping bag, cooking stove, and warm water bottles are probably the lone cruiser's best friends. A fire probably takes too much energy and time except in the best circumstances. Breathing the steam from a pot of hot water with a towel over your head may be an excellent means of regaining heat while you lie in your sleeping bag with the stove nearby heating another potful. (In fact, a device for administering warm breathing vapor is one of the frontline treatments used by emergency medical technicians.)

Near-Drowning in Cold Water

Perhaps as a throwback to marine mammalian relatives, humans have the recently discovered ability to survive underwater in a comatose state for an hour or longer. In water colder than seventy degrees Fahrenheit (twenty degrees centigrade), the body processes slow, thus requiring less oxygen. Consequently, supposedly drowned victims can be revived from this state, where previously they were assumed dead.

Such near-drowning might result quickly from a capsize in very cold water; the body cools quickly and rapidly shuts down its processes. Or, it might be the continuation of the later stages of hypothermia. In either case, the victim *looks* dead; there is no pulse or breathing.

Assume that the person is alive and revivable, though it may take long, hard, and discouraging work to make it happen. Both artificial respiration and CPR (the latter only if *no* pulse is found and medical help will not be available in the near future) must be administered continuously, along with hypothermia treatment. Do not stop until the victim is revived or until medical help arrives. Victims of near drowning have reported being aware of and hearing people working on them. Though unable to respond they may regain the will to recover knowing that help is at hand. Once recovered, the victim's temperature equilibrium will have been severely disturbed, so special protection and treatment will be necessary for several days.

Suggested Reading

Wilkerson, James, ed. *Hypothermia, Frostbite and Other Cold Injuries.* Seattle: The Mountaineers, 1986.

—*Medicine for Mountaineering, 4th Edition.* Seattle: The Mountaineers, 1993.

18

Nautical Charts and Navigation

Marine navigation's peculiarities make it somewhat more complex than terrestrial route finding. The beginner may be perplexed by the symbols and conventions used on marine maps (called charts). The ability to read charts and to key them to features in the surroundings is essential for orientation and to avoid potential hazards. Occasionally, the paddler must navigate toward a destination that cannot be seen from the departure point, and at times he may lose sight of *all* visual references. Far more typically, there are landforms, however distant and tedious to identify, from which to take visual cues. Because the water itself may move (due to currents), where it takes the paddler is often not apparent, and sometimes it may negate all of the paddler's efforts without his knowledge. Hence, an eye trained to evaluate drift and paddling progress from subtle changes in distant landforms is one of the most valuable navigation aids.

This chapter is a primer for marine navigation. For a comprehensive survey of nautical navigation lore as it relates to the sea kayaker, I strongly recommend David Burch's *Fundamentals of Kayak Navigation* (see end of chapter).

Nautical Chart Systems and Other Navigation Resources

Nautical charts are published by the National Ocean Service (NOS), a division of the U.S. National Oceanographic and Atmospheric Administration (NOAA), and by the Canadian Hydrographic Service in Canada. They can be ordered from these agencies (see Appendix) or purchased more conveniently from marine chandleries and bookstores if you have them in your area. Both U.S. and Canadian chart systems publish indexes, which the agencies or chart dealers provide free. These include a map that shows the area covered by each chart. Most areas are covered by two or even three charts with different scales.

Coverage of Mexico is a bit irregular, and the charts for that area are somewhat more difficult to obtain. The Defense Mapping Agency (DMA), within the U.S. Department of Defense, publishes charts for Mexico as well as other parts of the world. British Admiralty (BA) charts provide similar coverage. Indexes for DMA and BA charts are comprehensive and not free, though you might ask a chart dealer to copy the page(s) you need. Mexico publishes its own charts, though the agency responsible for them has been somewhat unresponsive to orders from the United States in recent years. You will probably do best pursuing DMA or BA charts, but allow at least a month for ordering. If you are driving to Baja California for kayaking, chart dealers in San Diego are well stocked with charts for the west coast of Mexico.

Of course, there is a great deal about paddling destinations that charts do not show, such as weather patterns and accommodations or campgrounds on shore. The chart-publishing agencies provide detailed books on coastlines and waterways, called *U.S. Coast Pilots* for the United States and *Sailing Directions* for Canada or other countries. Though most of the contents are not particularly helpful to kayakers, you can learn a lot about paddling conditions from these books. They include discussions of tides and currents and seasonal weather patterns and tables that show fair- and bad-weather wind directions, frequency of gales, average precipitation, wind speeds, sea temperature, and days with fog for each month. Additionally, they point out hazards such as dangerous breaking seas that may occur at a river mouth at certain stages of the tide. If you do not care to purchase the books, look for them at the library and copy the parts of particular relevance.

If you paddle in an area with significant tides, you should also have the appropriate tide tables for the area. If the tides produce currents in the area (which can be learned from *U.S. Coast Pilots* or *Sailing Directions*), current tables that show speeds and directions are essential. (See "Tides, Currents, and Weather.")

Privately published cruising guides may be the best sources for locating parks (which often are not identified on charts or in *U.S. Coast Pilots* or *Sailing Directions*), accommodations, and places where landings are forbidden (such as wildlife refuges). A number of regional guides for kayaks also are available.

Chart Scales and Detail

Small-scale charts are those that cover a large area with minimal detail (a way to remember this designation is that any landmark looks small on a small-scale chart). An example is a 1:250,000 scale chart, which means that a foot on the cart equals 250,000 feet in the area depicted by the chart. *Large-scale charts* cover a smaller area but offer more detail (and any landmark looks larger than on a small-scale chart). A typical scale for a large-scale chart is 1:40,000—a very useful degree of detail for sea kayakers.

Nautical charts are expensive (perhaps three times as costly as a comparable topographic map), and choosing charts to cover the area you want to paddle is a question of how much detail you are willing to pay for. You can usually get by with a small-scale chart, but you might appreciate having the two or more large-scale charts that cover the same area. Ask to see your choices at the chart dealer's (customers typically inspect their chart options before buying them).

The need for detail depends on the nature of the shorelines you will traverse. If there are many offshore islands or complex channels, a large-scale chart (perhaps 1:40,000) is much better for staying oriented (trying to study such complex waterways on a small-scale chart leads to eye strain). A smaller scale (such as 1:80,000 or 1:100,000) will be adequate where coastlines are straight and offshore features are few or large. In developed areas, where launching and landing sites are dictated by the location of parks and public facilities, you will not need the chart detail to pick out natural landing sites.

Latitude, Longitude, and Distance Scales

Positions of places described in *U.S. Coast Pilots, Sailing Directions,* and in tidal current tables are described in terms of latitude and longitude. Distances on charts are easily ascertained from latitude scales, so understanding latitude and longitude measures is important for coastal navigation. Latitude is the distance north or south of the equator (measured in degrees starting at 0 degrees at the equator and ending at 90 degrees at the poles). Longitude is measured in degrees east or west of Greenwich, England (up to 180 degrees, halfway around the globe). Degrees of latitude or longitude are further divided into 60 minutes, which in turn are divided into 60 seconds. Minutes are designated by the apostrophe (') and seconds by the double apostrophe (").

One minute of latitude is equal to one nautical mile. This mile, which equals 1.15 statute miles or 6,000 feet, is most convenient to use in sea travel for a number of reasons. First, the common measure of speed, *knots,* means nautical miles per hour (and four knots is therefore about the same as four and a half miles per hour because nautical miles are larger than statute miles). Wind speeds and current velocities are reported in knots in marine weather reports and current tables.

Since each minute of latitude is equal to one nautical mile, the north-south edges of your chart—where degrees and minutes of latitude are indicated—usually are the most convenient distance scale on your chart (see fig. 18–1). (Some charts include a distance scale, but the side edges are often more convenient to use on a folded chart.) To find the size of a nautical mile on your chart, look for notations of degrees and minutes, such as 47° 30', which are marked at intervals of 5' or more depending on the chart scale. Be careful not to confuse degrees with minutes (remember that the latter is marked by an apostrophe). From these, you should be able to determine the size of a minute along the side edge. For instance, if you see 47° 30' at one place and 25' farther down the edge, these are 5' or 5 nautical miles apart; there should be five intervals marked between them, each corresponding to a minute (or nautical mile).

Longitude—the east-west measure shown on the top and bottom edges—*cannot be used for measuring nautical miles.* In chart projections, longitude measures converge toward the poles, and you will note that a minute of longitude (on the bottom and top edge of the chart) is much smaller than a minute of latitude on a chart showing a place at 47 degrees North latitude (Puget Sound).

There also will be occasions when you will need to locate features on your chart from a latitude-longitude position. Examples are features described in *U.S. Coast Pilots* or locations of predicted strength and flow direction in current tables. A position described as 49° 20' North (latitude) 124° 15' West (longitude) is accurate to the nearest nautical mile (a minute of latitude); seconds (which equal 100 feet of latitude) usually are not included in the position description. I suggest some practice with charts and positions from *U.S. Coast Pilots* or current tables so that you understand the system and can pick out the minutes of latitude and longitude on your charts.

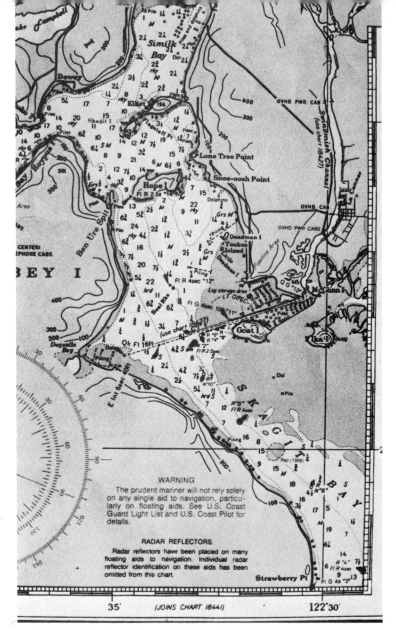

Fig. 18–1. The corner of this chart includes latitudes (sides of chart) from 48° 18' (the degrees of latitude are not shown on this portion) to 48° 27', a distance of nine nautical miles (because 1 minute of latitude equals 1 nautical mile). Longitude covers from 122° 29' (*right edge of photo*) to 122° 37' (*left*). The position of Hope Island (to the nearest nautical mile) is 48° 24' N (latitude) 122° 34' W (longitude).

Chart Symbols

The chart symbols described here are those that are most helpful to a kayaker. Both the Canadian and U.S. chart agencies publish a complete index of chart symbols in a pamphlet entitled *Chart No. 1,* available at nominal cost at most chart dealers.

Depths of water are indicated in either fathoms (6 feet) or meters. These soundings measure the depth at extreme low tides. Looking from deepest to shallow water you may see light dotted lines that surround areas of a certain depth, such as 100 fathoms. In more shallow water, the area of water less than a given depth, often 10 fathoms or meters, is shown in light blue. Areas of shallowest water (thought still covered at low tide) are shown in darker blue.

Where there is a significant tide, areas that the tide covers and uncovers (the intertidal area) is usually shown in a green-brown color. All water depths are shown to the average lowest tide level, so there are no depth soundings shown for the intertidal zone. Only on extreme minus tides that occur for a few hours each month will you find water depths less than what is shown or the intertidal area larger than the green area.

In shallow-water areas, you may see numbers with a subscript, such as 2_4. If the chart uses fathoms, this means 2 fathoms and 4 feet (16 feet); if the chart is metric, the depth is 2.4 meters.

Of course, shallow waters are of most interest to kayakers because the routes they take are often close to shore (see fig. 18–2). The symbols for rocks and islands in shallow-water areas are also the trickiest to learn. Rocks that are below the lowest tide level are shown as small crosses. If the rock is awash at low tide, there will be four dots in the corner of the cross. Intertidal rocks—exposed at low tide but covered at high tide—are shown as asterisks. If the height of this rock has been charted, a number will be shown in parentheses with a bar under it. This shows the height of the rock above the lowest tide (in feet if depths are in fathoms or in meters on metric charts). This is called the "drying height," and some charts will show "Dries 4 feet" instead of the same number in parentheses above the bar. If the rock is large enough, it will be shown as an enclosed green-brown area.

Rocks *above* the intertidal zone (never covered at high tide) are shown as an asterisk with the number in parentheses, but there is *no bar* under it. Here the height means either feet or meters above the *high*-tide level. If the rock is large enough it will be shown as an enclosed yellow area.

These intertidal and above-tide offshore rocks are your most significant landmarks on most coastal routes. For outer coast paddling, it is important to keep track of and avoid rocks below the surface as they are likely spots for intermittent breakers. Submerged intertidal rocks (asterisks) will be more likely to break than the deeper rocks (crosses).

The intertidal area may also be large areas of sand, rock, mud,

Fig. 18–2. These coastline chart symbols are on a 1:40,000-scale Canadian chart. Distance from right to left is just over 1 nautical mile. Foreshores (intertidal areas): *A*, rocky; *B*, sandy; *C*, boulders and gravel; *D*, rock 2 feet higher than high tide; *E*, intertidal rock exposed 12 feet at low tide; *F*, subtidal rock (depth not specified); *G*, shallow area with water depth 2 fathoms and 1 foot (13 feet); *H*, kelp beds; *I*, light buoy that flashes red and is marked "E98."

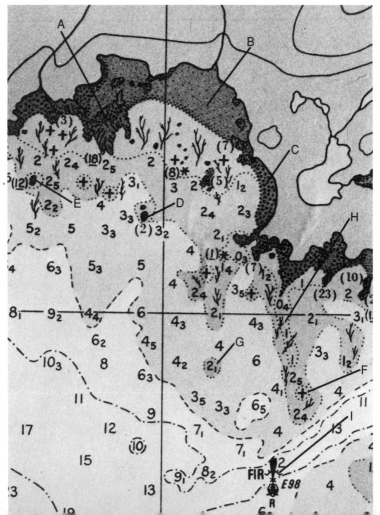

boulders, or mixtures. This area, shown in green, is called the *fore-shore* (see fig. 18–2). Whenever you go ashore, you will be concerned about both the size and composition of the foreshore. The water's edge moves most quickly in large foreshores such as tide flats, and beached kayaks may end up some distance from shore in a short time. If you choose a campsite at high tide that is fronted by a big foreshore, you may have to carry your boat and gear some distance if you aim for a low-tide launch the next morning.

Foreshore composition is also important for landings; sand or gravel beaches are preferable to boulders, especially where there is a shore break from waves or swells. In some places beaches come and go, and the foreshore composition shown is what happened to be there at the time of the survey.

Small-scale charts tend to generalize foreshore composition, and you will find that large-scale Canadian charts do a better job of showing the composition in little coves than do their U.S. counterparts of the same scale. The U.S. system relies on written composition descriptions like "sand and gravel," whereas the Canadian charts have a discrete symbol for each type that can be applied much more specifically (see Canadian *Chart No. 1*).

Lights and buoys are often handy for staying oriented, even though you may not travel at night nor need to stay in the deep channels that the buoys delineate. Lights on shore, which may be manned lighthouses or (more likely) a small tower with a battery-powered light, are usually painted white and easy to see from a distance. On the chart they appear as elongated purple diamonds much like an exclamation mark (see fig. 18–2). Nearby will be a legend that indicates the flash interval (e.g., "Fl 3 sec"), and the height above high tide in either feet or meters (which helps night navigators determine the distance from which the light can be seen).

Buoy systems are too complex for general description, so use *Chart No. 1* to decipher those on your charts. Though kayaks rarely need to follow the channels buoys mark or avoid the hazards they pinpoint, knowing which buoy you are passing may be your best means of staying oriented. Knowing its meaning may also help you predict the route of that aircraft carrier coming down the channel.

Buoys or fixed markers on the water usually are either green, red, or black. Red markers usually are placed on the right side of channels as you follow them inland or toward a port (hence, "red right returning" is a good rule to remember). Left-side buoys are either green or black. Right-side buoys often also have a cone-shaped top and are called "nuns" (marked N on the chart); left-side buoys have a flat top and are called "cans" (marked C on the chart). There may also be a number on both the buoy or marker and also on the chart in quotation marks. If there is a light on the buoy, it will show on the chart as a purple diamond as for terrestrial lights.

Charts also show what landforms look like from on the water, usually with contour lines as on topographic maps, symbols for cliffs or man-made features such as radio masts, or a description such as "conspicuous white streak" on a mountainside.

Navigation Under Way

Though navigators in large vessels do chart measurements and calculations as they go along, the kayak navigator cannot afford to. Propulsion depends on paddling, and any interruption of your cadence for figuring delays the ongoing passage and may complicate it because of drift. Hence, do course calculations on shore before beginning a passage (which means doing calculations for contingency plans at that time, too); memorize or write down the calculations so they can be checked while paddling.

Putting the chart in an easily accessible and visible place on the boat is important. You can keep the chart stowed for an occasional look when paddling along regular shorelines or areas you

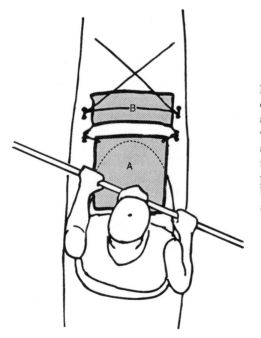

Fig. 18–3. A, this chart-case arrangement allows close-up chart viewing while paddling and, B, folds forward for exit from the cockpit and under the deck bungees during rough and windy weather.

know well, but in unfamiliar, complex shore terrain, it should be in constant view to help you stay oriented as you go along.

Most mariners shudder at the things kayakers do to charts. In larger vessels, charts are rolled for storage and flattened for display; in a kayak, charts must be either folded or cut up small enough to be manageable. They can be cut into pieces (quarters, sixths, or eighths, depending on the chart size) and laminated in plastic, perhaps back to back with another piece. I like to keep my charts intact and fold them as needed to show the area being paddled. They last well if kept dry and sprayed with a fixative to help protect them from abrasion, particularly at the folded corners. The folded chart should be inserted in a plastic bag or chart case with a zip closure or roll-down seal. This can then be placed under the deck lines just ahead of the cockpit (though I find that position too far away for detailed reading). I use a chart case, about 12 inches by 18 inches, with grommets at the corners. The case is clipped at its forward corners to strap eyes at the front of the cockpit. Fold the chart case back over the sprayskirt for easy viewing while paddling, and tuck it forward of the cockpit and under the deck lines for getting in and out of the boat or in rough water and wind (see fig. 18–3).

Courses, tidal current times and strengths, or other data needed while paddling a particular route can be written in pencil on the chart, on a separate slip of paper inserted into the chart case, or in grease pencil on the case itself. Some paddlers write such figures on adhesive tape and put it on their hand or on the paddle shaft.

Navigation by Dead Reckoning (Following a Compass Course for a Specified Time)

Dead reckoning is steering a compass course for a specified time and speed. For instance, to paddle through fog to an island 3 miles north of you through still water, a dead-reckoned course steered north at three knots for an hour should get you there. This technique is used to reach destinations you cannot see from your departure point and when there are no fixed reference points along the way. The procedure is essentially the same whether you are paddling a 2-mile channel crossing in fog or a 50-mile passage in clear weather to an island below the horizon.

Dead reckoning in kayaks involves a large element of guesswork. Kayaks are slow, the paddler cannot know exactly how fast he is paddling, kayaks are hard to steer along an exact compass bearing, and the degree of drift from current and wind is usually to some extent unknown. Most sea kayakers will not attempt a long dead-reckoned crossing in order to reach a small island in an empty sea. They prefer to wait until visibility improves. Dead reckoning certainly is practical, however, for crossings when the landfall is too big to miss.

The compass bearing of a dead-reckoned course to be steered can be taken off the chart or noted when visibility is clear (such as the night before a morning crossing when fog is expected). Assume a paddling speed (you should clock yourself over comparable and measurable distances on the chart to find yours) and estimate your crossing time by dividing the distance to be covered by your speed. Both course and time should be worked out on shore before you begin, if possible.

A conspicuous feature on marine charts is the *compass rose* (see fig. 18–5): a red or purple numbered circle that allows you to find what compass course you have to steer to get from one place to another on the chart. There may be from four to eight of these scattered around the chart to make it easy to determine a course at any point on the chart.

Anyone with orienteering experience using topographic maps is familiar with the headaches of declination: the difference between true and magnetic north. Though true north is at the north pole, the compass actually points to the magnetic pole near Hudson's Bay, Canada. On topographic maps, only true headings are shown, and declination must be added or subtracted to correct for the difference between true and magnetic bearings at that location.

Fortunately, declination is no problem on nautical charts because the inner ring of numbers on the compass rose shows magnetic bearings (the outer ring is true bearings). *As long as you use that inner ring, no corrections from chart to compass are needed.* (The outer true bearings are provided because large steel ships use gyroscopic compasses, which use true bearings.)

The first step in working out a course to be steered is to mark the course on your chart using a pencil and some straight edge. (This usually will be from your departure point to the destination. See below and "Tides, Currents, and Weather" for information on adjusting the course for current or wind drift.)

Next, get the corresponding course on the inner (magnetic) ring of the compass rose. The easiest way is to lay a straight edge (the edge of a book will do) over the center of the rose and turn it until it is parallel with the course you drew in the first step. Then read your course from the point where the straight edge intersects the inner circle. (Be sure to take it from the proper side of the circle; the opposite side has the course from your destination *back* to the departure point.) With the vagaries of kayak steering and susceptibility to drift, one degree of accuracy is usually plenty. Navigators on larger vessels use special rules and protractors for doing this precisely, but these are not practical to carry in kayaks. With practice, the parallel line method described should serve well enough.

A hiker's compass also can be used as a protractor to pick up courses from the compass rose. See figure 18–4 for two methods. To verify this procedure, check it with the parallel-line method. If there is an error, check for anything magnetic under the chart that may be disturbing the compass.

Next, estimate the paddling time to your destination by dividing distance in nautical miles measured on the chart by your speed in knots. Note the time when you depart, and you will know when to worry about an error or unexpected drift if the destination does not appear. Assume a speed you can sustain for the entire period (based on previous time-over-distance trials). For me, three knots proves a good speed for distances from 3 to 10 miles or so (allowing for short rests) with a laden kayak.

If there is a significant current flowing perpendicular to your course, you will need an adjustment to your course to compensate for the amount you are *set* (i.e., carried with the current). Determining tidal current strength is discussed in "Tides, Currents, and Weather." At this point I will assume that you know what to expect out there. Keep in mind that speed estimates derived from current references are based on one point in a channel, and currents elsewhere may produce a different overall speed than predicted.

A rule of thumb suggested by Burch (*Fundamentals of Kayak Navigation*) prescribes that you adjust your course upstream by six degrees for a current one-tenth your paddling speed. Thus a third of a knot current would require six degrees of upstream adjustment if you paddle three knots; likewise, thirty degrees of offset would be required in a one-and-a-half-knot current at the same paddling speed (one and a half divided by three equals five-tenths, times six degrees equals thirty). This rule works only for currents less than half your speed; stronger ones present an inauspicious situation for a dead-reckoned passage anyhow.

Wind-caused drift is a more difficult factor to anticipate. If the wind is strong enough to require a dead-reckoning course adjustment, do not attempt the passage unless the destination is large.

Steering with a Compass

Steering with a mounted marine compass is easy: keep the desired course number centered over the mark that faces toward you. Without visual cues for orientation (as in fog or out of sight of land), steering with a compass takes a little getting used to. People new at it tend to turn the boat the wrong way when the compass goes off course; they see the *needle* or the central card in a marine compass as moving, whereas, in fact, the boat has revolved. Instead, visualize the compass housing revolving around the stationary needle or compass card, and you will develop the right response to bring yourself back on course.

The hiker's compass takes more work to set up for course steering than the marine compass, but it is more versatile. Uses of the hiker's compass for steering, taking bearings, and picking up courses from the chart are shown in figure 18–4.

If you have used a compass with topographic maps, these procedures should be no problem for you. If you have not, borrow a hiker's compass to try it. If it causes difficulty, you may be better off with the more straightforward (but expensive) marine compass.

Checking Compass Procedures and Magnetic Disturbance

Whether you use a marine or hiker's compass, confirm that you are taking courses off your chart correctly and that you are using the compass to steer the proper course. The exercise described next should be practiced before you attempt any navigation in fog or other reduced visibility, particularly with the more complex hiker's compass.

On a paddling outing, pick a destination, with visible and identifiable land features, which you can find on your chart. Using the chart and compass rose, determine the bearing you need to steer to reach each feature from your location and mark it on the chart. Then get into the boat and aim toward each feature—the compass should agree with the chart bearing. If it does not, did you use the outer true baring ring on the compass rose instead of the inner magnetic bearings? If you have a hiker's compass, check that you rotated the bezel to the proper mark, that you set the long edge of the card parallel to the boat's direction of travel, and aligned the *north* end of the needle with the alignment mark beneath it (as described in figure 18–4).

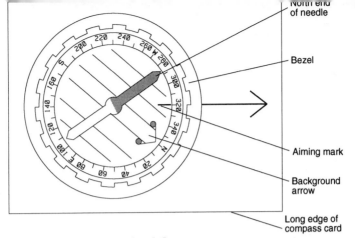

Fig. 18–4. Navigation with a hiker's compass.

Steering a course: Tie the compass lanyard to a point on your deck and lay the compass on your sprayskirt. Turn the bezel until the desired course number aligns with the aiming mark on the compass card (set to 320° in the example). Align the compass card's long edge parallel to the boat's axis with the aiming mark toward the bow. Turn the boat until the north end of the needle (usually red) is aligned over the background arrow (or between the two fluorescent marks on the bezel on some compasses). Steer to keep the arrow in that position.

Taking a bearing on a distant point of land: Aim the long edge of the compass card toward the distant object, with the aiming mark and arrow facing the object. Turn the bezel until the north end of the needle lies over the background arrow. Read the bearing from the bezel at the aiming mark.

Taking a course off the chart with the compass (oriented chart method): This and the next procedure use the compass as a protractor, and they are useful when your desired course is some distance from a compass rose. Zero the compass by turning the bezel until "N" (sometimes marked "0") lies over the aiming mark. Lay the long edge of the card on the north axis of the magnetic (inner) ring of the compass rose, being sure that the aiming mark or arrow is toward the north end of the compass rose. Turn the chart (with the compass on it) until the north end of the needle lies over the background arrow, which is also aligned with the aiming mark. *Without moving the chart,* move the compass to the desired course line, placing the edge on that course line, with the aiming mark and arrow toward the destination. Turn the bezel until aligning the needle with the background arrow, and read the course at the aiming mark.

Taking a course off the chart with the compass (non-oriented chart method): This method does not require orienting the chart to north, but the procedure may be harder to remember because it is less intuitive. The chart can be oriented in any direction. Lay the long edge of the card on the course to be steered on the chart, aiming mark toward the destination. Turn the bezel until the needle aligns with the background arrow. *Without moving the chart or adjusting the compass,* move the compass to the magnetic ring of the compass rose, aligning the edge with the north axis, aiming mark toward north on the rose. Read the course at the north end of the needle.

Also, check for magnetic disturbance caused by equipment in your boat or on your person that could seriously scramble your compass navigation. This check need be done only once unless you move your compass to a new location or change the loading plan for your boat.

Checking for magnetic disturbance is similar to the exercise above. But since magnetic disturbance is not necessarily the same in all directions, four course bearings roughly at ninety degrees to each other should be checked. This can be done at one fixed point (such as a buoy) where you can check bearings on four objects against what the chart says they should be (set this up in advance on shore). Or, if you know the route you will be paddling, pick out four locations where you can check one of each of the four bearing quadrants conveniently (such as from a marker on a point to a buoy).

Navigation by Piloting
(Using Visible Reference Points)

Piloting is the art of tracking your location through things you can see around you. I call it an art because much of it comes from a practiced eye. For instance, looking at a forested mountainside a mile away, I perceive that I am slowly being set by a current, yet I am not sure what I saw that made me sense that. Likewise, I can tell when a half-knot current is with me or against me as I paddle along the same mountainside, but I cannot explain exactly what I see that tells me so. If I stop and watch carefully, I will see changes in the view of the mountainside from which I got my cues. But because I have spent untold hours paying attention to the passing scenery, my eyes have their own intuitive way of doing it. With practice, so will yours. But start with some basic piloting procedures.

The key is to start out and stay oriented on your chart—always be able to point to it with assurance and say, "I'm right here." In most places, where shorelines are fairly linear and islands not too numerous, that job is easy. But in a maze of islands and channels, losing track of what is what leads to disorientation, which in turn leads to *lost*.

Whenever coming around a point of land opens up a new vista ahead, immediately try to identify all the newly visible features on your chart. Be sure of them. Use checks such as "If that's Clark Island, then I should see Matia Island just behind and right from my position." If you do not, suspect your assumption about Clark

Island (or your position). To head out in one direction on a false assumption about the surrounding landforms may cost you untold time and frustration.

Imagine that a dozen islands come into view ahead of you around a point, and all the islands look about the same. On the chart, your intended course takes you between two of them. But which is which?

To orient yourself, locate an identifiable feature on the chart, such as a light or a conspicuous cliff, that you can see from your position. If one such feature can be spotted, identifying each island successively to either side becomes fairly easy. If nothing is readily identifiable, try starting at one edge of the newly visible seascape. Your position on the chart should indicate features that define the right and left edges of your view, usually landforms closest to you on either side. Once these are identified from the real view, work toward the middle, carefully picking out each feature that corresponds to the chart.

If all else fails to orient you, your compass can save the day (here the convenience of the mounted marine compass is a real asset). Determine the bearing from where you are to where you need to go (if a compass rose is nearby and visible on the chart, try estimating the bearing by eyeballing it so that you can keep paddling) and then steer that course; you should be pointing at the proper place.

Ranges

Ranges are simply an alignment of one feature in front of another. (In Britain, ranges are called transits.) If you see that two features are lined up, you can locate your position on the chart as somewhere along a real or imaginary line drawn through them. Another such range on two other features will fix your position where the two lines cross. (See fig. 18–5.)

Range markers are sometimes used as a navigation aid in a narrow channel surrounded by shoals; a vessel keeps the two markers aligned in order to keep to the deep channel as it approaches the markers. *Natural ranges* are the same, except that any visible features—hills, points, buoys, towers—are used.

Though I never draw real range lines on my chart, I do frequent eyeball range checks whenever paddling offshore to confirm my position. As I paddle along, I note distant features as they come into alignment and then extend an imaginary line through them on the chart.

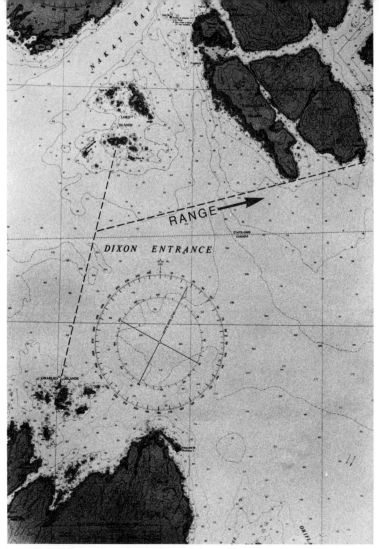

Fig. 18–5. Using ranges to verify your position. Passing the halfway point of this five-mile crossing between the groups of small islands could be noted by taking a range on the two points to the right. Drift from the course could be checked with ranges through the islands to conspicuous points in the bay beyond or by using the bow-stern check on both island groups (see figure 19–5). Also note the compass rose with true bearings (outer ring) and magnetic bearings (inner ring).

Ranges also are handy for checking drift caused by tidal currents, and they can be used to determine the right amount of course correction to offset the drift (tactics and methods for compensating for currents are found in "Tides, Currents, and

Weather"). Any two features you can spot repeatedly will work; you need not identify them on the chart. The point here is to observe ranges for changes over time. Such changes might be apparent immediately or perhaps only evident after watching for a minute or so. (See fig. 18–6.) Usually I try to fix a range in my mind (perhaps by a mental note, "the big tree on the crest of the island is right over the boulder on the shore"). Then I check it later to see if that comparison has changed.

Diligent practice with ranges may give you some surprising abilities. Glancing at a range on a point and distant hill, you might conclude without hesitation that the current is carrying you to the right—how did you know that? A comparison done over a few moments' interval will confirm what your intuition told you right away.

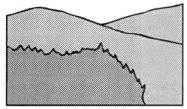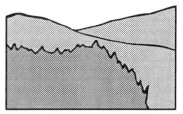

Fig. 18–6. *Left,* a mental note of the alignment of the tallest tree on the point with the hillside intersections beyond can be used to watch for drift. *Right,* A check a few moments later shows drift to the left. Forward progress is indicated by the rising foreground gradually eclipsing the background.

Suggested Reading

Burch, David. *Fundamentals of Kayak Navigation,* Second Edition. Old Saybrook, CT: The Globe Pequot Press, 1993.

19

Tides, Currents, and Weather

Tides are the major forces in the marine paddling environment, and understanding the forces that drive them is valuable for safety and convenience as well as your own edification. Though you can simply look up the tide's movements without ever knowing anything about what affects the cycles, awareness of the variations in tidal patterns and the causes could help you avoid mistaken assumptions that lead to trouble. For instance, one should not assume that the successor to a small tide will also be small—in some circumstances it may be very large. Likewise, do not expect tidal currents to operate on the same schedule as the tides in all cases.

Tidal Cycles

The attraction of both the moon and the sun creates tides, though the sun has about one quarter of the moon's effect due to distance. The moon's attraction produces bulges in the water levels because the water slides sideways (rather than being lifted). One bulge faces toward the moon, and there is another on the *far* side of the earth. (This one occurs because the earth itself is attracted toward the moon and is more or less pulled away from the water in that area.)

These two bulges produce the *semidiurnal* tidal pattern found in many parts of the world: two cycles per day, with six hours between the highs and lows. The tides move about fifty minutes later each day because of the moon's twenty-eight-day revolution around the earth (when the earth completes one revolution, and the daily tidal cycle would be expected to repeat, the moon would have moved on, causing the time lag).

Because the tides result from horizontal water movement over a large area, many ocean basins have a natural oscillation that produces large tides in some parts and small ones in others, much like water sloshing back and forth in a dishpan, with large height changes at the sides and little at the pivot point in the middle. One of the most dramatic examples is the northeast coast of North America, where tides funnel into the Bay of Fundy, Canada, forcing the front of the tide up to a 50-foot range (the difference between high and low tide) in the Minas Basin area. To the south, the pivot point (or node) of this oscillating system near Nantucket Island has a very small tidal range.

Some inland bays and waterways (including the Bay of Fundy) develop significant internal differences in tidal range as the tide moves into them. This occurs because the tide moves like a wave, which heightens as it passes through narrow or shallow waterways. Cook Inlet in Southcentral Alaska has a normal range of 18 feet at the entrance and 33 feet in Turnagain Arm near Anchorage (the progress of the wave here can be seen by the five-hour delay in the tides between these two points). Likewise, Mexico's Sea of Cortez tides rise and fall 5 feet near its entrance and 23 feet to the north end at the mouth of the Colorado River.

The semidiurnal pattern (two tidal cycles per day) predominates on both the Atlantic and Pacific coasts of North America. However, the Gulf of Mexico's natural oscillation rhythm causes one of the cycles to nearly vanish, resulting in a *diurnal* tide, with an interval of little change during the period when the other cycle would normally occur.

At certain times during the month, places with semidiurnal tides may closely resemble the Gulf of Mexico's tide, caused by *lunar declination*. The moon's orbit around the earth is tilted in comparison to the earth's axis; at one time the moon will be far north of the equator, and fourteen days later, far south of it. When the moon is in the northern portion of its orbit (north declination), the tidal bulge on the side of the earth toward the moon is located in the northern hemisphere, and the bulge on the opposite side is centered in the southern hemisphere. Hence, North America's waters get the effects of one bulge but largely miss the effects of the other. The result is a large diurnal inequality: one big tide and another small one (or even none at all). The same happens when the moon moves to south declination, except that we get the effects of the bulge from the far side from the moon. In between, when the moon is over the equator, we get the shoulders of both bulges equally, and tides are more even and of an intermediate size.

Hence, lunar declination is very important for trip planning where tides (and resulting currents) are significant. During maximum declination, part of the day will have large tides, which may have an interval as long as nine hours instead of the normal six. The remaining period will have much less activity (but with intervals of as little as two hours). Many tide tables include a calendar showing lunar cycles such as maximum declination periods. The effects of such factors on the tides are often delayed a few days.

Lunar calendars also show the times of *perigee*, when the moon's orbit is closest to the earth, and the tides are up to 20 percent larger than normal. Perigee is particularly significant on inside waters.

The sun's weaker effect also causes tidal movement. When it is in alignment with the moon—and we see either a full or new moon—tides are significantly larger than average, called *spring tides* (which have nothing to do with the season). When the sun and the moon are out of alignment (appearing as half moons), *neap tides* significantly smaller than average occur. Be especially careful at the times of solstice (late December and June), when the maximum declination of the *sun* enhances the sizes of spring tides.

All of these effects—lunar declination, perigee, and spring tides—occur on independent cycles, which sometimes coincide. For instance, in an area with semidiurnal tides, a spring tide coinciding with maximum declination and perigee will result in one very large tidal exchange and another smaller one during the day. If tidal currents are a potential hazard, be cautious while paddling during that time.

Tidal Currents

Though the strength of a current is related to the size of the tides, topography of the waterways is most important. Strong currents are most likely where the tide fills two adjacent bodies of water unevenly, producing a difference in water levels and a powerful downhill flow. In Washington State, currents up to eight knots may occur in Deception Pass because the tidal wave takes two hours in sweeping around Whidbey Island to deliver tides to the east side of the pass. Thus, when it is high tide on the west side, it is still two hours before the high on the east. The water level is therefore lower on the east side, and the strong downhill flow from west to east produces the pass's flood current.

In such places, the kayaker may time his paddling for *slack*—the period of least activity when the currents slow and turn to the other direction. Whether you do so depends on the nature of the current and channel as well as your boat-handling skills. As demonstrated for Deception Pass, tide tables for either the east or west sides of the pass would be an hour or so in error in predicting slack water in the pass. Other places may have an even bigger disparity between tide and current timing.

One such example is Nakwakto Rapids in British Columbia, some of the fastest-moving salt water in the world. This quarter-mile-wide channel connects the open Pacific with the 100-odd miles of nearly landlocked waterways composing Seymour Inlet. Nakwakto cannot pass enough water to significantly alter the level of Seymour Inlet, and it has a tidal range of only 6 feet compared with the 18-foot range on the Pacific side. Hence, the Pacific side water level rises past the Seymour Inlet level at midtide and remains higher through high tide and through the beginning of the ebbing tide. The two levels are again equal at midtide. Slacks before the Nakwakto flood and ebb currents, therefore, happen at the midtide level of the Pacific cycle.

Though currents can certainly be dangerous, they are primarily an efficiency consideration in most places; it is far easier and faster to travel with a favorable current. Examples would be the five-knot currents through New York Harbor's Hell's Gate Narrows, or Cape Cod Canal's four-knot flow. Many rivers on the U.S. Eastern Seaboard have two- or three-knot reversing tidal currents in their lower reaches. For kayaks and sailboats, travel against the current in many channels of Washington State's San Juan Islands and neighboring British Columbia's Gulf Islands is all but impossible. In Southeast Alaska, kayaks can hitch a 20-mile ride through Wrangell Narrows in a single tide cycle, using both flood and ebb, with the proper timing.

Some channels become dangerous only when the direction of the current opposes the wind direction. Still other places, including Deception Pass and Nakwakto Rapids, produce dangerous hydraulics that should be avoided by anyone not prepared for and experienced with such heavy going. British Columbia has many such passages; the Sea of Cortez (Baja) has a tidal maelstrom called *Sale Si Puedes,* translated as "Get out if you can." More on such hazards follows, but first you must know how to predict currents at any given time.

The flow direction of a tidal current depends on whether the tide is flooding or ebbing; and the current's strength or speed is related to the range of the ongoing tidal exchange. The direction of the current is marked on some nautical charts with a fletched arrow for the flood current or an unfletched one for the ebb (or alternatively, the letters F or E). There may also be a speed in knots indicated, which is an average for all tide sizes unless otherwise noted. Since tidal ranges can vary greatly depending on lunar and solar conditions, the current strength may fluctuate substantially from the average.

Predicting Currents

The timing and the strength of currents are predicted with annual tables designed for that purpose (tides themselves may be very poor indicators of currents). In Canada, current and tide schedules are published together in regional volumes by the Canadian Hydrographic Service. In the United States, the National Oceanic and Atmospheric Administration publishes separate coastal current tables in a volume for the Pacific coast and another for the Atlantic and Gulf coasts. With a few wording differences, the U.S. and Canadian current tables are identical in function and format. (These can be purchased from chart dealers or ordered from the agencies. See Appendix.)

Current tables have two important parts. The first is a set of daily predictions for currents in certain major waterways. You can look in these tables, for instance, to find the times of slack water and maximum currents in Deception Pass or Cape Cod Canal on May 12 of the current year. The second part determines currents at other local places, using time and speed corrections to be applied to the daily predictions for the major waterways in the first set of tables. The example in the Appendix demonstrates how this is done. (These do not account for daylight saving time.)

The tables give predictions for the time of slack and the time and speed of the maximum current (which should be about three hours later, though the interval can vary greatly). Because slack is the safest time to paddle if the current may be hazardous, it is valuable to know how fast it builds up speed after the slack (see fig. 19–1). Assuming a normal six-hour tide cycle (the interval between slacks), currents one half hour after slack will accelerate to 20 to 25 percent of the maximum speed that is predicted to follow. They attain about 50 percent of their speed one hour after slack and 90 percent two hours after slack. The same applies to deceleration before the slack. Thus if currents before and after a slack attained

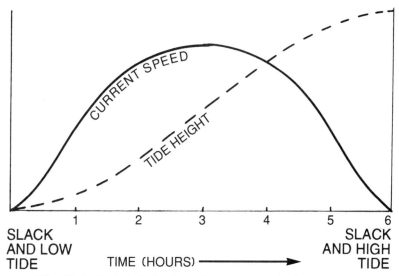

SLACK
AND LOW
TIDE

TIME (HOURS) ⟶

SLACK
AND HIGH
TIDE

Fig. 19–1. Typical tide heights and current strengths during a normal flood tide. Note that current accelerates faster than would be expected from tide rise. In the first hour, the current attains about half its strength, while the tide height rises only about a twelfth of its range. Although times of slack and tide changes are shown as being the same here, they may be quite different in some channels.

maximum speeds of six knots, there would be a two-hour window of time during which currents would be three knots or less and a one-hour window with currents one and a half to two knots or less.

Though current tables are the most precise resource for predicting currents at any time, they are tedious to use, especially in complex waterways where you are trying to see the overall picture of current flows for planning a route. In the Northwest, one private publisher has extracted the information from the tables and applied it to a chart, making route planning much easier.

Current *charts* present a much more vivid picture of current flows, using arrows and correction factors to calculate speeds based either on tide or current tables. Such current charts are published both by NOAA and by the Canadian Hydrographic Services for such places as Puget Sound, the San Juan and Gulf islands, San Francisco Bay, Chesapeake Bay, New York Harbor, Long Island Sound, and others.

Most current charts come in sets, one for each hour relative to the state of the tide (thus there are eleven hourly charts for a twelve-hour tide cycle). (See figure 19–2.) A few have multiple sets of hourly charts depending on the size of the ongoing tidal range. Most kayakers find current charts the most convenient to use (assuming one is available for their paddling destination). But where currents are very strong in tide-race passages, and where times of slack must be predicted accurately, the current *tables* are more reliable.

In publications, currents are always defined by the direction they are flowing *toward*. Winds, on the other hand, are defined by where they are *coming from*. Hence, a south wind and a 180° current would be in opposition to each other.

Fig. 19–2. This page of a current chart depicts currents in Washington's San Juan Islands and British Columbia's Gulf Islands at the last hour of a large flood tide, based on Vancouver tides (top of range). Note the circling eddies, some of which comprise the strongest currents at this time. (*From the Canadian Hydrographic Service's* Current Atlas: Juan de Fuca Strait to Strait of Georgia.)

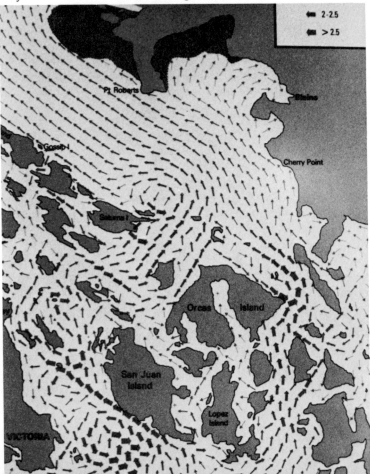

Hazards from Currents

Rough surface conditions created by currents can be a result of either wind waves made worse by a current or patches of turbulent water produced by currents even on the calmest days. In its most severe form, strong currents in the confinement of tide races can produce abrupt differences in the direction of flow (called *eddylines*), whirlpools, boils, and other heavy hydraulics that challenge the safety of the most competent paddler.

The most common problem is waves made steeper, larger, and closer together by wind blowing against an opposing current. This is called a *weather tide* (from the mariner's expression meaning that the current associated with that tide flows "to weather," or upwind). Seas are usually much rougher when the wind and the current oppose each other. With even a moderate wind, a tide change bringing an opposing current (one-knot speed is enough) can produce dramatic results: bigger, shorter-interval, and steeper seas that are more likely to break. Observing the change in current gives the impression that the wind had increased.

When the current flows in the same direction as the waves, seas will be abnormally long and smooth. This is the best time to paddle, as long as you keep in mind what can happen when the current turns.

How bad the seas will become during the weather tide depends on the current speed (a five-knot current can nearly double the size of waves flowing against it), wind strength, and the length (*fetch*) of open water over which waves can build. Unless there is a current flowing against wind over open water, paddling during the weather tide is not necessarily dangerous. If a particular passage along your route is a concern, plan to cover it when the current flow will most likely be the same as the wind direction (remembering that wind forecasts and current tables define wind and current in terms of origin and destination, respectively, as noted earlier).

Along the outer coast, watch out for ocean swells running in opposition to a strong current, which may cause powerful breakers even in deep water. This hazard is covered in more detail in "Paddling the Outer Coast."

Tide rips are patches of closely spaced and sometimes breaking waves caused by a change in speed or direction of current (see fig. 19–3). They may occur in calm weather, but wind waves or even boat wakes advancing against the current into them usually make them much worse. Though milder ones are a good place for fishing (because bait are brought to the surface and fish follow), many tide rips are severe enough to discourage small craft. Some are well known, such as the Plum Gut rip in Long Island Sound or the Bonita rip near San Francisco's Golden Gate Bridge. The Pacific Northwest has countless tide rip locations. The worst may be marked on U.S. charts as "tide rips" (sometimes with an explanation of the conditions that make them the worst). Canadian charts refer to rips as *overfalls* (a largely synonymous term) and mark them with wavy lines. But in general, do not count on your charts to show all tide rips.

Fig. 19–3. Tide rip. This one is caused by a current flowing over submerged sea cliffs at least 50 feet below the surface. Note that the wind is calm.

Tide rips are likely wherever confinement by bottom topography or collision with another current force a current to change direction or speed. When a current passes over a shoal, it must speed up to pass the same volume of water through the smaller space. When it speeds up, it absorbs surface turbulence (hence, water is often smoothest just upstream from a shoal or narrows). But when it slows down after entering deeper or less constricted space, energy is given up in the form of surface turbulence. Tide rips are possible downstream from such shoals, points (particularly when there is a spit offshore), or narrows. The same phenomenon occurs on white-water rivers in the form of standing waves at the bottom of a rapids.

Such rips can form on perfectly calm days. But if wind waves or boat wakes are attempting to advance upstream into the area where the current locally speeds up, they are slowed and steepened just as with the more general "weather tide" situation. At some point the waves may not be able to advance at all (usually within the tide rip), and they become breaking standing waves, which make the rip much worse. The same can occur with boat or ship wakes attempting to propagate upstream into a rip area.

Colliding currents can produce substantial tide rips, even in deep water, probably because of rapid changes in speed when one current contacts the other. Likewise, rips may form along eddylines (boundaries between two currents flowing in opposite directions), apparently because of turbulence created by friction and because waves seem unable to cross eddylines readily. Waves advancing into areas along an eddyline sometimes seem to rebound as from a sea cliff, and the reflected waves crossing the oncoming ones make very unsettling conditions. Boat and ship wakes can produce temporarily dangerous conditions if the eddyline is strong enough to stop and trap them.

In general, I have found that flows of at least two knots are needed to produce significant rips, though local portions of a channel (as where water speeds up over a shoal) may have faster speeds than predicted for the channel as a whole. Most tide rips are little cause for concern if you have developed reasonably good paddling skills and sense of balance in your boat. Others produce waves that any kayaker avoids. The best tactic with tide rips is to keep a sharp eye out ahead and go around ones that look too challenging. In calm weather even at a distance, rips make themselves known by noise like a river rapids, and they appear as a dark patch on the surface, perhaps flecked with white breaking waves. In windy weather, water and wind sounds and other whitecaps camouflage rips and make them difficult to spot at a distance.

When riding downstream on a current, try to spot tide rips well ahead of time. You will have less time for evasive action. If you find yourself unable to avoid being pulled through a rip, stop trying to get away and head into it. Keep up a fast and short paddling cadence in the rip so that each stroke can be turned into a small high brace to counter whatever the irregular waves do to your balance. Remember that the current will likely carry you out the other side if you can pay attention to keeping your stability.

Tactics for Paddling Across Currents

Crossing channels while a current is running is frequently necessary. If the current speed is as strong as or greater than your paddling speed, you will have no choice but to be swept down-stream by the time you reach the other side. In weaker currents, you have the choice of heading straight across and accepting some drift or adjusting your course to counter it.

Offsetting downstream drift is done by *ferrying*—adjusting your course upstream just enough to equal the current's speed (see fig. 19–4). This is usually the best tactic when you wish to avoid something down current, such as a tide rip area or open water. As you paddle across, find the best ferrying angle by taking a range (see "Nautical Charts and Navigation") on two aligned objects ahead (such as a tree along shore and another on a hillside behind it). Slowly turn your boat upstream until you can hold these two range markers in position, one behind the other. If the nearest one seems to move upstream relative to the more distant one, then you are drifting down current and need more upstream angle. If the nearer object moves downstream, you have more angle than you need and could cross faster with less angle. Current speeds change across a channel, so adjust as needed to get across with the least effort.

In long crossings of 2 miles or more, ranges on the far shore

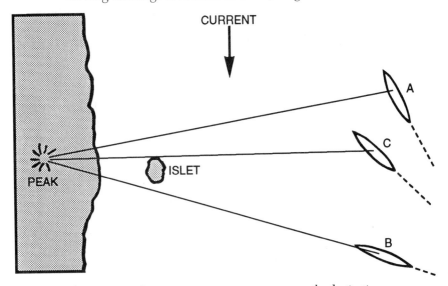

Fig. 19–4. To ferry across a current, use a range on the destination shore to determine the ferry angle (alignment of the edge of the islet with the peak beyond). Boat *A* is angled too far upstream; the islet would appear to be drifting downstream from this postion. Boat *B* needs more angle and would see the islet move upstream relative to the peak. Boat *C* finds the right angle to hold the range.

may be difficult to distinguish, particularly at the start. Instead, use ranges on the departed shore until near midchannel. Once you are a mile or so offshore, the effects of the current are difficult to detect without some subtle observations over time. One technique is to aim your boat toward a feature on the far shore and then sight back to note a feature over your stern on the shore behind you (or you can do this using the paddle held fore and aft). Paddle on for a few minutes, then aim toward the same feature ahead and check behind again. Where your stern (or paddle blade) now points relative to the last check gives an indication of drift during the interim. (See fig. 19–5.)

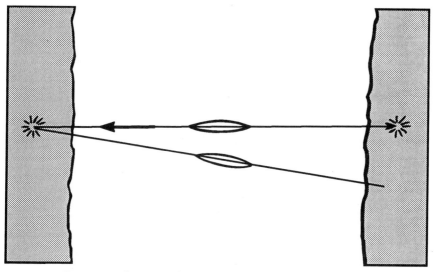

Fig. 19–5. A bow-stern drift check is used when the crossing distance is too great for accurate ranges. Aim toward a feature, sight over the stern and note one on the shore behind. Later aim toward the same feature and check behind again.

A mounted marine compass also is handy for checking drift. Aim toward a feature ahead, note the compass bearing, and then check again later for a change.

Sometimes your main objective is to finish a crossing as quickly as possible by aiming straight across rather than ferrying, regardless of where you end up. This might be necessary when there is an impending weather change or ship traffic along the crossing. If a wind were blowing in the same direction as the current flow, which would require hard paddling into the wind if you ferried, you could head straight across or perhaps even a little downwind to get to the other side with less effort.

If you need to get to the point on the far side across from your departure point, this across-and-down tactic may still be less work in the long run than ferrying. You may find an extensive eddy system (see below) to use to get upstream (see below), and you may find shelter along shore for paddling upwind.

Using Eddies to Paddle Up Current

Unless you are willing to wait, paddling against the current is sometimes necessary. But because kayaks are nimble, shallow-draft craft, the current can often be avoided by finding along-shore routes where it is minimal or even flowing your way.

In general, currents in a channel flow fastest in deeper water, where there is less friction with the bottom. The exception is where water is squeezed over a shallows or around an along-shore obstruction, where the current will likely be faster than elsewhere. But overall, the easiest upstream route usually is as close to the shore as you can paddle without running aground.

Where the shoreline is irregular, eddies will develop (see fig. 19–6). Being heavy (salt water is heavier than fresh water), flowing water is unable to make abrupt turns to follow a shoreline (such as the downstream side of a point). Hence, the flow breaks off and continues straight downstream, leaving an eddy of still water just below the obstruction. Some of this separated water is constantly

Fig. 19–6. Eddy hopping. The kayak builds inertia in the eddy backflow and is now crossing the eddyline, ruddering hard left and sweeping right to keep the bow upstream as it enters the main current. A downstream lean is needed at this point to counter the tendency to tip toward the current.

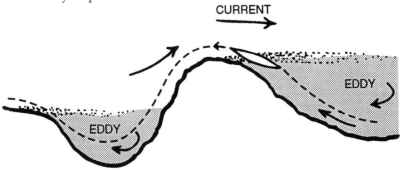

being pulled away by the nearby flow, creating a low-pressure area. To fill it, water flows upstream within the eddy, creating a *backeddy*.

An eddy on the downstream side of a point usually has a circular flow within it—water flows upstream toward the point along shore, toward the main stream just below the point, and then slowly downstream just inside the eddyline that marks the boundary with the main current. Eddylines are usually a zone rather than a well-defined line and are composed of swirls of water going in different directions. The abrupt and unpredictable flows within eddy boundaries make them likely spots for a capsize.

Eddy sizes can range from a few yards to miles. Little ones can be just right for a rest before tackling a stretch against the current. The big ones can give you a gentle but sizable upstream lift. Large eddies are rarely obvious; spotting them and finding the most favorable (or least unfavorable) route within them is a challenge that lends a nice sense of finesse to your upstream progress.

Slow-moving water (though still fast enough to significantly assist your progress over a distance) requires that you read subtle cues to detect its direction. One indicator on the Pacific coast is kelp lying on the surface. One end is anchored to the bottom, the other end has a ball-like float (a kelp head). The kelp head lies toward the downstream side. Changes in flow direction can be felt through your paddle as you go along. A sense of sluggish resistance to the blades tells that you have entered a current flowing your way, which you will feel until you overcome the inertia and catch up with the flow. Likewise, a feeling of less resistance and easy, quick strokes is a bad sign, since you have just entered an opposing flow, which will soon slow you down. Of course, these paddle cues only occur in changing flows; otherwise you will feel no resistance or help from paddling in a current.

At certain places, such as when rounding points, there is no choice but to fight the current upstream for a distance until another eddy can be found; and the flow against you may be faster than elsewhere for a short way. A current flowing faster than you can paddle can be beaten for a short distance, however, by building up speed and inertia within the downstream eddy.

Seek out any backeddy flow to add to your speed. Aim to cross the eddyline close to the point and obliquely so that your bow will be heading upstream as much as possible as you enter the opposing flow. If you enter the current while pointing out too much, it will grab your bow and swing it downstream, leaving you paddling across the current with little chance of upstream progress. If this happens, keep swinging downstream and re-enter the eddy you just left to try again. A rudder is very helpful for keeping on course as you cross the eddyline, since you can rudder hard toward shore to counteract the current's tendency to shove your bow out, while putting all of your paddling energy into getting upstream.

Tide Races and Dangerous Hydraulics

Fig. 19–7. Nakwakto Rapids, British Columbia, ebb current (*Kelly Tjaden*)

Particularly fast water—usually where the current converges through a narrows—can produce conditions attractive only to expert white-water paddlers, and a few tide races could intimidate even them (see fig. 19–7). The north Atlantic coast has the reversing falls at the mouth of the Saint John River in New Brunswick and Maine's Old Sow whirlpool near Eastport. In British Columbia, the whirlpools of Dent Rapids attain diameters of 100 feet with vortexes 12 feet deep! Speed of the current is only part of the picture (at least five knots or so is required for significant effects); underwater and alongshore obstructions produce changes in water direction and associated turbulence.

With all such dangerous passages, the safest transit time is around slack. (Caution: some tide-race currents accelerate faster than the rules of thumb presented earlier.) Second best is working upstream along shoreside eddies. I have found that the current usually prevents me from getting upstream into dangerous conditions (I cannot hop the eddies), as long as I am watchful of getting swept back into dangerous midcurrent situations when hopping from one eddy to the next. Riding downstream into a tide race is most dangerous because of the limited time you have to avoid a quickly approaching hazard, and you may not be able to get out of the current into eddies when you have to. In general, the eddies are the safest place to be, except that most of the dangerous hazards occur along eddylines, and boils *can* erupt in the middle of them without warning! Even the smoothest midchannel flow will likely lead to a series of standing waves wherever currents slow after a fast sluice.

Whirlpools are most likely along strong eddylines. These form as sections of the swirling, corrugated eddy zone, which are broken off and swept downstream along the eddyline. This body of water begins to spin, torqued by the opposite forces on each side like a pencil twirled between your palms. The centrifugal force of the spinning water throws it toward the outside, forming the depressed vortex in the middle. Contrary to what you see over your bathtub drain, downward sucking action is not necessarily a component of whirlpools, though your boat would likely slide down the incline of a whirlpool's dish to be trapped in the middle.

If you do find yourself approaching a whirlpool while riding down current, aim for the main-current side, as the upstream side of the whirlpool will be revolving in that direction, helping to deflect you around it. If you cannot avoid going into the vortex, be ready with quick braces to each side, but do not leave the paddle in the water because the direction will be changing and swirling erratically. The main effect, besides erratic water, is disorientation as you spin around. Remember that most whirlpools are short-lived and transient, moving down along the eddyline until they eventually drift off and dissipate.

Potentially strong downwelling and upwelling currents are possible wherever moving water is deflected by underwater shelves or collides with water moving in different directions. Upwellings are manifested in boils—domes of water that may erupt intermittently and can build several feet over the surface, with water spreading rapidly outward as water rises to the surface. Though I have never experienced a ride on a big boil, the probable difficulty would be dropping over the edge of the outflow (perhaps a fall several feet high); a strong brace and lean to the upward side as on a breaking wave would be critical.

All of these phenomena are most sensibly observed from the security of shore, and they are well worth a spectator's visit to particular tide races on a big spring tide. For the competent, risk-oriented white-water paddler, moving salt water produces the same hydraulic phenomena as river white water, except that sheer volume and the greater weight of salt water may increase the power. And finally, beware of abrading yourself on the large barnacles that may favor these intertidal rocks because of the increased aeration in the water.

20

Paddling the Outer Coast

The ocean's living energy makes the outer coast my favorite saltwater environment. Sea birds, whales, and intertidal life are often more prolific here than on inside waters. The power of the open ocean gives a sense of wilderness even when paddling short distances off developed shores. It commands the paddler's attention and also demands his energy—daily paddling distances are rarely as great as on more placid inland waters. Though my best experiences have been on the Pacific Ocean's outer coast, my most frightening ones have occurred there, too.

The *swell*—a large, fast-moving wave—defines this paddling zone. Swells are storm waves created by disturbances perhaps a thousand miles away. Traveling at speeds from twenty to fifty knots over vast distances, the swell that arrives at your location often tells more about recent distant conditions rather than conditions where you are. Swell sizes can vary tremendously over a period of hours with no relation to the local weather trend.

The outer coast is usually windier than inside waters due to the more exposed open spaces over which winds can develop. With wind comes wind waves, which may run opposite to the swell direction (swell direction is usually fairly constant). When marine weather forecasts talk about *seas,* they are referring to the state of locally created wind waves. Forecasts usually report the size and direction of the seas in addition to those of the swells (though seas are sometimes reported as combined wind wave and swell heights).

In deep water, swells are like rounded moving hills that cause few problems other than seasickness. But when they enter shallow water, their tremendous energy may be expended in breaking, and it is in your best interest to avoid being there at that time. If you watch as swells arrive at a beach and turn into breakers, you will see that they vary considerably in size. Certain depths will allow the smaller swells to pass by harmlessly, but the big ones will turn into breakers. Sea kayakers sometimes watch for a pattern in the sizes and sprint through the break area when the waves are smallest. Unfortunately, swell size patterns are not always so predictable, and trying to time your movements to the smallest ones can be hazardous. If a big one catches you in any one of the number of the bad situations described in this chapter, the result can be disastrous unless you have the skills to ride a breaker.

Before leaving the beach, surfers look for *sets*—groups of large waves that arrive together—and study the pattern of whatever set is out there in order to make best use of it. Any kayaker about to enter the surf zone should do this, too. The number of waves in a set can vary, and sometimes there are no sets at all, with swells arriving in truly random sizes. This situation occurs when the storm creating the swells is close by, or when the storm is at your location (in which case all waves are big). The more distant the disturbance, the greater the time and space for the swells to sort themselves out into some pattern as they travel. But even in the best-defined sets, wave sizes and patterns of arrival are always somewhat erratic.

While watching for a pattern, do not expect to be able to count waves in a set. More likely you will sense an overall length of

Fig. 20–1. Swells in the gap between Howell and Cree Islands (British Columbia) took one kayaker's life in 1987. Distance between islands is less than one quarter of a nautical mile. The shallows and intertidal rock in midchannel were probably responsible for the intermittent breakers that caused the capsize.

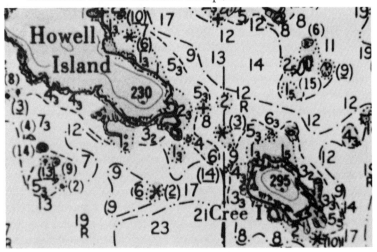

the cycle, which will vary somewhat. Look for the patterns, such as two or three big waves in succession, and also for the exceptions. The longer you observe, the better. Try to imagine going through the break zone as you watch it to decide the best start time.

In the Pacific Northwest, the temptation to catch a lull and shoot through the many narrow, shallow openings between islands, gaps in reef systems, or sea arches that are exposed to the ocean swell gets some of us in trouble. In Vancouver Island's Broken Group Islands (see fig. 20–1), playing the odds with swell sets between islets resulted in the loss of a kayak and a kayaker's life in two separate incidents within one year.

Some years ago, I nearly met my own nemesis in Alaska the same way when I tried to take a shortcut through a gap in an extensive reef. I watched until I thought I saw the pattern and then headed in when the time seemed right. It was not: a big breaker picked me up and swept me along, breaking over my stern and against my back. My bracing reflex failed me (it has since improved), and I felt powerless to do anything. Fortunately, I was carried on to deeper water where the breaker smoothed out before I lost complete control.

Offshore Breakers

A more subtle trap from variation in swell size is the intermittent offshore breaker, colloquially called a "boomer" (see fig. 20–2). Boomers often occur in "rock gardens"—areas of wildly different depths with underwater rocky pinnacles and reefs. Much of the area may be covered with steepening (but not breaking) swells as these begin to "feel the bottom." Rocks that are exposed are the least of the problem because you can see and avoid them. Rocks just below the surface are likewise clearly marked by constant breakers. But the boomer is a rock just deep enough to let smaller swells pass, only to cause a nasty break on the big ones. You might be paddling toward a boomer rock, seeing nothing as the small swells go by, and then get nailed by a big one.

Avoiding boomers in rocky areas takes careful attention. If you have a large-scale chart, spot the rocks on it and locate them visually if they are exposed or breaking. Intertidal rocks, marked as asterisks, are more likely candidates than subtidal ones, indicated by plus signs (if the tide is very low, then the latter are the prime boomer candidates). If you see one on the chart but cannot locate it visually, suspect a boomer, and watch the area carefully to see

SWELLS

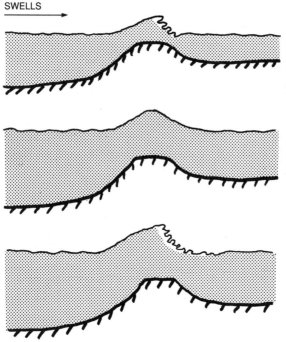

Fig. 20–2. Boomer. *Top,* on lower tides, this rock breaks on almost all swell sizes and is easy to spot. *Middle and bottom,* at higher tides only the largest swells break, making it a trap for the unwary.

what happens on big waves. If it does break occasionally, keep track of the location and avoid it. If you cannot locate it, steer a wide berth. Watch for telltale patches of foam (which may drift with the wind or current) that marks boomers. The presence of kelp may also indicate a shallow rocky area.

Surge and Reflected Waves

A steep shoreline will allow close paddling, because the swells will not begin to break until they are on the rocks. But bear in mind that the biggest ones may break farther out, as with offshore boomers. Also be alert for *surge*—the in-and-out movement of the water associated with the passage of swells. If you paddle in close to a rock at the point when the surge is moving outward, you may find yourself dashed onto the rocks on the next breaking swell. If you feel yourself being sucked away from a rock by a strong surge, *do not resist it!* It precedes a big swell that will put you ashore if you stay close in.

Swells are reflected back from near-vertical shorelines such as a sea cliff or a man-made sea wall. These reflected swells produce a condition called *clapotis,* or waves that pass through each other in opposite directions. The result is an area of irregular *standing waves,* which erupt quickly and unpredictably. If small, these "haystack" waves are at best uncomfortable and hard to paddle through. If large, they may inundate you, toss you into the air, and present a good likelihood for upset (see the Porcher Island tale at the end of this chapter for a haystack experience).

Though reflected waves can travel a considerable distance, they lose their force to oncoming waves. Hence, you may find a course a few hundred yards away from such steep shorelines much more comfortable than an inshore route.

Currents and Breakers

Though currents in most outer coast areas are milder than the ones in more confined inside waterways, they can interact with swells to produce very dangerous breaking seas. Breaking seas can occur at a river's mouth where there is a strong outflow or at an entrance channel with a strong ebb current. As with tide rips, discussed in the chapter on currents, swells flowing against an opposing current steepen and may break if they are slowed sufficiently, even in very deep water. Because swells are fast-moving waves, they require a significant current to cause breakers, but when they do, avoid them. Be cautious during the time of ebb currents—the situation most likely to oppose the swell movement. River currents generally are fastest during ebbing tides, and the water is shallower and more likely to break over bars when the tide is out.

Getting Ashore Through Surf

Most sea kayaks (and the majority of sea kayakers as well) are not at home in the surf. The average cruising kayak is particularly cranky when going toward shore with surf; it refuses to stay perpendicular to the waves and turns sideways into a broach. Then, the paddler is dependent on a strong lean and brace to keep upright as he is swept shoreward sideways. A load of gear can make the process far more awkward. Unless you want a challenge from the surf, seek a landing point where the surf is smallest.

Wave *refraction* may help you land. This bending of waves along a shoreline can diffuse their power, resulting in smaller surf in some places. Wherever the sea bottom shoals upward gradually and regularly toward a shoreline, swells obliquely approaching the

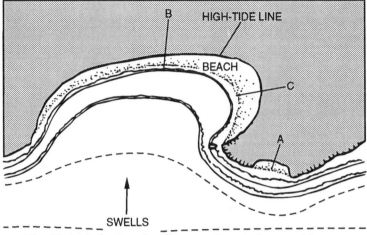

Fig. 20–3. Refraction of swells coming from the bottom of the illustration affect surf size on these beaches. Surf would be largest at A because of swells bending inward in that area. It would be much smaller at B and least at C, especially at high tide when the swells refract farther before breaking.

shoreline will attempt to bend around to strike it perpendicularly. Such refraction occurs because a swell slows (as well as steepens) when it enters shallow water. Hence, a wave approaching obliquely starts to bend around as the nearest end first slows, while the other end continues faster in deep water until it encounters the shallows.

In a bay rimmed by a beach, waves entering will refract to both sides to strike the beach perpendicularly (assuming that the bottom shoals evenly and gradually throughout the bay). As figure 20–3 shows, the waves' energy spreads sideways, diffusing the energy of the surf where it has refracted the most. The gentlest surf is often found on concave beaches, particularly at the ends behind rocks or headlands (see fig. 20–4).

Refraction can also *intensify* surf on beaches near a point or other convex shorelines because refraction bends waves inward, concentrating the energy and producing the largest surf. Sometimes these can be anticipated by inspecting the chart; otherwise it takes a firsthand look to see the condition of the surf.

Though waves may have refracted ninety degrees to wrap around an island, the back side, farthest from the prevailing swell direction, may be a rough landing place. Swells refracting around both sides may collide in haystacks and irregularly large surf in this area. An island close to shore may have a sand or gravel strip called a *tombolo* connecting it to shore. If the tide is out, the tombolo stops the waves from intersecting; this will be a good place to land. At high tide, it may be the worst, as surf collides over it from *both* directions.

The steepness of the bottom in the surf zone has a strong effect on the character of the surf. A very slowly shoaling beach will force swells to begin breaking gradually at some distance from shore. The breaking process occurs repeatedly in successively smaller sets over a distance, producing a more extensive surf zone—but probably less intense breaking energy—and a wide inshore area of largely dissipated waves (called "soup"), which allow easy exit onto the beach.

The worst situation occurs on a steep beach that produces "dumping" surf. Here, waves do not break until they are almost on

Fig. 20–4. The area just above Fan Point would be a bad one for boomers and surf, as refraction in the shallows steepens and focuses swells (coming from upper left) on the area. The cove just below and behind the point should have less surf due to refraction, but would be a poor landing area at high tide because of colliding surf crossing the tombolo.

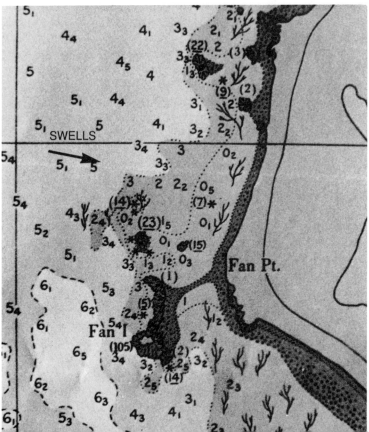

shore, then rear up and overtop in a crash onto the beach. You may be able to time a sprint to shore between such waves, but will be faced with exiting your boat and the break zone before a wave gets you. Because such beaches are steep, beached boats often slide backward into the next wave.

You may find the least surf in places of outflowing water called *rip currents* (which have no relation to tide rips). Surf tends to pile up water along shore, particularly on shallow beaches. This water establishes channels of return flow at intervals along a beach. Because the water is often deepest in these rip currents, waves are less likely to break (or they break farther in where you may be able to miss them by cutting to the side). Some rip channels are poor routes, as the opposing current will slow your shoreward progress somewhat and, if it is strong and the channel shallow, cause the waves to stack up close together and break.

Generally, the best procedure for getting ashore through surf is by following the back side of a wave as far as possible. You will get no assistance in progressing forward from the wave you are following, and it is not likely that you can stay behind one wave all the way in. You probably will need to let another wave overtake you before catching its back side. Your main concern is to avoid surfing ahead on the front of overtaking waves, which can make you lose control and broach. Stopping or reversing your direction by back-paddling will allow the boat to punch backward through quite large breaking waves without being surfed; this is an important tactic if you find yourself in the way of an approaching one. Be sure that you are pointing squarely down wave, duck forward, and you can get through intact. Then, paddle ahead hard to follow its back side as far as you can.

Timing your traverse through a surf zone to coincide with the smallest swells in a set (if you can see such a pattern) is difficult if the surf zone is broad—it may take too long to get through it during the lull. But in a dumping surf, this is vital. Watch for a pattern and then start in just as the last large wave breaks to give yourself as much time as possible to get ashore before the big ones repeat.

From seaward, surf is difficult to observe because you are looking at the backs of the waves. A group should send the most experienced member in first to watch the surf from on shore. That paddler can signal the timing for other members to come in and help them get ashore quickly. The signals devised by the American White-Water Affiliation work well for directing paddlers' timing from a distance: arms or a paddle held horizontally (out to the sides) means stop or wait; arms or the paddle held vertically over-head means come ahead.

One caution about beaching your boat in surf: get out and stand on the *seaward* side. Propelled even by a small surf, a kayak (particularly a laden or waterlogged one) can break your legs, knock you down, and run right over you.

Launching Through Surf

Time your launch for the smallest wave sets, if any, and then paddle hard out through it as fast as possible. Launching is generally easier than getting ashore through the surf zone (see fig. 20–5.) In a group, the most experienced paddler is the last to leave the beach. The second most skilled should launch first. Launching is easy on flat beaches with a broad zone of "soup" (spent waves). There boats can be boarded floating, and there is no urgency in attaching sprayskirts and getting ready. On steeper beaches, paddlers should enter their boats and put on their skirts just above the shore break. The last paddler launches each one after the biggest waves.

Momentum is critical for penetrating oncoming surf. Without it, the wave may surf you backward. So keep paddling, stopping

Fig. 20–5. Launching through surf. Keep up forward inertia to punch through the waves.

only when a wave forces you to lift your paddle overhead to clear it. Do not hold the paddle shaft in front of your face as you go through surf—it could hit you hard.

The last paddler or a solo cruiser has a harder time getting launched from a steep beach fast enough to time his start to the wave sets. (On a flatter beach, the "soup" area provides a relatively quiet place for a shallow-water launch and getting ready to head into the surf.) Position the boat just above the average shore break, but where it will be floated off by the wash from big waves; you will have to hold the boat in position while you get ready. Once sealed in, catch the last big wave's backwash, pushing with one hand and the paddle. The problems will be getting up speed to catch the backwash and staying straight to penetrate the first wave without being surfed back.

Paddlers in a K-2 have an easier job, as the front paddler can get sealed in while the stern paddler holds position. Then the bow paddler can hold position in the backwash or even start paddling out while the rear partner gets buttoned up.

Surfing

Cruising sea kayaks have limited potential for surf play, and fiberglass kayaks are vulnerable to damage. Surfing practice with a white-water kayak or wave or surf skis is preferable. Always wear a helmet, avoid beaches with rocks, and watch for logs in the surf (they can be lethal). If you should capsize in the surf, bend forward immediately to avoid being pushed backward against the bottom, which can result in neck or back injuries. Try to pick a flat beach that will allow you to stand and walk ashore after capsizes in moderate surf. Keep clear of other boaters in the surf; a collision with a down-wave boater is extremely difficult to avoid and can cause grave injury.

Face the beach and wait for a wave that is to your liking (back-paddle through those you wish to pass up). Then start paddling forward in the trough to build momentum to catch the forward face of the wave.

Surfing straight ahead on the forward edge of a wave is exhilarating and demanding, depending on the type of boat. It is possible to cross the entire surf zone on the face of a single wave, even with a cruising boat. After catching a wave, turns to either side may be headed off by leaning toward the turn (this is effective for some kayaks) and by a stern rudder with the paddle, which is best done on the side you wish to turn toward, so that prying outward achieves the effect. On a wave that is just beginning to break and still has a curving forward side, a lightly laden cruising kayak can be kept running straight ahead, provided that leaning and ruddering are used promptly to head off any turning tendencies. But on steeper faces of breaking waves, the bow will dig in deeply (perhaps to the point of ramming into the bottom, called *pearling*), and a broach is inevitable.

Fig. 20–6. Surfing broached.

Broached surfing is not difficult once you get used to it; and it has its own particular thrills (see fig. 20–6). A breaking wave usually delivers a one-two punch that can capsize you in either direction. If you are sitting neutrally or leaning away from the wave, the first effect will capsize you on the down-wave side—the standard wave capsize. Surviving that, the force of the wave will shove the boat sideways, capsizing you into the wave (this is the most common capsize direction in the broken waves of the inner surf zone). Hence, lean and brace into the wave just before it hits you. The boat will be snatched away from beneath you and flipped on its side (perhaps lifting you out of the seat if you are not well secured). Your upper body will fall into the surf and, for a split second, you will feel helpless. Then, as you, your boat, and your paddle blade accelerate to the speed of the wave, the brace begins to work and it will support you on the surface of the wave. (See fig. 20–7.) A low

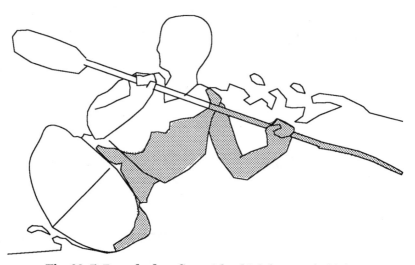

Fig. 20–7. Broached surfing with a high brace. The blade planes in the wave as both boat and wave move through the largely stationary water. Even more lean will be required in bigger waves.

brace works well in smaller waves and is less stressful and tiring than a high brace. In bigger waves a high brace is needed to let the paddle plane closer to the surface.

Spending twenty or thirty seconds on a wave in this manner is an indescribable sensation. On bigger waves, the kayak hull circulates up and down on the breaking wave face, taking you up and down with it through the white water like a washing machine. Just keep up the brace, and you will stay at the surface most of the time. You have little control over where you are heading in this position, though you should keep an eye out over your shoulder at what you are approaching.

Rescues in Surf

As in any heavily breaking sea, rescuing in a surf is a challenging situation for either group or solo recoveries. Chances are that a capsized kayak will be surfed ashore before recoveries can be done. In smaller surf, another paddler may be able to position himself to assist a recovery (having the rescuer on the down-wave side is preferable), though the recovering kayak will take on a lot of water and will be vulnerable to another capsize. Positioning yourself by a capsized boat in larger surf is both difficult and dangerous. You may be surfed well past the other boat; an approach from the down-wave side may be easiest. (I watched one individual recovery with the solo paddle-wing procedure when others were having trouble getting near him.)

If re-entry is not possible, the other option is to carry the individual ashore on the back of another boat. Carrying the victim on deck makes easier paddling but it is the least stable; otherwise the victim can grasp the stern grab loop and be pulled into the water. If it does not head for shore on its own, the empty kayak should be towed in with a towline, giving it enough room to avoid a collision (this is a slow procedure; the kayak will be swamped and probably inverted).

An Outer Coast Tale

To reach remote places beckoning me from the chart, I sometimes have let my respect for the outer coast's power lapse. Near northern British Columbia's Porcher Island, I learned how a "go for it" sense of self-confidence can be deflated to a more appropriate and realistic level of humility and caution.

Porcher Island's west coast is a spectacular 15-mile stretch of gravel and sand beaches interspersed with rocky points. The northern tip of the Queen Charlotte Islands lies only 30 miles west across Hecate Strait, but they cannot be seen from sea level and do nothing to diminish the swells sweeping down from Dixon Entrance into the strait.

I was drawn to this wild coast while paddling south from Alaska. Because I had to carry so many, my charts of the area were small-scale ones that omitted or miniaturized a great deal of the information about the coast, and the causes of some of my problems were not apparent until I perused a large-scale chart at home.

I approached the northern end of the coast late one afternoon via a protected route from the north and peeked out of the little entrance from which I planned to turn south along the west side the next morning. A strong high pressure system, which had dominated the coast for the past week, provided sunny weather but daily twenty-knot northwesterlies. I could see that it was rough, but negotiable, and I camped nearby with plans for an early morning departure. The weather forecast called for more of the same the next day.

The breezy but cloudless morning was so like the previous

days of this weather pattern that I did not bother to listen to the updated forecast. Had I listened, I would have heard that the swells had increased from low to moderate. I would soon see the consequence of that!

As soon as I cleared the entrance, I knew this would be a high-energy day. The swells were very big, but with the wind in the same direction, conditions seemed reasonable. The strong breeze at my back pushed me swiftly south.

Within the first hour of my passage south along the coast, the wind increased to thirty knots by my estimate, and I knew I was committed to whatever lay ahead. Shortly I approached the first of three points along my route. A mile offshore were some rocks that I hoped would shelter me somewhat from the swell. Instead, the swells began to heap up and steepen! The biggest ones began to break, seemingly at random.

Though it was not apparent from my chart, I had entered a huge shelf of shallows no more than 4 fathoms (24 feet) deep and often as shallow as 2 fathoms (12 feet). The entire area was a huge breeding ground for boomers as the big swells felt the bottom. In retrospect, I would have been better off to steer for the deeper water offshore of some rocks about a mile out. But with my inadequate chart and an instinctive desire to say close to shore, I saw no course but to continue downwind and hope for improvement.

Unfortunately, it got worse. A mile beyond was a rocky point that rebounded the steepened swells, creating huge haystack waves that erupted at random almost anywhere. I could only hope that one would not choose my location as I rounded the point, straining to give it some distance. But one eventually found me. It was like a waterfall in reverse, water rising all around me as the wave pushed up faster than my heavy boat could rise. Disoriented, I came down on my side with a crash as the wave dropped away. A low brace pushed me back to upright.

Fortunately, I cleared the point before another chanced on me, and I passed into somewhat deeper water. But I was thoroughly shaken. I thought of going ashore, but the heavy surf would have damaged my boat on the cobble beaches or dumped me offshore. I was still committed to the next 8 miles or so and hoped that the worst was over (though I had little reason to believe that). I felt the "weak in the knees" sensation to the point of wondering if I could stand.

Another hour passed with continued steep swells but no haystacks. Still thoroughly cowed, I paddled on toward where I hoped the gradually eastward-curving coastline would give me smoother going as the northwest swells refracted to follow.

Ahead were huge kelp beds. Normally, kelp is a welcome shelter from wind waves, but they do nothing to smooth swells of this magnitude. I found myself careening down the face of big rollers and looking down at big floating mats in the troughs. Bumping over them, I knew that should my bow dive under one of these fire-hose-size strands, I would surely go over with poor chances of recovery. From each swell peak I looked for gaps in the bed, but it stretched endlessly.

After another hour of such sleigh rides, I rounded Cape George, where the shore made an eastward turn, and the deep water prevented the swells from refracting to follow. At last, I was back in safer conditions and could land.

I still do not know whether my "go for it" nature would have overcome caution had I known the dangerous conditions affecting what was to come. I did not expect so much wind and certainly had not reckoned on the power of big swells in shallow water and the endless kelp. Some day I will return, hoping that gentler swells and winds, which also frequent the summer coast, will allow me to explore ashore at my leisure. But when I do, it will be with large-scale charts of such outside waters, the latest forecasts, and some better sense.

21

Trip Planning and Travel Safety

Planning to paddle a particular route starts with calculating how long it will take to cover it comfortably and an assessment of what problems you might encounter along the way. Then consider how those potential problems would affect your safety and ability to complete the route or return. A go or no-go decision rests on whether you accept the risks that might challenge your abilities or those of your companions.

Estimating Daily Traveling Distances

Most day trips are planned for 10 nautical miles (11½ statute miles) or less with the usual transit times to and from the launch point taken into consideration. If you account for breaks and short lunches, an estimated overall traveling speed of two knots is about right (a 10-mile route usually takes about five hours). How assiduously you keep moving is more important than paddling speed, and your own overall estimate may be quite different than mine if you are perseverant.

On multiday trips, experienced paddlers in reasonable conditions may manage 15- or 20-mile days, depending on winds, waves, or loading. Paddling 20 miles against any breeze over ten knots is an ordeal I would not wish to commit to. The turbulence of outer coast paddling in swells usually cuts my range by as much as a quarter, and a heavy load of gear has about the same effect in all conditions.

A long-distance day means many hours of sitting, and the parts of your body associated with sitting suffer more from fatigue than the paddling muscles. Getting out to rest once an hour or so makes a big difference, regardless of the comfort of the seat. On extended trips I find daily distances of more than 15 miles difficult to sustain for three days or longer in a row (though I may manage 20-mile days intermittently). My longest day was 35 miles, but the next day I suffered because of it. Nonetheless, strong paddlers can knock off 40-mile days on a regular basis.

The biggest planning concern for a trip more than a few days long is how much distance to commit to in a given period. A tight schedule predisposes you to pressing on, perhaps in conditions that would be more prudent to wait out. When planning my Alaska and British Columbia itineraries, I build in time for rest and exploration on shore and adverse weather and come up with an overall average daily distance of 12 nautical miles, measured in daily straight-line segments on a small-scale map or chart. This allows one day out of four as a rest day or a day when weather might prevent much progress. This itinerary is tenable for two weeks or more of travel, and it often leaves time toward the end. I prefer to get a bit ahead of my schedule so that bad weather at the end does not make me late, especially if I have a ferry to catch (for instance, at Pelican, Alaska, where the ferry departs every two weeks).

Exposed Routes:
Wind, Swells, Currents, or Marine Traffic

While some uncertainty always remains about likely difficulties along a particular route, keeping in mind its *exposure* to various hazards may help you judge any probable risks. An exposed route is one that presents a good chance of challenging paddling conditions or of some hazards. Such conditions are brought on by winds, currents, ocean swells, or even marine traffic. The risks are even greater if the exposed route forces you to go back, or worse, to continue under bad conditions. The distance from land during a crossing, a sea cliff, or the surf could prevent you from seeking safety on shore and thus leave you committed to a destination or the starting point.

Exposure to rough seas created by wind can be judged in light of the forecasted wind direction and the *fetch*—the amount of open water upwind from your route over which wind waves can build up. Hence, a particular route can have a significant exposure to southerly seas but be quite protected from northerly ones.

Exposure to turbulence created by currents depends on the

strength of the current flow (which is predictable) and on channel features (the effects of which are less predictable). Generally, a current speed of under two knots does not produce much turbulence on its own; but wind waves running against a current of that speed (the "weather tide" condition) can make rough going. Some routes avoid the worst current hazards by following the shore closely or sometimes by staying to midchannel, but these hazards are hard to foresee by looking at the chart.

Marine traffic poses a risk because a kayak is a tiny, easily missed object, which is difficult to see from the bridge of a ship. A kayak also moves at a speed one quarter to one sixth of that of a ship (most ships maintain from fifteen- to twenty-knot speeds on inland waterways). Many container ships have a blind spot from the bridge, which extends a half mile in front of the bow. And if a kayak were spotted directly in the ship's path, such a vessel could not throw its engines in reverse or make a sharp turn; doing so would send it out of control. It is the paddler's responsibility to stay out of the way or make sure that he is seen in plenty of time. Major waterways have shipping traffic lanes, which are clearly marked on the chart. You may cross them, but you must avoid interfering with traffic. You may not cross within a half mile of the bow of a moving ship, and you must keep a quarter of a mile away to the sides. Even more distance is prudent.

Short of displaying distress signals, making yourself visible to a ship is a problem. A kayak without a radar reflector will not show up on a radar screen, though there are small folding reflectors that can be hung from a mast or fishing pole (or even fashioned into a hat). If concerned about whether a ship bearing down on you has seen you, your best option is a call on your VHF radio (channel 13 is often monitored by ships) in plenty of time for them to spot you and take easy evasive action. But remember that you may be liable for any delays or damage you cause them in avoiding you.

If a route has exposed segments that may be risky to traverse, consider other options: go another way if there is one, turn back, wait for things to improve, or use some alternative land route. On a day trip, you might carry at least the bare essentials for overnight camping to make the waiting option realistic. Do not be forced to continue under conditions that might put you in trouble. If there are roads on shore, perhaps sending one member of the party to hitchhike back to the car would be worth the grief saved in going on.

On an extended trip, it might be wise to add extra time to the trip itinerary if there are exposed portions along the route. For instance, I usually add an extra day's traveling time for each open-water crossing over 5 miles on my trips in Alaska.

Forecasting Marine Weather

Though some radio and television stations include marine weather forecasts, the best are the continuous VHF broadcasts provided by NOAA in the United States and the Coast Guard in Canada. You can receive these broadcasts in most coastal regions and many large inland waters of North America. In the United States all broadcasts are on three frequencies (WX1 to WX3) in the 162 MHz range. Canada uses these and also WX4 (at 161 MHz, also called channel 21B) for its forecasts. You can get them on multiband (AM-FM-VHF-shortwave) radios, on AM-FM radios that include a "weather band," or on a small, inexpensive radio that tunes only to WX1 to WX3. Handheld marine VHF transceivers will pick up all weather frequencies and often receive them clearly when the other radios cannot.

Marine forecasts for the next twenty-four hours focus on wind speeds and directions and probably seas (size of wind waves, sometimes combined with swell height) for various areas. They also include visibility limits from fog or drizzle and, for the outer coast, swell size and direction.

A forecast for "light and variable" winds (meaning variable in direction) or one for "five to fifteen knots" (usually including a probable direction) is as auspicious for paddling as you will hear, and it could develop into a flat calm all day or become fairly rough. Fifteen-knot winds blowing for some time over a long fetch can produce waves that will give you some exercise and probably get you a bit wet, though they are rarely dangerous to paddlers with good boat-handling skills as long as an adverse current is not involved.

The next strongest typical forecast, "ten to twenty knots," may produce difficult conditions depending on your direction of travel and the exposure of the route. If the twenty-knot winds really do develop, seas over a long fetch can be quite rough. Making significant progress against a wind that strong is difficult (wind resistance increases as a square of the wind speed). A Small Craft Advisory is issued if winds are expected to range between twenty-one and thirty-three knots. This forecast is a good reason to stay on the beach unless you are willing to challenge your good paddling skills or unless your route is well protected from the predicted wind direction. Gale Warnings for winds stronger than thirty-three knots or Storm Warnings (over forty-seven knots) are never a good time for paddling except in specially controlled practice conditions.

In addition to the forecast, the report also includes local observations taken several times daily at places around the region, including communities and manned or automated light stations along the coast. Automated stations usually report the wind speed and direction; manned stations also include visibility limits, sea and swell sizes and directions, and cloud cover. These reports are often handy for anticipating conditions along your planned route if you know where each reporting station is located (see the *U.S. Coast Pilots* or the Canadian *Sailing Directions,* as well as charts). For instance, if there is fog in the morning, listen to the local reports to find out how extensive it is, which may tell you how soon it is likely to burn off. Or, if you are about to paddle on the outer coast, reports of swell size are an important consideration.

For a long trip in an unfamiliar area, knowing about the weather patterns or likely weather conditions (whether to expect headwinds or tailwinds, for example) in the area for the month of your visit will help you to plan your distances. The *U.S. Coast Pilots*, the Canadian or U.S. Defense Mapping Agency, or British Admiralty *Sailing Directions* have good weather summaries and tables of weather statistics by month. Elements of interest include wind directions (expressed as a percent of days having winds from each sector and days of no wind) and the average strength associated with each direction. Many areas have a direction from which the strongest winds blow (usually associated with bad weather). (Remember that winds are defined by where they come from, as opposed to currents, which are designated by the direction they flow toward.)

These reports may also include local situations that produce fast and violent wind changes or episodic gales such as the Sea of Cortez's *"chubascos."* Environment Canada publishes a booklet with descriptions of local weather hazards that plague particular spots along the British Columbia coast (they are planning to publish one for the Atlantic coast).

Convoluted mountainous coastlines usually develop characteristic strong winds as prevailing winds get funneled though channel valleys, over low saddles between peaks and ranges, or around the sides of high islands. These winds may bend as much as ninety degrees from the prevailing direction to follow channels. Very strong gusts are possible in inlets on the lee (downwind) side of mountains as air is pushed over the peaks and then drops rapidly into the inlets. Paddling along the lee side of Alaska's Prince of Wales Island, while a prevailing twenty-knot wind was flowing onto the windward side, I encountered gusts up to forty knots in each little inlet I crossed and little wind in between. And in winter, cold air trapped in the interior behind coastal ranges can produce sudden and violent *katabatic* winds in coastal inlets (forecasts usually warn of the possibility).

In warm climates, the sea breeze is a likely development on sunny days. As the land heats during the day, warmed air over it rises, creating a low-pressure area and drawing cooler marine air in to fill it. These onshore winds typically develop in late morning or early afternoon and continue until a few hours before sunset. The pattern may occur on a very local basis, with light winds blowing onshore within a mile or so of a land mass, or on a region-wide scale. In either case, mornings are almost always the calmest times of day (unless some other weather system moves through and exerts its own influence on winds). Crossing open water or places of greatest exposure should therefore be done as early as possible, or second best, at the end of the day.

Group Travel

There is safety in numbers, though you should keep in mind that it becomes "every man for himself" when conditions are bad enough. Using the "buddy system" is even more important in sea kayaking than for other activities. Having a partner prevents a paddler from wandering to the fringe of the group's route and getting missed should he capsize.

All members of a group should stay within voice communication of each other, which may be quite a short distance in windy weather. Whistles or compressed-air horns are helpful for getting attention. If two members carry radios, position them at the front and the back of the traveling party. The following paddle and arm signals (adopted by the American White-Water Affiliation) can be used at a distance:

• STOP Hold paddle horizontally overhead and move it up and down, or hold arms out to the side and move them in a flying motion. Usually used to regroup, for a conference, or to wait for a lull in surf.

• HELP/EMERGENCY Hold paddle vertically overhead and wave it, or wave arm in a circular motion overhead.

• COME AHEAD Hold paddle or arms overhead or to one side if you are directing members via a particular course. Most often used in surf landings or departures.

The following whistle signals were developed by the Association of North Atlantic Kayakers (ANorAK): one blast attracts attention for a visual signal; two blasts gathers or recalls the group; and three blasts indicates need for emergency assistance.

Decisions made while traveling in a group *must* be based on the least skilled or least confident member. More than one inexperienced sea kayaker has been led into a capsize situation by a more seasoned kayaker who was paddling into conditions that were easy for him. New paddlers lack the experience to judge conditions in relation to their abilities, and experienced paddlers forget what it is like to have only rudimentary boating skills. The burden of group leadership is to distinguish between party members' perceptions of what they can handle and their real abilities (either overconfidence or lack of confidence). It is a mistake to push a timid individual even if it seems like a reasonable challenge to his or her boat-handling skills; you may end up with someone in midchannel who is too terrified to deal with conditions effectively.

As many boats as possible should have towlines available on deck. Towlines are best attached to cleats near the cockpits on both boats so that they are releasable from either end. A short line just long enough for the towed boat to clear the towing boat's stern gives the best control, but a longer line will be necessary in rough seas to prevent collisions as the towed boat surfs ahead. If one member is incapacitated to the point of being unstable, someone can pull alongside to support him while another boat pulls the pair.

Sometimes individuals need the reassurance and presence of others to paddle out of a trying situation like a rough crossing. Perhaps just keeping the more experienced boaters on the upwind side will be enough to give the impression of some shelter. Keep together, as density certainly gives the impression of safety in numbers.

22

Cruising

Outfitting Your Boat for Cruising

Many paddlers like to add attachment points and deck lines that are handy for cruising. Here are some to consider.

Deck Bungees

This network of shock cord—standard on most hardshell boats—holds all sorts of things to your deck. On the foredeck, it might hold your chart, bilge pump, a furled kite or sail, and small articles of clothing you take on and off as you paddle. The deck just aft of the cockpit usually is reserved for the strong network that holds the paddle-float attachment for self-rescue. Farthest aft is the system for attaching a spare breakdown paddle.

Bungees are attached with a fitting called a *strap eye* made either from plastic, brass, or stainless steel (all are probably strong enough). These are secured with a stainless flathead machine screw and nylox lock nut backed up by a washer under the deck. Use a bedding compound to prevent leaks in all such installations. The shock cord needs to be replaced about every other year.

Painters

Painters are bow and stern lines used to tie the boat to a dock, to tow it (or a special line may be used for that), and perhaps to attach it to your car. My own painters are quite short, running from the grab loops to a cleat located just behind and to the side of my cockpit (in a position where it will not interfere with my elbow while paddling), resulting in a longer bow line. Each is tied at the grab loop with a bowline knot and another at the other end slips over the cleat. I also use this cleat as an attachment point for towing other boats.

A much longer bow painter can be stowed as follows. One end is secure at the bow. The free end leads aft to loop around a cleat forward of the cockpit, then forward to the bow where it passes through a bungie loop secured to the bow. It then leads aft again to hook over the cleat. The bungie loop keeps everything tight and allows you to secure the end with a bowline loop over the cleat. The painter can be used at full length or at one-third length by removing only the end loop from the cleat.

Attachment Points Inside the Hull

It is nice to be able to secure equipment against washing away in a capsize or to keep it from rolling around in the bilge. Attachment points in the hull also allow you to fill spaces in the sides of the cockpit, which otherwise are empty.

Folding boats, which have limited accessible space in the ends but are usually somewhat wider than hard shells, benefit from webbing straps, which lead around the longitudinal frame members to hold items in dry bags up in the side spaces. Otherwise these bags would roll toward the center and interfere with the paddler. Compress the bags into place by cinching the loops; they will stay in place in the event of a capsize.

Inside attachment points for a fiberglass boat should be done with fiberglass. Plastic or stainless D-rings can be glassed in with mat; wax the D-ring first to allow it to turn freely. Or, use a half section of three-quarter-inch PVC pipe, cut about an inch long. This little C-shaped piece can be glassed over to the inside of the hull with mat (being careful to avoid getting material at the ends where it will harden into sharp edges that would cut the bungee

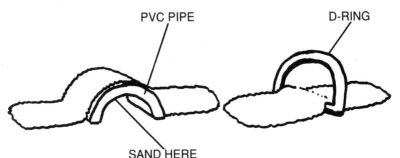

Fig. 22–1. Two methods for fiberglassed interior attachment points: PVC pipe and D-ring.

cord). Be sure to sand the inside of the hull where glassing will be done and the inside corners of the pipe piece to round them. (See fig. 22–1.)

One of the most popular places to add bungees is under the deck just forward of the cockpit, which is a good place to stow the bilge pump (rather than on the deck or next to the seat), a radio, or other small items. First be sure that your boat has enough room to let your legs and feet slide in and out easily. This area should not accommodate bulky items. Two lengths of bungee about 8 to 10 inches long should be sufficient. To aid sliding things in and out, install a thin sheet of polyethylene, fiberglass, or aluminum under the bungees and push your stowed items in between it and the deck. Keep it light.

Another spot is under the rear deck just aft of the cockpit (assuming there is no rear bulkhead in the way). This is a good place to stow a paddle jacket, keeping it out of any water in the bilge and accessible by reaching behind you from the cockpit. A plastic sheet as above may be helpful here to keep the jacket in place and to prevent it from snagging on other items as you pull it out.

You might also install attachment points beside and just ahead of the seat to hang small items such as a zippered bag (some paddlers hang a fanny pack here). Be sure that it does not interfere with the rudder controls.

Kites and Sails

A variety of specialized kayak sails and cloth parafoil kites are available commercially. Some include outrigger systems and sail designs that allow sailing upwind. Other spinnaker-type sails are practical for cruising on courses up to about thirty degrees from straight downwind. Some kayak sail rigs allow "reaching": sailing across the wind. Unless you are sailing for the sake of sailing, trying to go upwind makes little sense for cruising in a kayak. Windward sailing requires bulky leeboards or outriggers, greatly increases the risk of a capsize, and is probably slower than paddling. Sails are more useful than kites in light winds, but kites are safer when the wind gets strong, because they have less tipping force. Carrying both gives the greatest versatility.

Kites flown for cruising can be handheld, though you will welcome some way to tie it off to the deck, ensuring that it is quickly releasable. One way is to install a rearward-facing plastic hook (available at many sailing chandleries) on the deck to accept small

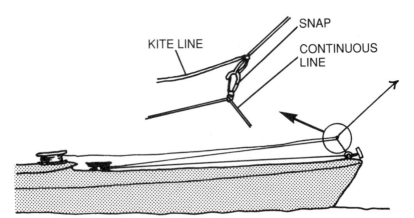

Fig. 22–2. This is a modification of the kite rig developed by Tom Schwartz (*Sea Kayaker,* Summer 1985) and Matt Broze. It helps steer the boat and keep it running straight in following seas. The continuous line runs through a cleat and the forward grab loop. A snap connects it to loops tied off at intervals in the kite line.

loops tied at regular points on the kite line, depending on how high the kite is to be flown. Excess line is kept on a reel or spool laid on the spray deck or under deck bungees while the kite is in use.

One arrangement (see fig. 22–2) lets the kite help to steer the boat while running downwind, which helps to prevent yawing toward a broach. This is accomplished by moving the attachment point toward the bow, using a continuous line that runs between the bow grab loop and a point near the cockpit. A small snap attached to this line can be clipped into loops tied at intervals in the kite line. Moving the snap and attached kite line forward tends to keep the bow pointing downwind. A knife kept handy on deck to cut the line in an emergency is prudent.

Kites can be adjusted for traveling when the wind blows predominantly from one side behind you. The adjustment compensates by making the kite fly off to one side from the wind so that it pulls straight ahead of your course. For instance, when we were traveling south in Baja, the wind was typically behind our left shoulders, and the kites flew off to the right of the bow. By tightening the tether lines on the left side, we made the kites veer off to the left of the wind direction and toward our bows. Likewise, kites can be adjusted for more lift (shorten the upper lines) or more downwind pull (using the lower lines), depending on typical wind strengths. These are tedious, sensitive, and trial-and-error

Fig. 22–3. My Chinese lug sail. A skimming low brace provides considerable stability while under sail. *(Kelly Tjaden)*

adjustments that are probably best done and tested ashore for conditions you expect to prevail for at least a day or two.

Sails require more installation work, and together with mast and spars (if any), are far bulkier. You *must* have a reflexive brace response (mine saved me on frequent occasions with my sail up). A strong skimming low brace serves as a good outrigger whenever you are sailing across the wind to some extent.

There are a variety of kayak sail rigs on the market. They vary greatly in size (and power and risk). I like a sail that allows paddling while under sail (see fig. 22-3); otherwise one ends up going *slower* when the sail is raised in lighter winds. Many spinnaker rigs either interfere with paddle action or use the paddle to position the sail. Masts can be stepped through a hole in the hull or against the front of the coaming (with a socket in the bilge to hold the foot) or attached flexibly to the deck. I have developed my own folding and removable mast step, which attaches on the deck to the existing strap eyes.

Outfitting and Stowing Gear for Cruising

In the appendix are three gear checklists: for day, weekend, and extended trips. Within each list, the most essential items come first, and the increasingly optional items fall toward the end. These lists are cumulative: items on the shorter trip lists are also assumed desirable for the longer trips. What you take from each list is flexible, depending on where you paddle and your own personal style. Few items will be required for a short paddle on the city's lake. Some people like to carry the basics for weekend camping on every day-trip outing where there is any chance of stranding due to weather.

Gear should be stowed in the boat with consideration for both convenience of access and weight distribution for good trim, though the latter is less important with day-trip gear. With a lot of gear, what goes where affects how much can be carried and how the boat performs.

The paddle jacket is an essential item to have at hand in the cockpit, because the advent of clouds and wind on a hot sunny day can produce a drop of thirty degrees (or more with the wind-chill factor). A shirt for sun protection might also be kept within reach. Either can be stowed alongside or behind the seat.

I keep a small dry-storage bag between my knees for items I use frequently, including a hiker's compass, pencil flares, folding knife, sunscreen, sunglasses, pocket camera and binoculars, wool hat, and snacks. This day bag must be kept small to fit in front of you and still allow easy leg entry and exit. On trips in remote country, I move some of the items to a small belt pouch, which is my shore survival kit and stays on me wherever I am. I also keep a half-liter water bottle handy next to the seat. Some men like another clearly identified one for urinating on long passages.

The radio usually rides alongside the seat or under the forward deck in its waterproof bag. The radio or an EPIRB and additional distress signals could be contained in their own dry bag behind the seat.

I also carry a larger dry bag on day trips. It goes either behind the seat or in the rear hatch. These are items I want on breaks ashore, including shoes, lunch, extra clothing (usually a complete change in case of capsize), extra charts, tide and current references, guidebooks, and the radio (unless it is in the cockpit with me).

Loading up for overnight or extended trips takes careful arrangement to ensure good boat trim and access to things you are likely to want during stops without taking out everything else. After a day or two of cruising, I fall into a mental loading plan that prescribes what goes where; this also serves as an inventory as I load (and has alerted me to items left at the camp on a few occasions).

Heavy items should be concentrated toward the middle section and positioned as low as possible in the hull for ballast. Light ends allow the boat to react to waves more quickly, keeping you drier. Try to preserve the normal fore-and-aft trim as much as possible with your loading plan. Bow heaviness is worst, as it makes for difficult steering.

If you carry water (I recommend one-gallon water bags either purchased or made from boxed beverages with a fabric cover added), stow these first in the bottom behind the seat (if they leak, you will be able to sponge it up). Elsewhere, try to load so that you can fit small items around bigger ones. Large bags, which leave unfilled spaces inaccessible, reduce your cargo capacity. A full boat is a compromise between the greater integral buoyancy (and convenience of handling) of items stowed in big dry bags and the greater capacity of loose small things.

If you run out of space, deck loads are a less desirable option, because they add windage and raise the center of gravity. Deck load light items such as a sleeping bag or pads in a dry bag or pots and pans in a mesh bag.

Kayak Camping

The impact on a camping area can be minimized by using existing campsites where possible and by using the intertidal zone for fires and toilet, unless the latter is provided elsewhere. In general, the flushing of tidal action and organic action of the ocean does a better job of processing human wastes than the soils on shore. Use the water-soluble toilet paper designed for portable toilets.

At least in the Northwest, most designated campsites do *not* have potable water. Many smaller island parks lack fresh-water wells, or they may be out of service during the busy season due to saltwater intrusion from overuse. Unless you are certain to find water, carry enough to get you through at least one day (usually one gallon per person if you use salt water for washing). Cooking with salt water can extend your freshwater reserves a little—use fifty/fifty when the water is to be poured off (noodles) or one-quarter salt water if it is not (rice).

Compared with backpacking, the advantages to kayak cookery are the ability to carry heavy things and to keep fresh foods longer. Soft ice chests that conform to hull interiors are available, and cold sea water will provide good cooling for foods stowed in the lower hull while traveling. (For tips on techniques and recipes that taste even better than food at home, I recommend Linda Daniel's *Kayak Cookery*.)

One aspect of kayak camping that I like less than its backpacking or bicycle touring counterpart is the time and effort required to break camp and get on the water in the morning. I find that two hours elapse between getting up and paddling away. Allow for this delay when planning early starts. Part of the problem is carrying the mountains of equipment that we kayakers indulge ourselves in. Some spartan discipline in what you take pays big dividends in trips to and from a distant low-tide beach. One or two large tote bags allow you to carry looser items and can reduce trips to and from camp.

Departure time can be cut by keeping breakfast simple and packing as much as possible the night before. If there are four or more members of your party, boats can be loaded at the campsite and carried by the group to the water's edge, which allows some loading the night before. Webbing straps with loops sewn in the end are very helpful for carrying loaded boats.

Cruising in Harmony with Wildlife

One of my most memorable wildlife contacts was while drifting within a few feet of a seal nursing a pup (the latter oblivious to my presence throughout), which I wrote about in the original *Coastal Kayaker*. But today I would keep my distance, having learned that this and other innocent encounters can have detrimental effects on these animals. In those days, the scarcity of paddlers trivialized our overall impacts. But sea kayaks are now numerous and far-ranging, and many marine wildlife managers are concerned that we could pose a real threat to wildlife populations.

Seemingly innocent visits from kayaks may change animal behaviors in ways that produce life-threatening stress, particularly for the young. For instance, approaching and disrupting a nesting colony of sea birds may allow other bird species to snatch eggs or hatchlings from unguarded nests. Hence, we should be most cautious during the spring and summer months, though the most critical times vary greatly by species. Some birds begin selecting nest sites in the late winter and are very easily driven away from scarce nesting habitats by intrusions. Raptors such as the bald eagle and peregrine falcon are especially sensitive during their nesting and rearing seasons.

Some critical nesting or haul-out rocks and islands have been set aside in the United States and Canada as wildlife refuges (usually as ecological reserves in the latter), and access is either restricted or prohibited. For instance, eighty-odd rocks and islands used by birds and harbor seals in Washington State compose the San Juan Islands National Wildlife Refuge. Access ashore is banned in all but two of these, and you are asked to stay 200 yards offshore from the others.

Unintentional impacts can be minimized through understanding the creatures you are likely to encounter. I particularly recommend the many articles about wildlife species in *Sea Kayaker* magazine, which you can locate through their periodical indexes. Below are some guidelines for interacting with marine mammals found in the Pacific Northwest.

To date there have been no incidents of orcas (killer whales) acting aggressively toward kayaks or accidentally bumping or upsetting one. The senses of these creatures are acute enough to know what and exactly where you are whenever they are close enough to matter. (One whale researcher did have his inflatable gently bumped by what was apparently a startled young orca awakening from a nap.)

How much kayaks interfere with the normal behavior of pods of orcas and the importance of such disruption is uncertain. The whales often appear to ignore nearby kayaks, though at times they seek them out for a closer look (see my own account in the introduction), and frequently they go out of their way to avoid contact. The best rule is to let them come to you and to avoid approaching within about 50 yards of them. If an orca group is coming toward you, your best chance for a good look at them is to stop paddling and keep your own group together and quiet. Avoid paddling in areas with rubbing beaches (where orcas traditionally rub themselves on submerged rocks), and be unobtrusive ashore there.

Orcas nap frequently while either stopped or moving slowly for a quarter of an hour or so. Experts agree that this is the time that they are most easily disturbed. Hence, if they are moving slowly enough for you to catch them, keep away.

Gray whales may be a significant hazard for kayaks. There have been at least two incidents—one in Mexico and the other in Monterey, California—in which kayaks were apparently intentionally upset by the whales. Gray whales have been known to play with objects on the surface, and a video was made of several whales bouncing an inflatable with a biologist aboard. Furthermore, the senses of grays are thought to be relatively poor compared to other whales. I and other kayakers have felt quite uncertain whether the huge beasts were really aware of us when very close. Consequently, I tap on my hull in hope of alerting them to me. In light of all this, keeping your distance is prudent.

At least in the Pacific Northwest, harbor seal populations are doing very well. Nonetheless, some marine biologists are concerned about the adverse effects of seals being repeatedly frightened off their intertidal haul-out rocks. During the pupping season, mothers and pups panicked into the water may become separated, and their critical nursing time is certainly reduced. (On the other hand, mothers may leave pups for as much as days to fish. Human odors from handling such an "orphaned" pup will cause the mother to shun it.) Adult seals need a good amount of sunbathing during the summer and fall molt, which can be disrupted by repeated intrusions.

Today I give hauled-out seals a much wider margin than I used to; some watch me warily, while others still dive for the water while I am quite a distance away. I try not to surprise them, and I settle for eye-to-eye contact from swimming seals, which are obviously much more at ease.

If you chance to encounter seals being chased by transient orcas (the sub-species that eats marine mammals, as opposed to resident orcas that live on salmon), be wary of terrified seals that might try to board you to escape. That has happened with whale-watching inflatables.

After being hunted almost to extinction by the nineteenth century, sea otters have made a very successful recovery following reintroduction along the Pacific coast. They are most often encountered floating on their backs close inshore along the outer coast, often in the kelp, and less likely found hauled out like seals. They are generally quite shy, diving or swimming away from your path. Simply continuing on is probably the best thing to do.

Sea lions are likely to be encountered throughout the Pacific coast. The primary detriment from contact with kayaks is, as with seals, while the animals are hauled out en masse on their rookeries. Kayaks approaching within a hundred yards or so may provoke a stampede for the water. Because sea lions are large and densely spaced on these rocks, pups may be trampled, injured, or killed in the process.

The excited and aggressive behavior of the lions when a kayaker approaches the rookery makes you anxious for your own safety, perhaps with good reason. Several years ago a canoe was capsized by sea lions in Alaska. I and others have been made to feel unwelcome by sea lions even where no rookeries were in sight, and many of us regard them as potentially the most dangerous of marine mammals. I give them a wide berth where possible.

Suggested Reading

Daniel, Linda. *Kayak Cookery: A Handbook of Provisions and Recipes.* Birmingham, AL: Menasha Ridge Press, 1997.

Appendix

Equipment Checklists

The three checklists below are *cumulative,* and each type of equipment is listed only once. If you are packing for a weekend trip, for example, check the day-trip list, too.

Though some of the items listed here are not necessary on every outing, you may wish to consider carrying them for safety or comfort depending on the destination and conditions. Some items are quite optional and depend on your preferences.

Day Trip

- ☐ Kayak
- ☐ Paddle
- ☐ Spare paddle
- ☐ Sprayskirt
- ☐ Buoyancy bags for both ends (optional if boat has bulkheads)
- ☐ Life vest
- ☐ Capsize recovery gear (paddle float, stirrup sling, etc.)
- ☐ Bilge pump
- ☐ Sponge
- ☐ Whistle (and/or compressed-air horn)
- ☐ Towline
- ☐ Chart and chart case
- ☐ Compass
- ☐ Tide and current tables
- ☐ Distress signals
- ☐ VHF radio transceiver
- ☐ Small dry bag (for items to be accessible in cockpit)
- ☐ Larger dry bag (for other items)

- ☐ Dry suit or wet suit
- ☐ Paddle jacket
- ☐ Wading footgear
- ☐ Paddling gloves (or pogies)
- ☐ Raingear
- ☐ Sun hat
- ☐ Sunglasses
- ☐ Sunscreen
- ☐ Basic first-aid kit:
    - ☐ Aspirin
    - ☐ Band-Aids
    - ☐ Ace bandage
    - ☐ Sterile compress
    - ☐ Adhesive tape
    - ☐ Zinc oxide ointment
    - ☐ Insect sting and snakebite kit
    - ☐ First-aid book
- ☐ Flashlight
- ☐ Change of shoes (if extensive stay at destination anticipated)
- ☐ Hat (for sun and/or warmth)
- ☐ Duct tape
- ☐ Water bottle
- ☐ Lunch and emergency food
- ☐ Change for phone calls
- ☐ Fire-starting implements
- ☐ Knife with screwdrivers
- ☐ Binoculars
- ☐ Camera
- ☐ Basic emergency shelter or hypothermia treatment:
    - ☐ Small tarp
    - ☐ Light sleeping bag
    - ☐ Chemical heat packs

Weekend Trip

- ☐ Repair kit:
    - ☐ Epoxy putty
    - ☐ Sewing items
    - ☐ Soft annealed wire
    - ☐ Reinforced strapping tape
    - ☐ Spare rudder cable and fittings
- ☐ Money for camping fees, if any

- ☐ Tent
- ☐ Sleeping bag in dry bag
- ☐ Ground pad
- ☐ Toilet articles
- ☐ Towel
- ☐ Extra clothing
- ☐ Personal gear bag
- ☐ Tote bag (for carrying loose gear to and from the beach)
- ☐ Hatchet and/or saw
- ☐ Garbage bag for packing out trash
- ☐ Food
- ☐ Water container (size depending on water availability)
- ☐ Condiments and spices
- ☐ Cooking set
- ☐ Eating utensils
- ☐ Cup
- ☐ Dish scrubber and soap
- ☐ Stove
- ☐ Fuel
- ☐ Tarp and tie lines
- ☐ Candles and/or lantern
- ☐ Insect repellent
- ☐ Weekend-level first-aid items:
    - ☐ Pain pills
    - ☐ Remedy for digestive upset
    - ☐ Fast-acting laxative and emetic (if shellfish to be eaten)
    - ☐ Burn ointment
    - ☐ Butterfly closures
    - ☐ Tweezers
    - ☐ Seasickness remedy
- ☐ Fishing gear
- ☐ Kite or sail

Extended Trip

- ☐ Class B EPIRB for remote coasts where VHF coverage is poor
- ☐ GPS
- ☐ Shore survival kit for wilderness coasts (basic shelter, fire, food, and signaling items in compact case to be carried on your person)
- ☐ Extended first-aid items:
    - ☐ Antibiotic pills

☐ Antibacterial ointment
☐ Pills for treating giardiasis
☐ Repair kit for extensive boat damage:
　—Fiberglass:
　　☐ Resin and catalyst
　　☐ Cloth or mat
　　☐ Disposable rubber gloves
　　☐ Plastic wrap
　—Folding:
　　☐ Hull patching adhesive and patches
　　☐ Heavy sewing: thread, needles, palm
　　☐ Epoxy glue for mending broken wooden parts
　—Inflatable:
　　☐ Patching adhesive and patches
　　☐ Spare valve and pump parts, if appropriate
　—General:
　　☐ Sandpaper (50 grit and 200 grit wet/dry)
　　☐ Small vice-grip pliers with cutters
　　☐ Piece of hacksaw blade
　　☐ Drill bits (held with vice grips or wrapped in tape by hand)
　　☐ Silicon lubricant (avoid contact with fiberglass)
　　☐ Sealant for cloth seams
　　☐ Sparse fastenings (bolts, nuts, and cotter pins as needed)
☐ Shower components
☐ Soap that will make suds in salt water ("sea soap")

Kayak Manufacturers

Ainsworth
P.O. Box 207.
Norwich, VT 05055
(802) 649-2952; Fax (902) 649-2254

Baldwin Boat Co.
RR 2, Box 268
Orrington, ME 04474
(207) 825-4439

Baltic Kayaks
330 McKinley Terrace
Centerport, NY 11721
(516) 673-4662; Fax (516) 673-8352

Betsie Bay Kayak
P.O. Box 1706
Frankfort, MI 49635
(616) 352-7774

Boreal Design
108 Amsterdam
Industrial Park
St. Augustin, Quebec, G3A 1V9, Canada
(418) 878-3099; Fax (418) 878-3459

Cal-Tek Engineering
36 Riverside Dr.
Kingston, MA 02364
(617) 585-5666

Current Designs
10124 McDonald Pk. Rd.
Sidney, British Columbia V8L 5X8, Canada
(604) 655-1822; Fax (604) 655-1596
e-mail: info@cdkayak.com
Web site: www.cdkayak.com

Dagger Canoe Co.
P.O. Box 1500
Harriman, TN 37748
(423) 882-0404; Fax (423) 882-8153

Easy Rider Canoe & Kayak Co.
P. O. Box 88108
Seattle, WA 98138
(425) 228-3633; Fax (425) 277-8778

Eddyline Kayaks
1344 Ashten Rd.
Burlington, WA 98233
(360) 757-2300

Englehart Products Inc. (EPI)
P.O. Box 377
Newbury, OH 44065
(216) 564-5565; Fax (216) 564-5515

Euro Kayaks/TG Canoe Livery
P.O. Box 177
Martindale, TX 78655
(512) 353-3946; Fax (512) 353-3947

Glenwa, Inc.
P.O. Box 3134
Gardena, CA 90247
(310) 327-9216; Fax (310) 327-8952
e-mail: cobrakayaks@worldnet.att.net
Web site: www.cobrakayaks.com

Great Canadian Canoe Co.
64 Worcester Providence Tpke. (Rt. 146)
Sutton, MA 01590
(508) 865-0010; Fax (508) 865-5220

Hop On Top Kayaks
P.O. Box 139
Jamestown, RI 02835
(401) 423-1815; Fax (401) 423-1815

Hydra Kayaks
5061 S. National Dr.
Knoxville, TN 37914
(800) 537-8888; Fax (305) 836-1296

Island Innovations Inc.
738 Selkirk Ave.
Victoria, British Columbia V9A 2T5, Canada
(250) 388-7466

Island Wave Skis
2729 South Atlantic Ave.
Cocoa Beach, FL 32931
(407) 783-5194; Fax (407) 783-5194

Janautica/Splashdance
Hwy 85 South
Niceville, FL 32578
(850) 678-1637; Fax (850) 678-1637
Web site: www.splashdance.com

Kiwi Kayak Co.
2454 Vista Del Monte
Concord, CA 94520
(510) 692-2041; Fax (510) 692-2042

Kruger Canoes
2906 Meister Lane
Lansing, MI 48906
(517) 323-2139

Mainstream Products, Inc.
182 Kayaker Way
Easley, SC 29642
(517) 323-2139

Mariner Kayaks, Inc.
2134 Westlake Ave. N.
Seattle, WA 98109
(206) 284-8404; Fax (206) 284-6046

Necky Kayaks, Ltd.
1100 Riverside Rd.

Abbotsford, British Columbia, Canada
(604) 850-1206; Fax (604) 850-3197

Nomad Kayaks
4918 boul. Rive Sud
Levis, Quebec G6W 5N6, Canada
(418) 838-0338; Fax (418) 838-0801

Northwest Kayaks, Inc.
15145 NE 90th St.
Redmond, WA 98052
(425) 869-1107; Fax (425) 869-9014

Ocean Kayak, Inc.
P.O. Box 5003
Ferndale, WA 98248
(800) 852-9257; Fax (360) 366-2628

Old Town Canoe Co.
58 Middle St.
Old Town, ME 04468
(207) 827-5513; Fax (207) 827-2779

P & H Designs/Impex International
1107 Station Rd., Unit 1
Bellport, NY 11713
(516) 286-1988; Fax (516) 286-1952

Pacific Water Sports Inc.
16055 Pacific Hwy. S.
Seattle, WA 98188
(206) 246-9358; Fax (206) 439-9040

Perception Inc.
P.O. Box 8002
Easley, SC 29641
(803) 859-7518; Fax (803) 855-5995

Phoenix Poke Boats, Inc.
P.O. Box 109
207 N. Broadway
Berea, KY 40403-0109
(606) 986-2336; Fax (606) 986-3277

Prijon/Wildwasser Sport USA
P.O. Box 4617
Boulder, CO 80306
(303) 444-2336; Fax (303) 444-2375

Pyranha/Impex International
1107 Station Rd.
Bellport, NY 11713
(516) 286-1988; Fax (516) 286-1952

Rainforest Designs Ltd.
P.O. Box 91
Maple Ridge, British Columbia V0M 1B0, Canada
(604) 467-9932; Fax (604) 467-8890

Seaward Kayaks Ltd.
RR 1, Site 16
Summerland, British Columbia V0H 1Z0, Canada
(800) 595-9755; Fax (250) 494-5200

Seda Products
926 Coolidge Ave.
National City, CA 91950
(619) 336-2444; Fax (619) 336-2405

Southern Exposure Sea Kayaks
P.O. Box 4530
Tequesta, FL 33469
(561) 575-4530; Fax (561) 744-9371

Superior Kayaks
P.O. Box 355
Whitelaw, WI 54247
(414) 732-3784

Swift Canoe & Kayak
RR #1 Oxtongue Lake
Dwight, Ontario P0A 1H0, Canada
(705) 635-1167

The Upstream Edge (Rockwood Outfitters)
699 Speedvale Ave. W.
Guelph, Ontario N1K 1E6, Canada
(519) 824-1415; Fax (519) 824-8750

Trent Canoe & Kayak
2350 Haines Rd.
Bldg. 28
Mississiga, Ontario L4Y 1Y6, Canada
(905) 273-9075; Fax (905) 275-3090

Tsunami
13732 Bear Mountain Rd.
Redding, CA 96003
(916) 275-4313; Fax (916) 275-3090

Valley Canoe Products/Great River Outfitters
3721 Shallow Brook
Bloomfield Hills, MI 48302
(248) 644-6909; Fax (248) 644-4960

Vermont Canoe Products
R.R. 1, Box 353A
Newport, VT 05855
(800) 454-2307; Fax (802) 754-2307

Walden Paddlers, Inc.
152 Commonwealth Ave.
Concord, MA 01742
(508) 371-3000

West Side Boat Shop
7661 Tanawanda Creek Rd.
Lockport, NY 14094
(716) 434-5755

Wet Willy Kayaks
6978 Hollywood St.
Coos Bay, OR 97420
(541) 888-8173

Wilderness Systems
P.O. Box 4339
Archdale, NC 27263
(910) 434-7470; Fax (910) 434-6912

Woodstrip Watercraft Co.
1818 Swamp Pike
Gilbertsville, PA 19525
(610) 326-9282

Paddle Manufacturers

Ainsworth
P.O. Box 207
Norwich, VT 05055
(802) 649-2952; Fax (802) 649-2254

Aqua-Bound Technology Ltd.
#1-9520 192nd St.
Surrey, British Columbia V4N 3R8, Canada
  In the U.S.:
  1160 Yew Ave
  Blaine, WA 98230
  (604) 882-2052; Fax (604) 882-9988

Backlund Paddles
26115 Clarksburg Rd.
Clarksburg, MD 20871
(301) 253-4947

Baldwin Boat Co.
RR2, Box 268
Orrington, ME 04474-9611
(207) 825-4439

Baltic Paddles
330 McKinley Terrace
Centerport, NY 11721
(516) 673-4662; Fax (516) 673-8352

Bending Branches
812 Prospect Ct.
Osceola, WI 54020
(715) 755-3405; Fax (715) 755-3406

Betsie Bay Kayak
P.O. Box 1706
Frankfort, MI 49635
(616) 352-7774

Boreal Design
P.O. Box 37
St. Augustin, Quebec G3A 1V9, Canada
(418) 878-3099; Fax (418) 878-3459

Carlisle Paddles, Inc.
P.O. Box 488
Grayling, MI 49738
(517) 348-9886; Fax (517) 348-8242

Camp Paddle Co.
2507 State Hwy. 7
Bainbridge, Ny 13733
(607) 967-8755
e-mail: campadle@tri.town.net

Caviness Woodworking Co., Inc.
P.O. Box 710
Calhoun City, MS 38916
(601) 628-5195; Fax (601) 628-8580

Clinch River Paddle Co.
2450 Jones Rd.
Lenoir City, TN 37771
(423) 986-9387

Cricket Paddles
17530 W. Hwy. 50
Maysville
Salida, CO 81201
(719) 539-5010

Current Designs
10124 McDonald Pk. Rd
Sidney, British Columbia V8L 5X8, Canada

In the U.S.:
We-No-Nah Canoe Co.
Box 247
Winona, MN 55987
(604) 655-1822; Fax (604) 655-1596
e-Mail: info@cdkayak.com
Web site: www.cdkayak.com

Dagger Canoe Co.
P.O. Box 1500
Harriman, TN 37748
(423) 882-0404

Epic Paddles, Inc.
6657 58th Ave. NE
Seattle, WA 98115
(206) 523-6306; Fax (206) 523-6306

Far Horizon/Doctor D's
P.O. Box 189
South Freeport, ME 04078
(207) 865-1244

Glenwa, Inc.
P.O. Box 3134
Gardena, CA 90247x
(310) 327-9216; Fax (310) 327-8952
e-mail: cobrakayaks@worldnet.att.net
Web site: www.cobrakayaks.com

Great Canadian Canoe Co.
64 Worcester Providence Tpke.
Sutton, MA 01590
(508) 865-0010; Fax (508) 865-5220

Grey Owl Paddles
62 Cowansview Rd.
Cambridge, Ontario N1R 7N3, Canada
(519) 622-0001; Fax (519) 622-0723

Impex International, Inc./Formula Paddles
1107 Station Rd.
Bellport, NY 11713
(516) 286-1988; Fax (516) 286-1952

Janautica/Splashdance
Hwy. 85 South
Niceville, FL 32578
(904) 678-1637; Fax (904) 678-1637

L'eau Vive
P.O. Box 18978
Boulder, CO 80308
(303) 417-1957; Fax (303) 417-1446

Lee's Value Right, Inc.
P.O. Box 19346
Minneapolis, MN 55419
(800) 758-1720
(612) 722-0057; Fax (612) 722-8040

Lendal Paddles/Great River Outfitters
3721 Shallow Brook
Bloomfield Hills, MI 48302
(248) 644-6909; Fax (248) 644-4960

Lightning Paddles
22800 S. Unger Rd.
Colton, OR 97017
(503) 824-2938; Fax (503) 824-6960

Malone of Maine
80 Second St.
South Portland, ME 04106
(207) 767-9776; Fax (207) 741-2477

Mitchell Paddles Inc.
RR 2, Box 922
Canaan, NH 03741
(603) 523-7004; Fax (603) 523-7363

Mohawk Paddles
963 North C.R. 427
Longwood, FL 32750
(407) 834-3233; Fax (407) 834-0292

Nimbus Paddles
4915 Chisholm St.
Delta, British Columbia V4K 2K6, Canada
(604) 526-2099; Fax (604) 522-1454

Norse Padle Company
Rd. 1, Box 242
Spring Mills, PA 16875
(814) 422-8844; Fax (814) 422-8336

Northwest Design Works
(See Werner Paddles)

North Woods Canoe Company Ltd.
Box 1419
Cochrane, Alberta, T0L 0W0, Canada
(403) 932-1948; Fax (403) 932-7123

Perception
P.O. Box 8002
Easley, SC 29641
(800) 595-2925; Fax (864)-855-5995

Prijon/Wildwasser Sport USA, Inc.
P.O. Box 4617
Boulder, CO 80306
(303) 444-2336; Fax (303) 444-2375

Sawyer Paddles & Oars
299 Rogue River Pkwy.
Talent, OR 97540
(541) 535-3606; Fax (541) 535-3621

Seda Products
926 Coolidge Ave.
National City, CA 91950
(619) 336-2444

Sidewinder Whitewater
1692 2nd Street
Richboro, PA 18954
(215) 598-3669

Silver Creek Paddles
677 Silvermine Rd.
Bryson City, NC 28713
(704) 488-9542
e-mail: silvrcrk@dnet.net

Superior Kayaks Inc.
108 Menasha
P.O. Box 355
Whitelaw, WI 54247
(414) 732-3784

Surfins
2227 Drake SW #10A
Huntsville, AL 33805
(205) 882-2227; Fax (205) 551-9494

Swift/Eddyline Kayak Works
1344 Ashten Rd.
Burlington, WA 98233
(360) 757-2300; Fax (360) 757-2302

Tomic Golf & Ski Mfg.
23102 Mariposa Ave.
Torrance, CA 90502
(310) 534-2532; Fax (310) 534-2532

Twogood Kayaks Hawaii, Inc.
345 Hahani St..
Kailua, HI 96734
(808) 262-5656; Fax (808) 261-3111
e-mail: twogood@alohoa.com

Venturesport, Inc.
P.O. Box 610145
Miami, FL 33261
(561) 395-1376

Werner Paddles
P.O. Box 1139
Sultan, WA 98294
(800) 275-3311; Fax (206) 290-1781

Whispering Waters
P.O. Box 497
Mt. Shasta, CA 96067
(916) 343-8681

Wood Strip Water Craft Co.
1818 Swamp Pike
Gilbertsville, PA 19525
(610) 326-9282

ZuZu Paddle Company, Inc.
P.O. Box 957
Flagstaff, AZ 86002
(520) 774-6535; Fax (520) 779-9466

General Sources of Paddling Equipment

Cascade Outfitters
P. O. Box 209
Springfield, OR 97477
(800) 223-7238
(503) 747-2272

Great River Outfitters
3721 Shallow Brook
Bloomfield Hills, MI 48302
(810) 683-4770

NOC Outfitter's Store
13077 Hwy. 19 West
Byson City, NC 28713
(800) 367-3521
(704) 488-6737
Fax (704) 488-8039

Northwest River Supplies
2009 South Maine
Moscow, Idaho 83843
(800) 635-5202
(208) 882-2383
Fax (208) 883-4787

Piragis Northwoods Company
105 North Central Avenue
Ely, MN 55731
(800) 223-6565

Calculating Currents Using NOAA's Tables

The example shown is for June 3, 1985, a day of particularly strong currents, at San Juan Island's Limestone Point, Washington State. In the lower portion of the table, corrections for Limestone Point (Spieden Channel) are based on daily predictions for San Juan Channel (the upper portion of the table). One hour is added to the calculations for daylight saving time. To calculate the first slack for Limestone Point, take the slack water time for San Juan Channel (A), minus the correction time for the minimum current before the ebb at Limestone Point (B), plus one hour for daylight saving time (DST).

0328 – 1 00 (1 hour 0 minutes) + 1 00 (DST) = 0328.

To calculate the maximum ebb current for Limestone Point, take the maximum current time for San Juan Channel (C), plus the maximum ebb current correction for Limestone Point (D), plus one hour for daylight saving time (DST).

0724 + 0 26 (minutes) + 1 00 (DST) = 0850.

To calculate the speed in knots for that time, take the maximum current velocity for San Juan Channel (E), multiplied by the ebb speed ratio for Limestone Point (F).

4.3 x 1.2 = 5.2.

To calculate when the next slack for Limestone Point will occur, take the next slack water time for San Juan Channel (G), minus the correction time for the minimum current before the flood for Limestone Point (H), plus one hour for daylight saving time (DST).

$$1047 + 0\ 23\ (\text{minutes}) + 1\ 00\ (\text{DST}) = 1210.$$

Note that the interval of this large exchange is almost nine hours. Though the afternoon flood current will be five knots in San Juan Channel, Spieden Channel will be slower than during the morning ebb. To calculate the speed in knots for that time, take the maximum current velocity for San Juan Channel (I), multiplied by the flood speed ratio for Limestone Point (J).

$$5.0 \times 0.7 = 3.2.$$

SAN JUAN CHANNEL (south entrance), WASHINGTON, 1985

F-Flood, Dir. 010° True   E-Ebb, Dir. 180° True

JUNE

Day	Slack Water Time	Maximum Current Time	Vel.
	h.m.	h.m.	knots
1 Sa	0214	0555	4.2E
	0922	1237	4.6F
	1630	1910	2.5E
	2210		
2 Su		0024	2.0F
	0250	0639	4.3E
	1004	1325	4.9F
	1726	2004	2.5E
	2309		
3 M		0113	1.6F
	0328 A	0724 C	4.3E E
	1047 G	1415	5.0F I
	1819	2057	2.5E

CURRENT DIFFERENCES AND OTHER CONSTANTS, 1985

NO.	PLACE	TIME DIFFERENCES				SPEED RATIOS	
		Min. before Flood	Flood	Min. before Ebb	Ebb	Flood	Ebb
		h. m.	h. m.	h. m.	h. m.		
	SAN JUAN CHANNEL	on SAN JUAN CHANNEL, p. 58					
1655	Cattle Point, 1.2 miles southeast of	+0 11	−0 20	+0 34	−0 01	0.3	0.9
1660	SAN JUAN CHANNEL (south entrance)	Daily Predictions					
1665	Kings Point, Lopez Island, 1 mile NNW of ...	+0 51	−0 07	+0 27	+0 36	0.6	0.5
1670	Pear Point, 1.1 miles east of	+0 40	+1 09	−0 10	+1 01	0.4	0.5
1675	Turn Rock Light, 1.9 miles northwest of	+1 19	+1 22	+0 20	−0 01	0.4	0.5
1680	Crane Island, south of, Wasp Passage	−0 10	+0 35	+0 29	+0 07	0.2	0.1
1685	Wasp Passage Light, 0.5 mile WSW of	+0 19	+0 28	+0 15	−0 15	0.5	0.4
1690	Spring Passage, south entrance	+0 04	−1 09	−0 43	−0 13	0.4	0.4
1695	Limestone Point, Spieden Channel	+0 23 H	−0 12	−1 00 B	+0 26 D	0.7 J	1.2 F

(Reprinted with permission from *Kayak Trips in Puget Sound and the San Juan Islands* by Randel Washburne, © The Mountaineers.)

Ordering Charts

Agencies Supplying Charts

U.S. NOAA:
Distribution Branch (N/CG33)
National Ocean Service
Riverside, MD 20737
Web site: www.nos.noaa.gov

U.S. DMA:
DMA Office of Distribution Services
Attn: DDCP
6500 Brooks Lane
Washington, DC 20315

Canadian:
Canadian Hydrographic Service
Department of Fisheries and Oceans
Institute of Ocean Sciences, Patricia Bay
9860 West Saanich Road, P.O. Box 6000
Sidney, B.C. V8L 4B2
Web site: www.chshg.dfo.ca

For any of the above or Mexican or British Admiralty:
Captain's Nautical Supplies
1914 Fourth Avenue
Seattle, WA 98101

Index